TRUE CRIME FILES

---

48 DISTURBING TRUE CRIME STORIES – THE ULTIMATE BINGE-WORTHY COLLECTION OF REAL CRIMES AND UNSOLVED MYSTERIES

SCOTT MATTHEWS

The true mystery of the world is the visible, not the invisible.

— Oscar Wilde

CONTENTS

PART I

TRUE CRIME FILES

24 DISTURBING TRUE CRIME STORIES OF MURDER, MYSTERY, AND MADNESS

INTRODUCTION

Every society is built on a fragile foundation of trust. We trust that our neighbors are who they say they are, that our leaders act in our interest, and that the world follows a predictable logic. But what happens when that trust is systematically dismantled? In *True Crime Files: 24 Disturbing True Crime Stories of Murder, Mystery, and Madness*, we step into the fractures where that foundation has crumbled, revealing a reality that is as fascinating as it is fearsome.

The cases ahead represent a global map of human transgression. This journey takes us from the unsettling discovery of a skull hidden in a child's toy in China to the high-pressure world of international deception, including Canada's infamous Busang Mirage. We aren't just looking at the act of crime but at the terrifying evolution of it. You will witness the psychological grip of the Gloriavale Christian Community, the cold-blooded calculations of the Lahori Psycho, and the lingering, taunting silence of the Jazz Murders.

While some stories explore the brutal finality of violence, others delve into the "madness" of the mind and the "mystery" of the unknown. We examine the chilling complexities of a family turned on itself in the Colt Clan case and the intellectual battle of a cipher that successfully defied the FBI's greatest minds. These are the accounts that challenge our understanding of morality—where cults sign contracts in blood and "princes" build empires on nothing but lies and audacity.

As you navigate these twenty-four files, you will find that the most disturbing monsters aren't always found in the shadows; sometimes, they are hiding in plain sight, protected by a badge, a religious robe, or a charming smile. The cases are real, the victims are many, and the truth is waiting to be uncovered.

Step inside, but be warned: once you see the world through these files, you can never look at it the same way again.

1

THE PLUSH THAT HID A SKULL

In 1999, Hong Kong police entered a Granville Road apartment after a teenage witness led them there. The flat was jarringly decorated floor-to-ceiling with Hello Kitty motifs — curtains, bedsheets, and a cluster of oversized plush toys.

Among those toys, officers found the most crucial piece of evidence: a large Hello Kitty mermaid doll with a human skull sewn inside. The remains were identified as Fan Man-yi.

Fan Man-yi's story is about how the spaces of pleasure and profit, drugs and sex, and the lure of easy money can intersect with organized crime to create an arena where a person can be stripped of their protections, their freedom, and finally their life.

Before the apartment and the mermaid doll, before the drug binges and the debt that spiraled out of control, there was a child who had been left behind. Fan Man-yi was abandoned in childhood and grew up in an orphanage until age fifteen, when the age limit forced her out. With no adoption and no home waiting, she was suddenly on her own. Homelessness came quickly. Addiction soon followed. To survive, she entered prostitution, working brothels to earn money for food and, increasingly, to feed a dependence that never stopped asking for more.

In her early twenties, she secured work as a dancer at the Empress Karaoke nightclub. There she met a client who would become her husband: a fellow drug user whose presence in her life did not halt her habits, and rather enabled them. They married in 1996 but it wasn't a happy marriage — he abused her. But despite the abuse, the couple stayed together long enough to have two sons. Even neighbors got used to the sounds of the children crying, and the adults arguing through the night. She lived in survival mode, with strain always present in the background.

By early 1997, the marriage couldn't halt the economic reality of her life. Fan returned to prostitution, working at the Romance Villa in Kowloon. It was there that she met a man whose name would become inseparable from her own in everything that followed.

Chan Man-lok was thirty-four, a wealthy figure with social pull and connections. He inhabited a world where crystal meth (ice) moved alongside money and sex. He was a dealer and a pimp, tied to the triads, and he had a circle of younger men orbiting him. For a woman in Fan's position, his presence promised cash and drugs in quantity. He paid her for long all-night sessions, supplied ice, and pulled her into the comfort of a circle that at first didn't feel like a trap.

Once she was inside that circle, the balances shifted. Comfort shaded into familiarity and soon enough, familiarity into vulnerability. In the hierarchy Chan maintained, there were underlings to do his bidding and women to supply sex and money. He was not someone to be messed with, or even associate with safely. Yet, in a moment that would become the hinge of the story, Fan did exactly that.

During a binge, Fan stole Chan's wallet. About $4,000 in cash changed hands. In ordinary street crime, it was a simple theft — money taken to feed a habit and buy dinner. Inside Chan's hierarchy, it was something else entirely: an affront that cost him face and challenged his control. The money mattered, but the insult mattered more. From that moment, the "debt" stopped being a balance to repay and became a pretext to punish.

Fan agreed to repay the $4,000 from her work but Chan refused the straightforward return of principal and demanded $10,000 in interest. She said she would need time. On the surface, it sounded conciliatory; to

Chan, it only sharpened the trespass. This was less about cash than audacity — less about the loss of money than the loss of face.

When the money didn't arrive on Chan's timetable, discipline gave way to punishment. The "debt" stopped functioning as a balance sheet and became the instrument that justified whatever came next.

In March 1999, Chan gave the order. Two of his men abducted Fan and brought her to his apartment on Granville Road. It was large, five bedrooms, decorated in Hello Kitty paraphernalia — curtains and sheets, wall décor and plush toys. The cuteness stood in absolute contrast to what would happen there. The plan, as he framed it, was straightforward: he would force her to work until she paid back the debt. The reality was that he kept moving the line. The interest kept climbing. The goalposts were never fixed. She could not reach a point where the debt was satisfied because satisfaction wasn't the point.

When the money did not appease him, punishment began. Control slid into violence and the cycle fed on itself. Beatings left her too injured to work, and her inability to work was treated as defiance that brought more beatings. The tempo matched the meth binges, with longer nights, thinner inhibitions, and spikes in irritability, impulsivity, and aggression. This was not a sudden outburst but a systematic abuse. The debt gave the pretext, the drug gave the fuel, and the group's shared indifference normalized it until laughing at her pain felt, to them, like part of the night's routine.

The core group that held Fan captive formed around Chan. There was Chan himself. There was Leung Wai-lun, a subordinate described as nineteen or twenty-one years old. There was twenty-six-years-old Leung Ching-cho. And then there was a fourteen-year-old girl known as Ah Fong, an alias for her real name. She had been groomed by Chan, described as the girlfriend of one of the underlings but also likely one of Chan's prostitutes. Young as she was, she joined in. She laughed. She invented new cruelties. She was part of the dynamic that normalized the harm and spread it around the room.

What they did to Fan was sustained, malicious, and relentless. They restrained her and beat her with whatever was at hand. There was sexual violence. They forced degrading acts and used heat and irritants to worsen her injuries. On one day, she was kicked in the head fifty times. When her legs and feet were already damaged, they struck them again to keep her from healing. They poured sauces and oils on her and turned the abuse into a cruel game, ordering her to smile and say she liked it, then threatening worse if she did not.

The humiliation kept escalating. They urinated on her and punished her when she gagged. Ah Fong forced further degrading acts meant to break her will. They wrapped her in electrical wire, hoisted her from a ceiling hook, and left her hanging through the night. Over time they stopped feeding her. The fluids they forced upon her became, grotesquely, the only intake her body received. Clients turned away from a woman so wounded she could barely stand. The men watched television, played video games, and treated her suffering as filler for hours that might otherwise have been dull. She drifted in and out of consciousness on the floor of her torturers while her husband and children waited somewhere else in the city, not knowing where she was or whether she would return.

One night, the group went out drinking. They tied Fan and left her on the bathroom floor, locking the door behind them. On April 15, 1999, after about a month of unspeakable torment, Fan died on the bathroom floor, alone and in pain. When they returned, Ah Fong went to use the bathroom and found the body. The men argued, first about what had caused her death, then about what to do next. Some believed she had overdosed, a conclusion that fit their assumptions about her drug use. Others did not settle on a single explanation. In practical terms, the argument paused nothing. They left the apartment to play arcade games indifferent to her death, and later returned to sleep, the body still behind the bathroom door.

The following day, high again, Chan gave the instruction that would turn the apartment from a scene of torture into a site of desecration. "She must be destroyed," he said. They carried her to the bathtub and dismembered her body to smaller parts that could be handled and moved, to more manageable parts. Decay and smell drove their next decisions. They boiled the parts on the stove. Chan woke Ah Fong up and sent her to put a bag of viscera into hot water to tamp down the odor. At the same time, Leong Xing Cho was boiling the head and called Ah Fong over to look.

She said she was scared and did not want to, but he told her to pretend she was watching TV. She took a quick peek and agreed it looked like something from a horror movie.

By then the process had dragged on for ten hours, and the group was getting hungry. As they tended to the pot and stirred from time to time, they started cooking noodles on the next burner. They used one spoon for both, alternating between the noodle pot and the other pot.

By the time their meal was over, the head was nothing but bones, and the skull was sewn into the head of a Hello Kitty plush — specifically a mermaid doll. Why that choice was made is not clear, and in a sense, the absence of a coherent reason is part of the horror. The object, already present among many cute objects in the apartment, became a container for what they had done. They kept other bits, a tooth and some organs, for no reason that has held up to telling. Most of the rest they disposed of in the building's garbage.

For a month, nothing happened. The flat stayed quiet. The men went on. The mermaid doll remained. Then Ah Fong walked into a police station in May and told officers she was being haunted by a ghost. It is a strange entry point into a homicide investigation, but it was the words she chose and the way she described the figure that made officers listen. The ghost, she said, had been tied with electrical wire and murdered. The haunting could have been dismissed as a teenager's nightmares, a story told to stir attention or sympathy. The details were too sharp for easy dismissal. She admitted that she had played a role in the death.

Officers followed her to the apartment. Inside, she pointed to the Hello Kitty mermaid doll. There, investigators found the skull. The rest of the flat held the residue of what the script describes: the refrigerator, the pots, the objects that, when arranged together, made the story legible in terrible clarity.

Police arrested the group and brought them to trial. The case turned on the ordinary questions of guilt and responsibility and also on the extraordinary atmosphere of cruelty that the testimony captured. Ah Fong took the deal offered. She testified against the others in exchange for immunity. She told the court she had been Chan's girlfriend, perhaps also his prostitute. When asked why they had done what they did, she said she thought it was for fun. She said she needed to speak to placate Fan's ghost, to unburden the guilt, to stop the haunting that pressed on her. Her testimony was not coy. She described the acts, the laughter, the games. The courtroom heard every detail.

The trial ran for six months. Material evidence came in as exhibits: the refrigerator where parts had been kept, the pots used in the cooking, the skull. The odor reached beyond the front rows. Psychiatrists examined the men and described them to the court as without remorse. The lack of a clean forensic path to cause of death made one part of the case unusually difficult. Given the state of the remains, the court could not assert a definite mechanism. The injuries alone could explain it; an overdose could also be consistent. Jurors were left to decide whether the defendants had killed with intent or whether they had caused death without the mental element that elevates homicide to murder.

In the end, the jury convicted them of manslaughter. They accepted that the men had caused Fan's death. They could not agree that intent had been proven beyond reasonable doubt. The guilty verdict was thus constrained, and yet the sentencing judge refused to minimize what had happened.

In December 2000, Justice Peter Nguyen sentenced the three men to life imprisonment with eligibility for parole after twenty years. His words carried a stark judgment on conduct that, in his view, stood apart. In recent years, he said, "Hong Kong's courts had not encountered such cruelty, depravity, callousness, brutality, violence, or viciousness. The public deserved protection from men like these."

In another jurisdiction, across the border in mainland China, executions might have followed swiftly. Hong Kong had no death penalty. Life with parole eligibility was the law's shape of permanent censure.

Outside the courtroom, Fan's husband spoke. Life sentences felt like a measure of justice, something he could assent to. He did not pretend that any sentence could repair what had been done. He said the words that anyone in his position might say when the formalities are over and the cameras go away: how can I ever forget.

Ah Fong, who had been fourteen when the events unfolded, walked away from criminal charges and into foster care. Her current whereabouts and the arc of her life after the case remain unknown.

The men appealed in 2003 but the sentences stood. Years passed. The apartment at thirty-one Granville Road was demolished in September 2012. The site, washed of its past in brick and glass, was rebuilt as a hotel in 2016, a place for travelers in a district that constantly remakes itself. By some dark irony, the precise location of the murder now houses a restaurant, a place designed for families and friends and the brief pleasures of a meal. In 2014, the skull that had been sewn into the doll's head — the only part of Fan's body that remained in official custody — was returned to her family. They had it cremated.

Time moved on inside prisons as well. A twenty-one parole horizon arrived in 2020. Leung Ching-cho was released in April 2014 after a court accepted that the evidence against him was insufficient, a post-conviction turn that pulled him out much earlier than the life sentence implied. He returned to the city, and not long afterward, he returned to the police's attention. In January 2022, employed as a waiter, he groped a ten-year-old girl's chest. A court later sentenced him to twelve months' imprisonment for that offense. But the status of the rest is unknown to the public.

The city's reaction mixed disbelief with fascination. Hong Kong's identity as a safe, modern city produced a cognitive dissonance with the facts. The trial's duration, the youth of the girl who took immunity, the way the men joked and cooked and stirred and ate — each detail stacked until the stack formed a portrait that felt both singular and instructive. The case moved quickly into culture. Films told the story in sensational terms. *Human Pork Chop* is a title that reflects the sensationalists' urge to make atrocities sound like jokes. *There's a Secret in My Soup* is a title that makes the mundane domestic sphere complicit in the act. Abroad, the case appeared in fictionalized form in an episode of *Bones*, an American drama series, showing that the story had crossed borders the way urban legends do, carried more by image than by nuance.

When the trial ended, the city did not forget. On Fan's birthday, people gather for a candlelight vigil in the center of Hong Kong to remember a woman whose life had been narrowed by abandonment and poverty long before her captors took her. The ritual is small compared with the spectacle of the trial, but it is truer to what memory should do. It takes a name that otherwise might be lost to the icon and places it in light. It separates the woman from the plush toy. It turns a story of degradation into, at least for an evening, a story of recognition and care.

2

THE DAY MONA DIDN'T COME HOME

On Saturday, May 31, 1975 — the first day of New Zealand's Queen's Birthday long weekend — eighteen-year-old Mona Elizabeth Blades left Hamilton intending to hitchhike home to Hastings. It was a last-minute plan. She had not told her parents she was coming because she wanted to surprise the family and bring color to an ordinary milestone: a first birthday for her nephew, marked by a small gift of tumbling plastic blocks. By Monday she was not back in Hamilton. On Tuesday, June 3, she did not arrive for her first day at her new dairy job. That was when her absence turned into a missing person report. Nearly 50 years on, the case remains open without a body, without belongings, and without a definitive account of what happened between Hamilton and Hastings.

Blades was born in 1957 in Hastings, daughter of Peter Blades and Wagamina Blades, with siblings Lillian and Tony. As a teenager she moved to Hamilton and lived with her sister Lillian, brother-in-law Tom, and their baby daughter Angela. She worked as a shop assistant and had secured a new position to begin on Tuesday after the long weekend.

She did not own a car. Her sister and brother-in-law could not make the 190-miles (about 308 kilometer) drive to Hastings. Hitchhiking was her solution, and it was not unusual in 1975 either. Long-distance public transport across the central North Island was sparse. Intercity buses connected towns on limited schedules; rail options were minimal. Car ownership was high and the roads were full of private traffic. For those without a vehicle, thumbing a ride was commonplace.

Tom dropped her on Cambridge Road, near State Highway 1 (SH1), the longest and most significant road in New Zealand, early that Saturday morning. She dressed for a winter day — a black duffle coat over a green rugby jersey with a white collar and a thorn jersey beneath, light green slacks, brown shoes with yellow laces. She carried a hitchhiker's brown bag and an older shoulder bag. The plan, unshared with her family, was straightforward: Hamilton to Hastings, roughly five and a half hours by bus, shorter if the rides went smoothly.

The first leg went as planned. A woman picked her up in Hamilton, drove her south to Taupo, about ninety miles (145 kilometers) along State Highway 1, and dropped her at the information centre. From there, the record becomes a series of sightings and statements that do not fully align.

Around 10:00 a.m., a witness reported seeing a young woman matching Blades's description, wearing a long green parka, at the corner of Lake Terrace and Titiraupenga Street. Shortly after, a woman working at the information centre recalled speaking with a young woman who planned to visit her parents in Hastings. This woman had left a pack by the centre's door when she came inside.

At 10:30 a.m., a man who knew Blades at the Waipahihi fruit shop saw her walk past. He later said he watched her join another female hitchhiker and saw both get into a dark blue or dark green station wagon heading toward State Highway 5 (SH5), the Napier road. Napier is about twelve miles (twenty kilometers) by road from Hastings. Those details would suggest progress toward her destination.

Yet between noon and 1:30 p.m., other witnesses placed a young woman matching Blades's description at the Spa Hotel in Taupo. Two said they saw her drinking with another girl. A third spoke to a woman who identified herself as Blades and said she got into a red Toyota station wagon outside the bottle shop there. That red Toyota was later reported in a convoy with a motorcycle group at a Taupo service station. In the same time frame, a female witness said she saw two people load a rolled piece of carpet into the back of a red Toyota station wagon.

The cluster of statements complicated the timeline. Police later reasoned that some witnesses may have seen different hitchhikers with similar builds and clothing. Even so, the names of streets, the makes and colors of cars, the times on the clock — those elements stuck to the record and narrowed the window in which Blades was last confidently moving toward Hastings.

The most consequential account from that morning pointed to State Highway 5, the road to Napier, and to a small Japanese station wagon. A truck driver said he saw Blades get into an orange Datsun 120Y station wagon around 10:00 a.m., heading in the direction of Napier. That statement, despite conflicts with the later Spa Hotel sightings, became the last official sighting widely accepted by police at the time.

The driver of the Datsun was described as a balding, large, middle-aged man. Witnesses watched the car veer off SH5 and turn onto Matea Road, a rural dirt track in Rangitaiki about thirty-four miles (about fifty-five kilometers) southeast of Taupo. One fencing contractor drove past and saw the driver and a woman matching Blades's description in the car. When he returned along the road a short time later, the Datsun was parked and empty. What happened in the interval between those two passes has never been established.

About six weeks later, the police received an unsigned letter from a young woman who had been hitchhiking on SH5 that same day. She wrote that she had been picked up by a man in an orange Datsun station wagon heading toward Napier. She felt uncomfortable with his behavior, asked to be let out, and he complied. An elderly couple picked her up soon after, and as they continued, they passed the same Datsun parked by the road. She caught part of the number plate: it began with H, ended with the number 4, and the second letter was either K, V, or E. Her parents told her not to get involved, so she sent the account anonymously. Police appealed publicly for the writer to come forward and provide more, but she did not.

Since the trip was a surprise, no one was waiting for Blades at a specific time. Her absence became clear on Monday when she had not returned to Hamilton, and again on Tuesday when she did not arrive for work. By then, two days had passed, and any immediate trace on roadside verges, in ditches or lay-bys, or along Matea Road was harder to read.

Police from Taupo, Rotorua, Hamilton, and Auckland searched more than 120 miles (about 200 kilometers) of roadway between Tokoroa and Napier. They canvassed the information centre and the Spa Hotel and re-interviewed drivers who might have been on SH1 and SH5 that morning. The size of the search force mirrored the size of the uncertainty.

One detail hampered the investigation from the outset. The initial missing-person notices carried a photograph of Blades with long hair, taken when she had been a bridesmaid. By late May 1975, her hair was in a shorter mullet style. The mismatch may have led some people to dismiss a memory of a short-haired hitchhiker as someone else. A witness said he had thought the hitchhiker he saw was a man because of the haircut. Decades later, in 2018, police released a computer-generated image depicting how she looked at the time with the shorter style. The correction came long after the days when a revised image might have freshened recollections.

The truck driver who reported the orange Datsun later changed aspects of his story on re-interview, and investigators noted the possibility that media coverage had altered his memory. That caution did not displace the central place his account has held in the narrative, but it framed it as a piece of evidence with limits.

Given the emphasis on the orange Datsun, the inquiry widened to everyone who owned, rented, or drove a 120Y station wagon matching the description. Over the six month open inquiry, police examined more than 500 such drivers. Among them were men whose names recur in discussions of the case.

One was John Freeman, who rented an orange Datsun over the long weekend when Blades disappeared. Two weeks later, after police went public about seeking a Datsun, Freeman shot and killed a student at St Cuthbert's College in Epsom, Auckland, and then killed himself. Apart from the rental, investigators found no evidence linking him to Blades's disappearance.

Another was Charlie Hughes, originally from Hamilton, who moved to Sydney and worked as a caretaker. In 1975 he drove an orange Datsun as a company vehicle while employed by a house-removal firm. Accounts at the time said he could not fully explain his movements over the long weekend, and odometer readings showed a distance consistent with a Hamilton–Napier–Hamilton trip. Hughes has repeatedly denied involvement, speaking to newspapers and television over the years to say he had nothing to do with Blades's disappearance. Police interviewed him multiple times in the 1970s and 1980s, again in 1997, and again in 2005. That year, Rotorua detectives flew to Sydney, questioned him for five hours, and collected a voluntary DNA sample. A broadcast on TVNZ's (Television New Zealand Limited) Sunday program suggested that Hughes had been the driver of a Datsun that picked up Blades. Those allegations did not ripen into charges.

A third suspect, unnamed publicly, owned an orange Datsun at the time and drew attention for that reason alone. A fourth was Mervyn Derrick Hinton, a former traffic officer. When asked about the case, he told police, "If you think it was me, prove it." In January 2012, officers drilled through the concrete laundry floor at Hinton's former home in Kawerau (Bay of Plenty), to a depth of about thirty inches (eighty centimeters), then probed another thirty inches (eighty centimeters) beneath. They found nothing. Hinton's daughter, Pauline Barrett, said she was not surprised; she maintained that her father had not owned an orange Datsun station wagon, but an orange Toyota Corolla, and that photographs proved the laundry floor concrete was poured before Blades disappeared. A former police sergeant, Tony Muller, who had been Hinton's friend, insisted that Hinton did own an orange Datsun in 1975 and had ordered both his cars repainted soon after Blades vanished. A 1978 photo from Barrett showed the Toyota still orange at that time. Hinton also did not resemble the balding, heavyset driver described near the Datsun; he had a full head of hair until his death. Muller alleged domestic abuse in Hinton's household; Barrett denied it. Hinton died in 2008. Muller has continued to point to him and speculated that Blades's remains might be under another section of the same house. None of those claims have produced evidence.

The emphasis on vehicle color and brand focused the search, but it also risked narrowing it too far. An orange station wagon on major routes during a long weekend was not rare enough to exclude other possibilities. The letter with the partial plate provided a thread that could not be pulled to its end.

In 2004, the case was reinvestigated. That same year, workers in Huntly, in the Waikato district, found a shallow grave under a garage floor bearing the name "Blades." The inscription raised immediate, painful speculation. Within days it became clear that the name had been set in concrete years earlier as a grim joke. The former property owner apologized to the family. The reinvestigation continued without a discovery.

The losses inside the family deepened the absence. Peter Blades died in 2004. The following year, Mona's brother Tony spoke publicly for the first time, telling the Daily Post that their mother thought about Mona every day, often crying, with no burial and no facts to let grief find its shape. In January 2011, Mona's mother died. The police review that had been reopened in 2004 wound down in 2006.

In 2018, the TVNZ program *Cold Case* reconsidered the investigation. Detectives on the broadcast argued that the original case had fixated too tightly on the orange Datsun. They highlighted the independent sighting of a red Toyota station wagon moving with a motorcycle convoy and suggested that this track had not been sufficiently explored at the time. The episode also floated the idea that Blades had affiliations in gang circles in Auckland and Hamilton and that gang members might have been traveling south toward a gathering in Wellington that weekend, moving through Taupo.

After the broadcast, police clarified their position. Detective Inspector Mark Loper said that the inquiry did not include associates of motorcycle groups. The official view did not adopt the gang theory. Even so, the program's retracing of the red Toyota sighting fit the original witness accounts from outside the Spa Hotel and the service station, which had placed a similar vehicle in company with bikers.

Public tips do not align themselves to official hypotheses. After the episode aired, a man told the Rotorua Daily Post that he had overheard members of Highway 61 — the outlaw motorcycle club founded in New Zealand in 1968 — talk about killing Blades. He said the conversation took place in an apartment in the Grey Lynn, Westmere area of Auckland in the 1970s. The friend he named as the speaker died in 2013. The witness said he had not come forward earlier because he believed from coverage that the orange Datsun driver was responsible, and the friend he heard did not drive an orange Datsun. Highway 61 has chapters in Taupo and Hastings and expanded to Brisbane in the 1980s. Over decades it has been linked to drug dealing, sexual violence, theft, and homicide. None of those general facts fill the gap in this specific case. The man's account added a rumor to a file already heavy with them.

The *Cold Case* broadcast had an enduring practical effect. It re-emphasized that the last hours in Taupo are the critical terrain. It questioned the assumption that Blades had left town that morning, a point the police now state directly. They believe she did not leave Taupo on the day she disappeared. That belief rests on how the sightings intersect and on the limits of the Datsun narrative. It does not, by itself, answer the two questions that structure every missing-person case: where is she, and who is responsible.

If you travel the same roads today, the distances haven't changed. Hamilton to Taupo remains a stretch along State Highway 1. Taupo to Napier remains State Highway 5, bending through forest and pasture. Matea Road remains a side turn into rural quiet. The lines between those places took an eighteen-year-old toward a home she did not reach. What happened along those lines has not been found in the ground or confirmed on paper. The case is still open. The questions are the same ones police asked in June 1975, although most of the people who asked them have long since retired. Somewhere there is an answer about the orange Datsun, about the red Toyota, about the woman who wrote a letter and folded her name away. Somewhere there is a place where the missing day ends.

3

BLOOD SIGNED "CONTRACT"

The story began in the middle of Indiana in the 1980s and ended, for one victim, in a field in DeKalb County in 1991. People had spent a decade arguing about Satanic cults and whether they existed as the public imagined them. In Franklin and Greenwood and at county fairs across Indiana and Ohio, a set of young men tried to make that image real. They chose the symbols that frightened people the most, said the words they believed would give them power, and carried violence with them as they moved from lot to lot. The names that matter are simple. Mark Goodwin. Keith Lawrence. David Lawrence. Jimmy Lee Pinnick. William Anthony Ault and Andrew Wright.

Mark Goodwin's interest in Satanism began when he was a student at Custer Baker Middle School in Franklin. He was about twelve when he started looking up the symbols he saw on album art — the inverted cross, the pentagram — and then moved from images to texts. He read widely, including Anton LaVey's *Satanic Bible*, and took the language at face value. By his mid-teens he had adopted Satanism as a personal identity and wanted others to share it. His family pushed back, especially his father who condemned the ideas outright. Some relatives tried to ignore the subject and wait for it to pass, some cut off contact but none of these stopped him. He collected friends and older acquaintances into a loose circle and then pressed it into a group with a name.

They called themselves Satan's Disciples. The membership was uneven: more males than females, ages ranging from pre-adult to mid-thirties, and a hierarchy that placed Goodwin at the center. He took the title of priest. The settings were barns on the rural edges of Franklin, Indiana, wooded patches that were easy to reach and hard to see into, and an old cemetery near Martinsville. The rituals followed a pattern. The men wore black ceremonial robes; the girls and women were required to wear black lingerie or nothing. The group drank heavily. Goodwin stayed sober and led the rite. He drew a pentagram on the ground, led an invocation to Satan, and said the chant would conjure demons to serve the group's will. Then they killed a cat and drained the blood into a chalice to drink it. The ritual ended in sex without rules.

The details are important for what happened later: the set piece of candles and chant; the idea that the right words could summon help; the idea that blood gave access to something beyond ordinary life; the requirement that the leader stand outside the fog of alcohol while others went along. They carried those assumptions forward. What Goodwin says he would not carry forward was talk of killing a baby as a "true" sacrifice. When some members raised that idea, he left. He was eighteen. He no longer had a group, and he had broken his relationships at home arguing about the person he wanted to be. He decided to reverse that decision on the surface. He told his family he was done with Satanism, moved back in, and hid his beliefs to keep a bed. For two years there were no rituals and no cult. The change was strategic, not ideological.

The next turn came through work. In 1991 Goodwin, then about twenty, took a job at a fast-food restaurant in Greenwood. Two brothers worked there as well, David and Keith Lawrence. Keith was the younger brother, about eighteen or nineteen. David was early twenties. The roles in the family were inverted. Keith led; David followed. Keith had been drawn into Satanism years earlier and had made it a framework for how to think and speak. He collected literature and treated the ideas as a philosophy. He once chased David through their house with a kitchen knife in an argument about beliefs. His parents sent him to a private school in Terre Haute for structure and distance. He came home changed in schedule, not in mind. David stayed close to him because, he said later, Keith was the only family member who treated him with respect. They were a unit. And in Greenwood's back room, one detail gave them away to Goodwin. Keith wore a pentagram necklace.

Goodwin asked about the symbol. Keith talked. The phrases and claims, which the brothers had been using for years, met a listener who wanted to hear them. Goodwin stepped back into the shape he had left. He and Keith wrote out a contract with Satan: twenty years of power in exchange for the soul, signed in blood. David was present but did not sign. The two who had agreed to the terms started going to cemeteries to hold séances, trying to speak with the dead. The efforts did not produce anything they could point to, but the routine mattered more than the result. It renewed a rhythm, it gave a role back to Goodwin and gave Keith a peer who treated his language seriously.

The families reacted the way they had before and the arguments started again. By May 1991 each young man was close to being put out. They chose mobility over another round of fights and signed on with a carnival operator. The choice solved several problems at once. They had jobs and beds, a reason to leave home without a fresh argument, and nights in towns where no one knew them. The routes ran through Indiana and into Ohio. In that circuit, they met a worker from Shelbyville named Jimmy Lee Pinnick.

Pinnick was older than the others at twenty-four. He came from an abusive home, had been in and out of trouble for years, and did not avoid violence. He introduced himself as a Satanist and was admitted into the group. At this point, the circle that moved with the show had a fourth presence near it who wanted in: a twenty-one-year-old worker named William Anthony Ault. He was interested in Satanism, eager for company, and kept at the edges because the three did not want him in the center.

Pinnick's presence changed the balance. He had a criminal history and a willingness to use it. The first death tied to the group came at the end of August. On August 30, 1991, a carnival worker named Andrew Wright, eighteen, from West Milton, Ohio, was found in a field near the Ohio Turnpike, stabbed and left. In the group's account to police, the motive was simple: Wright had been talking about Pinnick's past crimes, and Pinnick wanted him quiet. Pinnick and Keith lured him out, cut his throat, stabbed him, and left him there. No one arrested them then. The only people who knew were the killers, Goodwin and David, and Ault, who learned enough to use the knowledge as leverage. He wanted into the inner circle, and the information looked like a key.

A month later they told him he could join. There would be an initiation. The plan required a location, and a friend of the group named Brenda Ferguson found one: a secluded farm building near Auburn in DeKalb County. On September 25, 1991, after the DeKalb County Free Fair shut down for the night, she dropped the five men at the site. The ritual began with instructions to Ault to lie on a door that had been set up like an altar. They bound and gagged him. Keith read an invocation. Pinnick took a knife that belonged to Keith and made a long cut from the base of Ault's neck down through his abdomen. Keith, David, and Goodwin added their own cuts until an inverted cross was carved into Ault's chest and stomach. Goodwin attempted to cut out Ault's heart. Ault was still alive while all this was happening. Pinnick leaned in and asked whether he was ready to die. Ault whispered something no one has recovered. Pinnick cut his throat and ended it.

After the death, they moved the door into the field with Ault's body on it. They removed the head and hands and tried to burn them. Pinnick later said the head was meant for a friend of Keith's who wanted a skull. Whatever the intent, they left all of the remains at the site. Ferguson returned to pick them up. The group used the cash taken from Ault's pocket to buy food at Arby's and went back to work.

When the fair season ended, the circle broke along job lines. Pinnick returned to Shelbyville. The Lawrence brothers went to the Bahamas with a unit looking for winter work. Goodwin went to Florida and found a job in Hollywood.

Distance changed Goodwin's calculation. He no longer had the nightly presence of the group around him. Without the immediate pressure that comes from shared acts and shared language, he called home. On December 12, 1991, he told his father he had witnessed a torture killing in DeKalb County. His father went to the police. On December 13, officers found Ault's remains in the field, including the skull and hand fragments. On December 30, they arrested Goodwin at his home in Indianapolis and charged him with conspiracy to commit murder. That same day they arrested Pinnick in Shelbyville and charged him with murder. Pinnick confessed. He said he had made the first cut and the last, and he named the others. Goodwin at first said he had only witnessed the killing and would not go further. The names led to warrants for the Lawrence brothers. On January 10, 1992, Keith and David flew into Miami. Customs officers met them at the gate and took them into custody. They were returned to Indiana.

The motive the police settled on for Ault's death followed the earlier pattern. After Wright's killing, Ault knew enough to be a risk The initiation was a pretext for a silence they wanted to enforce. The men pleaded to a range of charges. Pinnick pleaded guilty to murder in Indiana and received sixty years. In Ohio, he pleaded guilty to the murder of Andrew Wright and received twenty-years-to-life. Keith pleaded guilty to conspiracy to commit murder and was sentenced to an indeterminate term of eight to thirty years, followed by twenty years of probation. David pleaded guilty to assisting a criminal and received eighty years. Goodwin pleaded guilty to assisting a criminal and to battery by means of a deadly weapon and received eighty years on each count, to be served concurrently.

In court, Goodwin addressed Ault's mother. He said he was ashamed. He said he did not really know her son but believed he was "good-hearted." She answered him. She said he should be ashamed. She asked what chance her son had now and told him she would not feel sorry for him. The exchange was brief and shaped by a fact that cannot be changed by words. Ault had been led into a building by people he wanted to call friends.

The years after the sentencing add coda rather than closure. Pinnick tried to appeal in 1995 and failed. Goodwin converted to Christianity in prison and told a reporter that Satanism was dangerous. He used Ault as an example of a person who "didn't make it," a formulation that puts the decision in the wrong place but the truth still stands: Ault did not make it because the group decided he would not. Keith's prison record included two college degrees and no major disciplinary problems. He was released in 2006 to begin his twenty-year probation. The county where he lived with his parents did not have an in-home detention program, so the conditions were eased to regular probation. In November that year, he pleaded guilty to public intoxication and received 180 days in jail. Two felony counts — criminal confinement and battery — were filed and then dismissed.

The final image worth holding is not the robes or the chant or the inverted cross cut into skin. It is the simple fact of movement. The group moved because the carnival moved. They used that to their advantage. They killed, ate a meal purchased with the victim's money, and went back to their posts. The people who welcomed families to the midway in the morning had spent part of the night in a field with a door and a knife and a body. The distance between those two facts is not large. It is a short drive and an early shift.

4

WEDNESDAY CALLS

Dorothy Jane Scott disappeared on May 28, 1980 after months of alarming phone calls from a man she did not know. Four years later, a construction worker uncovered her remains at Santa Ana Canyon Road. The calls, the disappearance from a hospital parking lot, the burned car, and the fragmentary recovery of her remains are the fixed points of a case that remains unsolved decades later. The record that survives is sparse and methodical: names, dates, distances, objects left behind. The gaps, including who placed the calls and who drove her car away from the hospital that night, have never been closed.

Dorothy was born on April 23, 1948, in Anaheim, California. In 1976 she gave birth to her son, Sean. She was a single mother; Sean's father, Dennis Terry, lived far away in Missouri and was not involved in day-to-day care. By 1980, Dorothy was thirty-two, Sean was four, and they lived with Dorothy's aunt, Shanti Scott, in Stanton, about twenty minutes from Anaheim, where Jacob and Vera still resided, her father and mother. Dorothy handled back-office duties for two adjoining businesses at 517 South Brookhurst Street — Swinger's Psych Shop and Custom John's Head Shop — co-owned in part by her father. The shops fit their era: rock music and posters, back-lit rooms, drug paraphernalia next door, the lingering color of 1960s and 1970s counterculture. Dorothy's role sat behind the scenes, keeping the operation organized.

Descriptions of her personality are consistent. Co-workers called her dependable and organized. Friends and family called her a devoted mother. She was a regular churchgoer, a quiet introvert. She did not drink, did not use drugs, did not date. Her routine centered on work and her child. Each day she dropped Sean at her parents' house, worked long hours, and returned to him at night.

In the first months of 1980, the routine was disrupted by anonymous calls to her home and workplace. The caller was a man. His voice was familiar enough that Dorothy told her mother and others she thought she knew it but was not able to name him. The content swung between declaration and threat. He said he loved her but also that he would kill her. He described how he would get her alone and dismember her so she could not be found. He said he was watching, then proved it by recounting what she had worn or done that day. On one occasion he told her to look outside; she found a dead rose on the windshield of her 1973 station wagon. The calls continued for months. One of the last calls unnerved her enough that she began karate lessons. She discussed buying a firearm with her mother and co-workers but before she can, she was abducted.

The day of her disappearance began with normal errands. On May 28, 1980, Dorothy dropped Sean at her parents' house and went to an employee meeting. During the meeting, co-worker Conrad Bostron appeared ill. He was sweating, unable to sit still, with an inflamed red rash on his arm. Seeing this, Dorothy insisted on taking him to the hospital and another co-worker, Pam Head, joined them. Dorothy drove her Toyota station wagon. First, they stopped at her parents' home so she could update them on the situation and check on Sean. She changed her scarf from a gray or black one to a red one, then continued on to University of California, Irvine Medical Center (UCI Medical Center).

The diagnosis justified the urgency. A black widow spider bite explained Conrad's symptoms and required monitoring. They remained at the hospital through the day and into the night, waiting. Dorothy and Pam stayed together in the lobby, reading and talking, leaving only for brief bathroom breaks. Around 11:00 p.m., Conrad was discharged. He was still unsteady, so Dorothy offered to bring the car around to the front entrance. Conrad and Pam went to the pharmacy to pick up his prescription. They expected to meet Dorothy at the curb within minutes.

When they reached the hospital entrance, Dorothy was not there. After roughly fifteen to twenty minutes of waiting, Pam and Conrad walked toward the lot where Dorothy had originally parked. Before they arrived, a car came fast toward them with its high beams on. The lights were bright enough to blind their eyes. The station wagon swerved, narrowly missing them, then turned out of the lot, switched off its headlights, turned right from the hospital, and disappeared. The two were left at the curb with no explanation. They considered that Dorothy might have had an emergency involving her son and needed to go home quickly before returning. They waited two hours but she did not come back. They called Jacob and Vera; the couple had not heard from their daughter. Pam decided to call the UCI police. The initial response reflected a standard posture toward missing adults: Dorothy was free to do whatever she wanted. However, the posture changed several hours later.

Between 4:30 and 5:00 a.m., authorities found Dorothy's station wagon in Santa Ana, about nine miles (fifteen kilometers) from the hospital, engulfed in flames in an alleyway. Dorothy was not inside the vehicle. Searches in the following days found no sign of her. The fire moved the case from uncertainty to suspicion, but there was still little to hold onto beyond a timeline and a burned car in a separate city.

The question of how the car got there acquired layers. There were mentions about another car leaving ahead of Dorothy's, turning the same way out of the hospital. Those mentions were not uniform. If true, the detail could suggest more than one person involved, one driving Dorothy's car and another leading or following, and a second vehicle available later to leave the scene where the Toyota was set on fire. If false, the possibilities narrow to a single driver who either disposed of the body first and then burned the car or set the fire and left on foot or via a waiting ride. No witnesses came forward to say they saw the car set alight, a person walking away, or suspicious activity in the alley. The interval between the hospital and the fire — four to five hours — left room for multiple scenarios and no firm answer.

The calls did not end with the disappearance. About a week later, Vera answered the house phone. The male caller asked whether she was related to Dorothy Scott. When she said yes, he said, "I've got her," and hung up. Police asked the family not to publicize the calls or the disappearance, to reduce false leads. After a week with no progress, Jacob spoke to the Santa Ana Register. The paper published a story and offered a $2,500 reward for information. On the day of publication, the paper's editor, Pat Riley, received a call from an anonymous male. The caller said, "I killed her. I killed Dorothy Scott. She was my love. I caught her cheating with another man. She denied having someone else. I killed her." He authenticated himself by referencing details that had not been released: that Dorothy had changed from a dark scarf to a red one, and that Conrad had suffered a spider bite and that Dorothy had taken him to UCI Medical Center. He also said Dorothy had called him from the hospital hours before her disappearance.

The claim that Dorothy phoned him did not align neatly with what Pam reported. She had been with Dorothy in the lobby all day and night except for brief bathroom breaks and said Dorothy had not made any calls. The point remains a gap. It is possible to imagine a call made in a restroom or during one of the short intervals when they were apart, but there are no phone records that settled the question either way.

Investigators contacted Dennis, Sean's father. Distance made him an unlikely suspect; he was over 3,500 miles (over 5,600 km) away in Missouri. Co-workers from the psych and head shops were questioned repeatedly and ruled out. Because Dorothy worked in the back office, it seemed unlikely a customer had fixated on her, though the possibility cannot be completely excluded on that basis alone. Sex offenders in the area were checked without result. Those in Dorothy's social circle described a woman without enemies and without an obvious person who disliked her enough to harm her.

Dorothy's parents and detectives turned to psychics. The case had little physical evidence and few leads. Months turned into years. The anony-mous male continued to call Vera almost every Wednesday afternoon. He used short phrases — "I've got her," "I killed her," "Where is Dorothy?" — a narrow set of statements that served only to remind the family of what they did not know. Police installed a recorder at the Scott residence. The voice was gruff and obviously disguised. No one recognized it. Efforts to trace the calls failed; he never stayed on the line long enough. The timing suggested he knew the family's routine and called when he expected Vera to be home. In April 1984, Jacob answered. The caller hung up. The calls stopped for a long period.

The break in the case came not from the phone or a confession but from a construction site. On August 6, 1984, a worker at Santa Ana Canyon Road uncovered the remains of a dog. Beneath that burial was a set of human remains: pelvis, arm, two thighs, and a skull. With the remains were a turquoise ring and a watch that had stopped at 12:30 a.m. on May 29, 1980, the night Dorothy disappeared. Vera recognized the ring as Dorothy's. Dental records confirmed the identification. An autopsy could not determine a cause of death due to decomposition and the partial nature of what was recovered. Shortly after the public announcement of the discovery, Jacob and Vera received one more call. The male voice asked, "Is Dorothy there?" There were no further answers in the years that followed.

The case remains cold. Jacob died in 1994. Vera died in 2002. There has been no official suspect named, and no arrest.

To this day, theories are still circulating. The first suspect is a man called Mike Butler. He was described as deeply religious, with alternative beliefs and possible involvement in cult-like activity. A frame that some see as consistent with the burial detail of a dog above Dorothy's remains, though the significance of that element is not established. He was an "army brat"; his mother was a New Zealand war bride, his father an Army captain. The family settled in Southern California after his father retired. He went to Fullerton Union High School and later California State University, majoring in English. He was athletic, voted MVP (Most Valuable Player) in cross-country. Drafted into the U.S. Army at age twenty, he served in Hohenfels, Germany, in 1967 after basic training. In Germany he wrote for Stars and Stripes News, an independent news organization that provides news and information to U.S. military communities around the world, and served as a public information and media officer, and photographer. After his service, he became a roadie for rock bands, including work with the Beach Boys and for his sister's band. His sister, an accomplished musician and singer, worked for a time at the Swinger's shop in Anaheim alongside Dorothy. Mike settled in Orange County and worked maintenance at a machine shop across the street from the shops where Dorothy and his sister worked. The proximity could explain a voice that sounded familiar to Dorothy without a clear name attached. It could also have given someone the opportunity to watch her routine. Mike Butler died on June 28, 2014 from health complications. If he was involved, his death would remove the possibility of any confession. The theory rests on proximity, a possible path to a familiar voice, and his background, which might align with elements around the burial.

A second theory compares the case to the Golden State Killer, also known as the East Area Rapist and linked to the Visalia Ransacker cases. The points of contact are the phone calls — pre-crime and, in at least one instance, a call a decade later — the stalking, and a focus on women in vulnerable domestic contexts. He moved to Southern California in 1979. Dorothy's case reads as personal in a way the Golden State Killer's pattern does not. The caller said he loved her and referred to a cheating accusation. Dorothy was taken from a hospital setting rather than attacked at home, which was the offender's usual pattern. The comparison highlights superficial similarities, but there are some clear divergences too.

The third theory is the most straightforward: a secret boyfriend or former boyfriend. This would fit the caller's claim of love, the "cheating" accusation, and the knowledge of Dorothy's day-to-day life. It would also explain a phone number and the ability to reach her parents' residence. The counter-points are also simple. People close to Dorothy said she did not date, worked long hours, and spent her evenings with Sean. She lived with her aunt. If she had been absent at night or asked her parents to take Sean more than usual, someone might have noticed. All that is known is what has been reported by the people around her; it cannot exclude a relationship that others did not see.

Across all the theories, the same fixed events define what can be said with certainty. Dorothy was harassed by a caller for months in early 1980. She took up self-defense classes and discussed buying a firearm. On May 28, 1980 she drove Conrad and Pam to UCI Medical Center, checked on her son in between, changed to a red scarf, and remained with Pam through the evening. At about 11:00 p.m. she left the lobby to retrieve her car. Within minutes her station wagon nearly struck her two co-workers under high beams, swerved, and drove off with the lights off, turning right out of the hospital. Hours later the car burned in Santa Ana. Calls to Vera and to the newspaper followed, including details that had not been public. For years, the same man phoned on Wednesdays and hung up when Jacob answered. In August 1984, Dorothy's remains were found beneath a dog burial at Santa Ana Canyon Road, with her turquoise ring and a watch stopped at 12:30 a.m. on May 29. The cause of death could not be determined.

The story does not end. It merely rests. The remains were identified. The parents died without resolution. Sean grew up with the public outline of events that surrounded his mother's disappearance. The person who called Vera on Wednesdays had a script that never varied much. Each sentence kept the family suspended in the moment after May 28, 1980. There is no closing legal paragraph to place here. There is only the record of what happened and the unanswered question of who dialed the phone and who drove away from the hospital entrance with the high beams pointed at two people waiting on the curb.

5

THE BUSANG MIRAGE

On December 13, 1993, a prospector in the jungles of Borneo said he had found what every mining investor hopes to hear: a strike big enough to change the map. The hills were volcanic, the theory familiar — gold often sits in and around ancient volcanic systems — and the core that went to the lab came back with grades that made sense to people who wanted to believe. The property was called Busang. The company tied to it was a small Canadian junior that traded like a thousand others until this set of results lifted it out of obscurity.

The person on the ground was Michael de Guzman, a Filipino geologist who had spent years in Indonesia without breaking into the upper tiers of major firms. The promoter who would carry the story to North American investors was David Walsh, a Western Canadian stock man who needed a property and a narrative. Between them stood John Felderhof, a risk-tolerant geologist of good reputation who had been associated with a real Indonesian mine. The roles were clear in practice: de Guzman controlled the site, the samples, and the day-to-day; Felderhof provided technical credibility; Walsh told the market what the labs seemed to be saying.

Junior mining shares are built on assays. Rock comes out of the ground, is split, crushed, and sent to a lab; a number comes back; analysts publish;

the stock moves. At Busang, the early numbers were strong. The company's market value climbed from the low single digits to levels juniors rarely reach. Each round of results appeared to extend the zone. Commentary from Bay Street and Wall Street amplified the effect: dispatches from Indonesia, comparisons to "elephant deposits," charts that made the hills and drill collars feel immediate. Money arrived. De Guzman cleared jungle, opened pads, and expanded drilling with better equipment. The more holes they reported, the more the equity rose. The logic was circular and, in that phase, effective.

Behind the numbers was a mechanism. De Guzman, knowing there was no gold in the rock, salted the samples. The method was simple and careful. Core pulled from the ground was supposed to be split in half, with one half archived on site for verification and the other half crushed and sent to labs. He brought crushed core into a locked shed and added fine gold to the pulp — initially from his wedding ring, later from small purchases of placer gold panned by locals in nearby rivers. He calculated how much to add to produce grades that looked plausible rather than spectacular, the kind of numbers that inspire confidence rather than suspicion. If a salted sample shows too much metal, geologists balk. If it looks right, the story holds.

Where an auditor expected to see half the core stored in tidy racks, de Guzman offered less than a tenth retained, with an explanation. He cited the "nugget effect," the genuine phenomenon in which coarse, unevenly distributed gold can produce erratic numbers from one split to the next, and argued that he needed to crush and assay all the material to get a proper average. To a visiting accountant, that rendered many cross-checks impossible. If half the core is gone, independent labs cannot re-assay against the original; if the only remaining material has been milled to dust, visual checks for coarse gold are meaningless. To address another potential tell, de Guzman's river-gold source was made to fit the story with a volcanic-pool theory: if the deposit had been remobilized by hydrothermal fluids, flake-like shapes could appear. The auditors accepted the framework. The company's website announced success. The stock lifted again.

As Busang 1 filled in, maps were redrawn to suggest scale. If gold was in a structure, perhaps it extended into the next. The company moved to "Busang 2," and when the drills there brought more strong lab numbers, Walsh sought listings beyond the junior Alberta exchange. NASDAQ and the Toronto Stock Exchange followed. Each regulatory milestone was framed as external validation: if the company could list there, then the company had cleared serious hurdles, and the core must be as good as reported. The stock approached $300 a share. The company's paper value touched roughly $6 billion. On paper, men who had struggled in their trades for years were rich. They sold some shares — enough to transform their circumstances, not so much as to abandon the narrative — and the market read that as insurance rather than a signal.

The Indonesian state, which had never been gentle with natural-resource concessions, made its own move. In August 1996, officials revoked Bre-X's exploration permit and opened the property to other firms. A fight among majors began, with Jakarta poised to pick its preferred partners and to keep a large share for the government. For a hoax that depended on a controlled worksite, this was the beginning of the end. Other geologists would drill their own holes within a few feet of de Guzman's collars. They would keep the chain of custody tight from rig to lab. They would cut, crush, and assay without letting local hands touch the pulp between steps.

Before that scrutiny arrived in full, there was an "accidental" fire. De Guzman's site records burned. In the narrative that followed, the loss of maps, logs, and residual samples helped obscure what had been done. The government imposed a new partnership. Freeport-McMoRan, an experienced operator in the region, took a controlling technical role. Bre-X's stake was cut to forty-five percent and the market punished the dilution. The company responded with a new, larger reserve estimate to offset the value erosion. Where analysts had been told to expect fifty plus million ounces, they were now told to expect 70 million. The stock, briefly rocked, found its footing. The shareholder meeting in Toronto in early 1997 had the look of a victory lap: the chief geologist delivering a slide deck, a promoter who could say he had kept the deal alive under pressure, and a room full of people whose brokerage statements supported the applause.

In Indonesia, Freeport's drills were spinning a few yards from the collars that had supposedly tapped the richest ore. Their samples contained no gold. The phone call that followed was direct: get back here and explain. Three years of releases, billions of dollars of paper value, and a series of almost cinematic milestones were about to meet a number that mattered, and that number was 0.

On the morning of the flight back to the site, de Guzman boarded a helicopter. It climbed over the rainforest. When the pilot looked into the rear, the seat was empty. De Guzman had gone out the door at 400 to 500 feet (about 120 to 160 meters). Three days later, the army announced that it had found his body, badly decomposed and partly scavenged by animals. The pilot had logged a GPS position; the delay made little sense to those who knew what that meant. The remains were not shown to his family. Then came the rumors: that he had been pushed, that he had staged the fall and vanished, that he was alive under another name. The official statement was suicide.

Freeport's twin holes kept returning nothing. Independent check drilling — tight security, strict custody — found no gold where Bre-X had claimed "pools" of it. The market's turn was swift. The "largest gold deposit in the world" could not survive side-by-side holes that showed barren rock. The stock that had been a vehicle for hope became, quickly, a zero. Investors who had put retirement money into a Canadian junior lost savings overnight.

In the aftermath, the principals scattered along predictable lines. Walsh, who had denied knowing about any fraud, moved to the Bahamas and died of a heart attack two years later. Felderhof maintained a comfortable life in the Cayman Islands, with the benefits of a jurisdiction that did not extradite Canadian white-collar defendants at the time. No one served a day in jail for the central act: selling salted assays as real. Bringing criminal charges would have meant proving intent — what executives knew and when. Each could claim, credibly to some, that they only relayed what the labs reported and that any wrongdoing lay with trusted subordinates. The one man who could have tied it all together — if he'd wanted — fell from a helicopter into the jungle.

The Bre-X collapse did change the plumbing of the market. Canadian regulators tightened technical disclosure standards in mining. The idea was to make it harder to repeat a con that depended on lax custody of core, thin archives, and third-party reports written off site with no direct verification. The appetite for a "company-making" deposit has never left the junior sector; neither has the dynamic in which a stock's rise is taken as proof that underlying facts must be sound. In Busang's case, the rise masked the absence of ore.

6

GLORIAVALE CHRISTIAN COMMUNITY

New Zealand's South Island is a landscape of almost unimaginable beauty, a place of glistening lakes and snow-capped mountains. Its scenery is so idyllic that it seems impossible for anything sinister to take root there. Yet, nestled in a valley on the island's remote west coast, a reclusive community lives entirely cut off from the modern world. This community is known as Gloriavale. What began decades ago as a small, enthusiastic group of devout Christians has, over the years, mutated into a secretive and disturbing cult, built around a twisted predator.

The Gloriavale Christian Community is currently home to about 600 men, women, and children. They live, work, and pray together, almost completely severed from outside society. Documentaries have offered a surface-level glimpse into their lives, showing children playing and families eating together. But even in these sanitized portrayals, the red flags are impossible to miss. The community practices arranged marriages. Everyone, including small children, is required to wear a uniform. Multiple families are forced to live together in cramped hostels. And at the center of it all is the leader, a man who wields ultimate authority over every life. The devotion he commands is absolute, with members stating they would lay down their lives for him.

This facade of pious harmony conceals a reality steeped in controversy and abuse. The people of Gloriavale are forced to live a lie, brainwashed into believing their twisted existence is the only path to heaven. From birth, they are taught that they are the chosen people and that if they ever leave, their souls are automatically damned to hell. It is a utopia custom-built for its founder, where people are treated like slaves, abuse is encouraged, and merely having an independent opinion risks severe punishment or exile. This is not a historical footnote; the group exists to this day, and as recently as July 2025, one of its leaders pleaded guilty to serious crimes.

The architect of this world was Neville Cooper. Born in 1926 in Queensland, Australia, he grew up under a strict father and a mean mother. After clashing with his father, who owned a fruit shop, he was kicked out at sixteen. A brief stint in the Air Force, compounded by his brother's death in the war, reportedly led to a mental health decline. Around age 21, while recovering at an aunt's house, Neville experienced a religious awakening. He claimed God told him his purpose was to preach the gospel as a minister.

He threw himself into the Bible, adopting extreme, hellfire-and-brimstone beliefs: any sin meant damnation, and women must be subservient to men. At his new church, he met Gloria Perry. He was twenty-one; she was fifteen or sixteen. Described as sweet and quiet, she was easy for him to control. They would go on to have sixteen children. At twenty-three, Neville started his own traveling ministry, "The Voice of Deliverance," preaching an energetic, charismatic message of piety or damnation from a large tent. He gained a following and a pilot's license, flying himself on missions. On Christmas Eve 1965, he survived a plane crash with three others, an event the media called a miracle. Neville believed it was a sign he was destined for more.

In 1967, he moved his family to New Zealand. He clashed with local church leaders, finding them insufficiently extreme and attempting to take over their congregations. In 1969, after a final falling out, he formed his own community with members who left to follow him, believing in his special connection to God. They became known as the "Cooperites." By the late 1970s, they settled at Springbank, on New Zealand's South Island, in a commune called the Christian Church at Springbank. From this point, Neville began to exert total control. His vision was a self-sustaining utopia, separated from the world. Followers had to sell all their possessions and give the money to the church.

He established a rigid hierarchy: he was the "Overseeing Shepherd," followed by "Shepherds," "Servants," and the general population, with women at the bottom. The community lived by a literal interpretation of the King James Bible. Individualism was forbidden. Members could not have their own opinions, choose their jobs, or marry who they loved. Neville ruled through fear and shame. The primary fear was eternal damnation. If any family member was deemed sinful, the entire family was publicly shamed, creating an environment where people would inform on their own relatives to stay in Neville's good graces.

Children were taught to fear the "evil" outside world. One former member recalled being told that as a child, she deserved to be "stoned with rocks constantly." They were taught that the more severe the sin, the hotter the flames. Lessons on the property included creationism, such as how dinosaurs fit on Noah's ark by Noah simply taking baby ones. No birthdays or holidays were celebrated.

The community was aggressively male-dominated. Women were taught to be completely subservient, existing only as a "help meet" for their husbands, who were their "head." Women wore a uniform of long skirts, high-necked, long-sleeved tops, and head coverings to show their subjugation. Pants, makeup, and jewelry were forbidden as vanity. Even when swimming, girls wore their dresses. The costume designer for *The Handmaid's Tale's* television adaptation later cited the cult as an inspiration. Neville's rationale was that men could not control themselves, so it was a woman's job not to tempt them. He had a particular fixation on elbows, which were never to be shown.

Life was run on a strict schedule of communal meals and assigned chores. Women would wake as early as 2:00 a.m. for cooking and cleaning, while children were forced into hard labor from as young as 5 years old. Any man who voiced dissent was forced into a "men's meeting," where leaders would berate him, sometimes for days, until he repented or was punished.

Marriages were arranged by Neville to manage "sexual urges." Wives were never allowed to refuse sex; upon marriage, they lost the right to say no. Consent was not a concept in the group. Neville believed girls were "considered a woman" as soon as they had their first period, around age twelve or thirteen, and that they were capable of being mothers then. One former member stated she was considered an adult at age 10. The only reason Neville made them wait until age sixteen was because of New Zealand's laws. These rules were codified in a cult-written book, *What We Believe*. When Neville implemented these rules, some original members left, but most remained, trapping their families in decades of abuse.

Neville was physically abusive to his own children, especially his sons, and likely his wife Gloria as well. He taught his followers to discipline their families the same way. Physical abuse was rampant, with most men beating their wives and children, a practice that was completely normalized. One former member described how being beaten by a violent father became the norm, and how he learned to take it without flinching or crying, turning his endurance into a source of pride. Teachers at the school would also beat children.

Alongside this, sexual abuse was pervasive. Neville sexualized everything, creating a bizarre contrast to the community's puritanical rules. Leaders and other men would openly grope girls serving meals, rubbing their bodies or untying their dresses as they passed, often in front of their own families. The girls, taught to never question a man and that they had no bodily autonomy, felt they had no choice but to let it happen. This behavior by the leaders signaled to other men that it was acceptable. The girls were made to feel it was their fault, as they had been taught men could not control themselves.

Neville's predation was methodical. He encouraged parents to have sex in front of their young children, as young as six or seven, to "educate" them. He held group "marriage counseling" where he would have couples lay out blankets and order them to have sex in front of each other, while he watched. He would invite newlywed couples to dinner, only to force the husband to lie next to Neville's wife, Gloria, and watch as Neville undressed and violated the new bride. He did this to his own son, Phil, and his wife, Sandy, who were terrified to refuse. This abuse caused severe issues within their marriage. This was not Phil's first experience; as a teenager, Phil had confided in Neville about pain in his testicles, and Neville had proceeded to assault his son under the pretense of an examination.

Another ritual involved a spa room on the property. Neville and other shepherds would get into the pool completely naked, put a pornographic movie on a projector, and then force teenage girls to strip down and get into the pool with them. This, he claimed, was part of their education, preparing them for marriage.

The arranged marriage process was a clinical ordeal. A man would request a wife, and the leaders would consult bloodline lists to avoid inbreeding, selecting a suitable girl. After "praying" on it, they would inform the man of God's "choice." Often, the couple did not even know each other. The man would then ask the woman for her hand, and she would go pray about it before returning with her "yes." This was just a formality, as the women had no real choice. After an engagement of about a month, a large wedding ceremony was held. After exchanging vows, the bride, now the man's property, had to sign a document effectively agreeing to be her husband's sex slave, waiving her right to ever refuse anything sexual. In the middle of the reception, the newly married couple would be led to a "honeymoon suite" to consummate the marriage immediately, sometimes with Neville present, before returning to the party.

Over the years, twelve of Neville's sixteen children managed to escape, but those who left were completely cut off from the members who remained. Inside the cult, women were expected to have as many babies as possible, as contraceptives were forbidden under any circumstances. Even if a doctor advised a woman not to have more children for life-threatening medical reasons, Neville would make the woman write a letter to her doctor rejecting the medical advice. When complications arose during childbirth, women were allowed to go to a hospital. But if the baby did not survive, the mother received no emotional support. She was expected to return to work immediately, with no time to grieve or recover. She was also made to believe the death was her fault, a punishment from God.

Former member Theo Pratt described how her mother, after delivering a stillborn son named Samuel at a hospital, was sent back to the commune with his body in a small box. While she was in bed, distraught, the leaders came to her room, not to offer sympathy, but to take Samuel's body. They refused to tell her where they were taking him. Stillborn babies were reportedly buried in a separate, overgrown, and forgotten part of the property. She was forced right back to work, expected to completely turn off her grief.

In the early 1990s, with the group expanding, Neville moved the cult to an even more isolated plot of land on the west coast, about an hour's drive from Greymouth. He had large hostels built, with several families forced to live together in very tight quarters. Just before the move, Neville's wife, Gloria, died of a brain tumor. He named the new commune the "Gloriavale Christian Community" in her honor. Neville himself remarried twice; his second wife, who was in her eighties, died shortly after, but his third wife, Ruth, was only seventeen years old when he was in his sixties. It was around this time that he had everyone change their names; he became "Hopeful Christian," while others adopted names like "Willing Disciple," "Steadfast Joy," and, for one baby girl, "Submissive."

Gloriavale is worth a lot of money. The cult owns several profitable businesses, including a massive dairy farm, an air service for short flights, and a deer processing business, which together bring in millions of dollars per year. The cult members, including children, operate all of these businesses, working upwards of 70 hours a week or more for zero pay. Neville built a community of worshippers who ran his profitable enterprises as slave labor. He claimed they were paid by receiving free rent, food, and healthcare, but if anyone left, they walked away with nothing.

Shortly after the move to Gloriavale, Neville's past caught up with him. A former member named Yvette Olsen, who had escaped the Springbank commune years earlier, courageously went to the police. She reported that in the early 1980s, when she was sixteen, she had developed a "secret friendship" with a fourteen-year-old boy named Tim. They ran away together but were tracked down and dragged back. Neville forced the teenagers to get married in a secret ceremony. For two years, he kept them separated and waged a campaign to destroy Yvette's self-worth, forcing her to call herself degrading names like "Harlot" and constantly beg for forgiveness.

After two years, Neville insisted they needed "marriage counseling" before they could live together, which he himself would conduct. During Yvette's private sessions, he subjected her to a bizarre and brutal assault for three days straight. He forced her to lie on a bed while he assaulted her with a long wooden object soaked in oil. He told her he had measured Tim's genitals to make sure the object was the right size. He threatened that if she tried to get up, he would ensure she and Tim could never be together. Yvette and Tim eventually escaped with their child. She decided to go to the police years later, after her niece confided that she had also been assaulted by a Gloriavale man.

Police raided Gloriavale in 1994, and Neville was arrested. He claimed he had simply given Yvette the object to use on herself as "therapy." Four other victims came forward, and Neville's own son, Phil, testified against his father about the sexual abuse he had endured. Neville was convicted of ten counts of indecent assault and sentenced to six years, but he appealed and was granted a new trial. This time, he was found guilty of only three charges and sentenced to five years, but he was released after serving less than two.

Because the followers were so cut off from the world, they had no idea what Neville was actually convicted of. The leaders fed them lies, pushing the narrative that Neville was being persecuted for spreading God's word. The leaders went to great lengths to maintain this ignorance, even going through old newspapers used to start fires and cutting out any articles they didn't want the followers to see. Neville continued to send orders from prison, and when he was released, he returned to Gloriavale as a hero who had suffered for his faith.

Tragedy continued to strike within the community. In June 2015, a fourteen-year-old girl named Prayer Ready, who had Down syndrome, died in one of the community's "isolation rooms." These rooms were used to quarantine the sick. Prayer was ill and had been sent to the room. Her dinner was delivered, but the food had not been cut into small pieces, which she required as she struggled to chew properly. Her mother, Sharon, was in the room but had her back turned and did not notice until

Prayer began to choke on a piece of meat. Sharon panicked. Another adult in the room tried to help but was unsuccessful. When they tried to get help, they found they were trapped; the door handles had been disabled. Eventually, someone climbed out of a window yelling for help. By the time help arrived, it was too late, and Prayer Ready was dead.

According to former members, it was common practice to disable the door handles, supposedly to prevent healthy children from wandering into the room. Concerns about this dangerous practice had been ignored in the past. An inquest ultimately ruled that the disabled handles played no part in Prayer's death because they had access to a window, a conclusion many disagreed with. The cult's leader, Hopeful Christian (Neville), later approached Prayer's grieving father, Clem. He told Clem that he could take comfort in the fact that now that Prayer was dead, she would not be sexually molested by anyone in the community. This comment deeply shook Clem.

In 2018, another death occurred under strange circumstances when Sincere Standtrue, a twenty-year-old man, was found unresponsive in the cult's paint shop where he worked. It is widely believed he died by suicide. Sincere's sister, Rose, has said he was treated horribly by the community. Sincere was deaf, and Neville would become angry when he couldn't hear orders. Other boys picked up on this and bullied Sincere, mocking him, calling him names, and locking him in bathroom stalls. He was also picked on by teachers. When he took his hearing aids out to stop the mockery, he got in more trouble for not being able to hear. He told his sister his boss had beaten him with a pipe, and there were reports he had been sexually abused as well.

Two months before his death, Sincere had been removed from his family's home and forced to live in the "men's room," a place seen as a disgrace, reserved for single men or those whose wives had escaped. Sincere had repeatedly asked the leaders to be assigned a wife but was always denied because he had not been allowed to sign the community's "commitment." v In a cult where a person's entire value was based on having a family, this denial would have been devastating, making him feel worthless. Rose now believes her brother, who was smart but struggled to verbalize, may have had autism. Instead of being supported, he was ostracized, isolated, and bullied. An inquest into his death, concluded in March 2025, ruled it accidental, likely caused by a "blacking out game" popular in the cult, a ruling his sister disputes.

Prayer Ready's sister, Connie, escaped the cult after her sister's death. In 2018, she went to the police with allegations of child abuse against her father, Clem. She stated he would severely beat all his children, including Prayer, sometimes for no reason. Clem later blamed his actions on the cult's culture, which encouraged violent discipline, and the exhaustion from working seventy-hour weeks. He pleaded guilty, received supervision, and was ordered to pay damages and attend counseling. This conviction was a turning point for Clem. He began to reassess the cult's teachings on violence and its sexual attitudes toward his wife and daughters. When he started asking questions, the leaders kicked him out. He and his wife, Sharon, unable to leave their children, grandchildren, and Prayer's grave, became "uninvited guests," living in an old building on the edge of the property.

The legal troubles mounted. After multiple investigations into forced labor were dismissed with the ruling that the members were "volunteers," former members brought multi-million dollar lawsuits in 2022 and 2023. The church argued the members signed the commitment of their own free will. The women argued they were born into the cult and conditioned since birth, groomed to be cheap labor and to provide unlimited sex. This time, the court agreed with the former members, ruling they were employees, not volunteers, a major victory that exposed decades of forced child labor.

Neville Cooper died of cancer in 2018 at the age of ninety-two. His son Phil remarked that his father would have to answer to God for the lives he destroyed and would likely go to hell. The cult, however, has endured, and the allegations of abuse have continued. In 2022, Joseph Hope was imprisoned for assaulting a girl under twelve, sometimes while his wife and children were in the same room. That same year, Timothy Disciple pleaded guilty to assaulting a twelve-year-old girl and two other young victims. Fervent Ben-Kenan was sentenced for abusing young girls in their beds at night between 2004 and 2018. Jonathan Benjamin was sentenced in 2024 to nearly twelve years in prison for abusing multiple children, one as young as five, between 1986 and 2017. When leaders found out about abuse, the offender was merely made to repent and apologize publicly.

The leaders, of course, were often offenders themselves. Howard Temple, an eighty-five-year-old former U.S. Navy engineer, took over as Overseeing Shepherd after Neville's death. In July 2025, Temple pleaded guilty to multiple charges of indecent assault against women and children. He also admitted that the community had a policy preventing members from reporting crimes to outside authorities. A new leader, forty-eight-year-old Steven Stanfast, has since taken over, claiming he is bringing real change.

Police investigations are reportedly ongoing. As of 2024, police have identified more than 138 victims of physical and sexual abuse and over 400 crimes, with many men charged or under investigation. This is not the full picture, as many are still too scared or brainwashed to come forward. Before his death, Neville had also established sister communes in India. Five girls from Gloriavale were sent to India to marry men in the new sect, populate the commune, and serve as manual labor, a situation that has prompted human trafficking concerns. A leader of the Indian sect, Faithful Stronghold, made a disturbing admission that Indian men are very forceful and that it is part of the culture to force themselves on women.

Despite the decades of abuse, people have been fleeing. The Gloriavale Leavers Support Trust was started in 2019 to help escapees, providing housing, financial aid, and emotional support. Former members, including Rosanna Overcomer and Pearl Valor, have been central to these efforts and the lawsuits. These women, once forced into uniforms and subjugation, are now seen wearing clothes they choose, looking confident and happy. Over the years, at least 300 people have left Gloriavale. But as of 2024, about 600 people remain, more than half of them children, and they are not safe.

7

NANJING UNIVERSITY MURDER

January 19, 1996 carried the kind of cold that tightens the jaw and shortens a person's stride. In Nanjing, a sanitation worker was still out on the pavements when most of the city stayed indoors. He worked a routine — keep the walkways clear, pull stray trash before it iced over — until a handbag near Hao Road in Xinjiekou pulled him off that route. It felt abandoned. When he opened it, he saw neat slices of cooked meat. The color and finish suggested pork. He took it home. Under a tap, piece by piece, he rinsed away grit. His hand closed on something rigid and unfamiliar. He pulled it free and saw a human finger. Two more lay among the meat. He stopped, called the police, and handed over the bag he had meant to turn into a stew.

Officers began with skepticism and then saw the same thing he had seen. No prank produced three human fingers. No ordinary household would discard so much prepared meat. The bag went straight to the station. Hours later, the examination result was plain: human remains.

Police widened their search. Around Nanjing University they found more, at the stadium, near the gate, outside a hospital, and along nearby roads. Each package had the same logic: plastic wrap; meat cut small; the look of cooked pork overlaying something else. Ten days later, clothing surfaced that investigators believed belonged to the victim. With mid-

1990s forensic tools, DNA was not practical in the way it is now, so they moved by accumulation. Muscle and hair provided limited markers, and clothing provided another set. The conclusion they reached was categorical: the victim was female. A name followed after outreach to families of missing persons and after a small mole on the right cheek helped confirm identity. The woman was Dao A-qing.

By the end of the initial sweep, the count of recovered fragments exceeded 2000. They were wrapped in plastic, distributed across multiple locations with a center of gravity near the university. The cuts were precise. The neck's dissection line was especially clean. Investigators concluded this was not amateur work. A butcher's hand, or a surgeon's, or at least someone with practiced familiarity with anatomy and a steady tolerance for the task.

One detail shaped both the investigation and the rumors that followed. Portions of the body had been cooked not once but over several days. That made time-of-death analysis less precise. It rendered the face unrecognizable. It destroyed some of the trace signatures investigators rely upon. And another fact pushed the case into a separate category of violence: the heart, liver, and spleen were missing.

Dao was born in March 1976 in Shanggao, Changyan District, Taizhou City, Jiangsu Province. She was the younger of two sisters. Her family's resources were limited. Winters required sharing a coat, and new clothes felt out of reach. Her older sister, Dao Ai-hua, left school to work so the younger sister could stay in class. Dao wanted to help as well but was told to study instead. In October 1995 she enrolled at Nanjing University's School of Adult Education, majoring in computer applications in the Department of Information Management. Her family could not send devices or extras. They kept losses and funerals to themselves so she could concentrate. Friends described her as introverted, orderly, and not given to display. She wore a small rotation of neat clothes, studied hard, and kept a narrow social circle for company when she needed it.

In early January 1996 she returned to her hometown for dinner with classmates, then came back to Nanjing the next day. On January 10, at about five p.m., classmates saw her leave the Gulou campus. In the hours before she walked out, a dormitory issue had flared: her roommate had used an induction cooker, a violation of rules. Dorm staff levied a fine and told Dao to pay half because the device had been used in her room. She objected but the staff did not yield. After that exchange, she left the building wearing a red coat with a black lining. It was exam week and her habit was to seal herself into study when pressure rose. Her bed was made before she left. Friends thought she might be taking a short break and would be back but she did not come back at all.

Her absence was reported to the dorm administration, which chose not to inform her family immediately. They limited the information to staff and a few students. Nine days later, the bag was found.

The first hours and days after identification built an investigative frame. The skill implied by the cuts suggested a person familiar with animals or bodies. The cooking suggested time in a place with a stove. The distribution suggested either an attempt to scatter attention or simply a practical means of disposal. Police considered the simplest profile that fit those elements. One internal outline, later described publicly, focused on a single, physically fit middle-aged man living alone with access to a kitchen. Officers searched the dorms and the perimeter that supported the campus, looking for someone who matched. Nothing came out of it.

A special task force set up inside the university worked for three months. The mid-1990s relied on paper ledgers and footwork. Public surveillance networks were rare. Buildings with cameras were the exception. The bags, the plastic wrap, and the handbag used to move the meat was ordinary. Even the printed bed sheet that later appeared in a police notice was ordinary enough that it did not single out a buyer. Officers canvassed students, staff, and teachers. They took statements, asked each student to account for the night Dao disappeared, then for the nights when bags were found. They sent notices to neighborhoods and to families of the missing, and asked for tips. Rumors ran in the space that evidence could not fill. The task force wound down when repeated passes over the same ground produced nothing new.

When a case resists resolution, theories multiply. Some began with the facts and widened their circle. Cooking, scattering, and removal of organs suggested an effort to erase traces and complicate identification. Others took the missing organs as a starting point and reached for broader systems. A widely repeated line of thought linked the case to the organ trade. A later paper by Xue Wang, cited in online discussions, described how executed prisoners had been a primary source of transplant organs since 1983 and how that system was officially abolished in 2015, leaving an even tighter supply. That pattern, plus the details of this case, made a fit that many found persuasive. No direct evidence supported the link. The theory persisted because it was comprehensive: it explained the missing organs, the skill, and the lack of a local suspect. Another group of discussions turned to cannibalism. That framing had a shock value that kept it alive in stories even when it made less sense of the logistics. If someone intended to eat, why leave so much behind? Scattering created witnesses. Silence would have been the easier path.

In the first months of the case, police released what they thought might prompt recognition: the kind of plastic bags, the model of handbag, the pattern on a bed sheet. They asked the public to look closely. Nothing returned that could be acted upon. Years later, the case took on a second life online. On March 21, 2007, a user named Shiliu Cha posted a detailed account. On May 28, 2008, anonymous users opened a "Dao A-qing bar" to collect what could be collected — press clippings, photos, routes, guesses. On June 19, a user with the name "Hey Misa" posted an analysis called "A Little Thought on the Nanjing Corpse Dismemberment Case," arguing that the killer likely knew Dao and might have been in love with her. The post spread widely and drew attention because it was organized and confident where most commentary was not. Some readers thought the author knew more than he claimed.

On June 24, 2008, Nanjing's Modern Express wrote about the online traffic. The police took interest. Shortly afterward, the "Hey Misa" posts disappeared. That absence provoked the usual conclusions. Later reporting said "Hey Misa" was a twenty-six-year-old male law student whose father had been a police officer, that he had agreed to cooperate if asked, and that his posts were largely speculation rather than evidence. Police asked the forum to remove the content; moderators complied. No arrest followed from those threads.

On July 4, 2008, a netizen using the name "Dao Hong Shuan" traveled at his own expense from Shandong to Nanjing and to Jiangyan, where he sought out Dao's parents. Her father received him. Her brother-in-law was wary and contacted the Jiangyan Public Security Bureau, which brought the visitor in for questioning. On July 13, after tips from other users, the same man wrote on his blog that a novelist, Wang Dain, whose 1998 book Jinyan Wu (The Memorial) had appeared two years after the killing, might be linked to the crime. The author publicly denied the claim, called it imaginative extrapolation built on rumors that had already been proven thin, and moved on. No formal action followed.

On January 19, 2016, a local WeChat account marked the date for a reason that had nothing to do with weather. Twenty years had passed since the remains were first recovered, the period that some read as the outer limit for prosecution. The message was stark: if the law's clock ran out, a confession would carry no legal consequence. The reaction was swift. The next afternoon, the Criminal Investigation Bureau of the Ministry of Public Security posted on Weibo that the case would continue to be investigated without an expiration date, and that it would be pursued to the end. Legal scholars argued over how statutes should apply in a case like this and how exceptions could be structured. The public message simplified the point. The work would continue.

In May 2022, a post on Weibo claimed the case was solved and tied that claim to an arrest in the separate Hulan police murder case. The link traveled quickly. It fit a pattern of hope and resolution that these cases attract. On May 30, the pattern collapsed. Dao's family, Nanjing police, and the Cyberspace Administration all said the rumor was false and that the case remained unsolved. The original poster was banned for spreading misinformation.

Nanjing University refunded Dao's tuition to her family. In March 2021, twenty-five years after the killing, Dao's sister filed a lawsuit in the Gulou District People's Court seeking 1.62 million yen in compensation, arguing that the university had failed to protect Dao, particularly after punishing her on January 10 and allowing her to leave alone, and pointing to the distribution of remains around campus as evidence that safety had not been adequately managed. A week later she withdrew the suit. No reason was made public. Dao's father visited the university four times over the years seeking updates, the last visit reported as either 2010 or 2022 depending on the source. During that visit, he requested assistance and received 10,000 yen after signing a letter promising not to seek further compensation connected to the case.

What the record cannot yet hold is a name. The suspect profiles have not matched a person the police could arrest and charge. The online energy has not delivered a lead the police could rely upon. The family's invitation to a hypothetical murderer — come forward, we will forgive — has not changed the silence. For those who study violent crime, this is a familiar shape: a limited set of physical facts, a narrowed set of possible motives, and a wide, durable field of interpretation that grows each time the date rolls around. At this point, even one person's choice to speak, or on a small, neglected detail found by someone patient enough to look again can bring so much to the light.

Yet, until that happens, the case remains what it has been for almost 30 years: a set of dates and places, a family that holds a name close, a university that still sits at the center of the map, and a winter story that began when a man on a late shift bent down to pick up a bag.

8

THE ORDER OF THE LION

In the pre-dawn darkness of May 21, 1990, a phone call shattered the quiet of Salida, California. At approximately 2:00 a.m., police were dispatched to a home on the corner of Mason and Elm Street, responding to a report of multiple murders. When officers arrived, they were confronted with a scene of incomprehensible brutality. They found the bodies of four victims: three men and one woman, later identified as thirty-five-year-old Dennis Colwell, twenty-five-year-old Richard Ritchie, fifty-one-year-old Franklin Raper, and twenty-three-year-old Darlene Paris. Raper, they would soon learn, was the owner of the home.

Amid the carnage, police located one survivor, a woman named Donna Alvarez. She was found in a state of profound shock, a blanket over her head, as if to block out the reality of what she had witnessed. As the attack began, Alvarez had managed to escape the main living area and ran into the garage. She burrowed under a pile of dirty clothes, remaining perfectly still until the sounds of violence subsided. When she believed the attackers were gone, she pried open the garage door, slipped out, and ran to a neighbor's house to call for help.

Donna told the officers she had been staying at Franklin Raper's home, a courtesy he often extended to those with nowhere else to go. She had been introduced to Raper by one of the other victims, Richard Ritchie. Her account of the attack was chaotic and terrifying. She said a group of people, all wearing camouflage, had burst into the house simultaneously through doors and windows, immediately assaulting everyone inside. She noted one man in particular, a white male in his mid-twenties, about six feet tall (about 182 centimeters), who was not wearing a mask and was holding a silver gun. His most distinct feature, she told them, was his afro-like hair.

This specific description stood out to the officers on the scene. While surveying the area, a detective noticed a local lingering nearby. The detective approached him and asked if he knew anyone who matched that description. He identified the person as "Jason," a man who lived at a place known locally as "the Camp."

The Camp, detectives learned, was an old labor camp now occupied by people living in campers and trailers. Neighbors of the Camp filled in more details. They told police the people living there were involved in some kind of weird military group and had a reputation for intimidating the people who lived there. The neighbors provided names: Gerald Cruz, David Beck, Ricky Vieira, and the man Donna had described, Jason LaMarsh.

The most critical piece of information came when the neighbors told police that one of the victims, Franklin Raper, had recently lived at the Camp himself. He had left after a major falling out with the other men and moved to the house on Elm Street. Suddenly, the investigation had a direct link between the victims and a secretive, militaristic group. Before heading to the Camp, detectives ran Jason LaMarsh's name through their system. He had a prior record, which meant they had a photo. They presented a lineup to Donna Alvarez, who immediately identified Jason LaMarsh as the unmasked attacker.

Armed with a positive identification, detectives drove to the Camp. No one was there, but the property itself offered immediate clues. They saw a small studio house toward the back of the property and, hanging on a clothesline, freshly washed camouflage clothing that matched Donna's description. As the officers were preparing to leave, a car pulled up. The driver, Gerald Cruz, got out and was met by the detectives. Cruz was perfectly calm, telling police he knew nothing about any murders. Before leaving to secure a search warrant, they asked him to confirm the names of the other residents. He listed David Beck, Jason LaMarsh, and Ricky Vieira.

With the warrant in hand, police returned and began a methodical search of the property. What they found inside the small house belonging to Gerald Cruz and his wife, Jennifer, began to paint a disturbing picture of the man who lived there. They discovered bomb-making materials, military manuals, and satanic literature, including *The Satanic Bible*. They also found a copy of *The Big Book of Secret Hiding Places*, a guide for concealing contraband. And then they found two items that provided a chilling glimpse into the group's internal dynamics: a strange wooden wheel divided into sections, each bearing a different form of punishment, and a collection of journals.

These journals, police realized, were the key. They contained disturbing entries that detailed the life of the group at the Camp, confirming the suspicions of the investigators. This was not just a military group; it was a cult, and Gerald Cruz was its leader.

Gerald Dean Cruz was born Gerald Dean Cox in Modesto, California, around March of 1962. His entire life was shrouded in confusion about his parentage. He was raised believing his mother was a woman named Hortencia Cruz and his father was Ascencio Cruz. Ascencio, however, had returned to Mexico before Gerald was born, unaware Hortencia was pregnant. In his absence, Hortencia listed a friend, Lawrence Cox, on the birth certificate. When Ascencio returned to Modesto two years later, he was shocked to learn he had a son.

Gerald grew up with the surname Cruz, but when he entered school, he was called Gerald Cox. This was how he learned of the discrepancy on his birth certificate, fueling a lifelong confusion. The truth was elusive; family members who testified at his trial years later gave conflicting accounts of his childhood. One half-sister, Marlene, claimed that Hortencia was not his mother at all. She testified that Gerald's real mother was Hope, another woman believed to be his older half-sister, and that his father was, in fact, Lawrence Cox.

According to Marlene, who was fourteen when Gerald was born, his childhood was one of severe abuse. She described Hortencia as a violent woman who was cruel to animals and children alike. Marlene and Hope, who apparently fought over whose responsibility it was to care for Gerald, would allegedly beat him with switches, ropes, electrical cords, umbrellas, and hangers.

This trauma at home was mirrored by torment at school. Gerald was bullied relentlessly for his clothes and his hair, and for the fact that he did not know who his real father was. This search for identity became a defining struggle. Experts who later studied him suggested that this void drove him to invent an identity for himself. He began to believe he was special, that he possessed special powers and abilities. These delusions, born from a childhood of abuse and confusion, morphed as he grew older, emerging in a sadistic desire for control.

Gerald's beliefs were eclectic and ever-changing, a hallmark of what psychologists would later call a "cult of personality." The group's doctrine was not fixed; it was simply whatever Gerald willed it to be. One moment he was focused on white supremacy and the idea of a "master race," the next he was immersed in black magic, the occult, and satanism. The only constant was his own authority. Having failed to succeed in mainstream society, he had withdrawn and, as one psychologist noted, "collected around himself a band of people almost like a Neanderthal clan."

He preyed on the vulnerable: the homeless, the lost, those disconnected from their families. He offered them a place to stay, the promise of a family, and a sense of belonging. For a short time, life for a new member would be good. But once Gerald sensed their complete psychological and physical dependence, his true nature would emerge.

By his early twenties, Gerald was living in a home in Modesto when he met Ricky Vieira. Ricky, likely fifteen or sixteen at the time, was a perfect target. He came from a terrible home life, abused by his father and neglected by his mother. He was desperate for an escape, and Gerald swooped in, offering him a home, a "family," and a new path. Ricky moved into Gerald's home, and for a little while, he felt he finally belonged.

Around the same time, in the mid-1980s, two of Gerald's childhood friends re-entered his life and became core members of the group. David Beck, who had known Gerald for years, had drifted away, gotten married, found success in his career, and become a devoutly religious man. But after a difficult divorce, Beck was lost. He reconnected with Gerald and soon became his second-in-command. Beck's family would later say he became a different person, changing from a happy, bubbly man into a withdrawn, zombie-like figure. Another old friend, Ron Willey, also reconnected with Gerald and Beck, getting drawn into the periphery of the emerging cult.

Another early recruit, Stephen Perkins, moved in around the same time as Ricky Vieira. With his inner circle formed, Gerald began to formalize his control. He gave the men journals — the same ones police would later find — and instructed them to write in them constantly. They were to detail their deepest fears, insecurities, and thoughts. Gerald would read their entries and use their vulnerabilities against them. He kept his own journal, in which he made the men cut their hands and leave a bloody fingerprint as a binding contract of their devotion.

He initiated weekly ceremonies where the men would dress in white robes resembling Ku Klux Klan (KKK) attire, light candles, chant, and speak in gibberish. The group's ideology was a chaotic mix of religion, military structure, and the occult. Almost immediately, the psychological control escalated to physical abuse. Gerald would make Ricky and Stephen stand perfectly still in a room while he punched them in the stomach as hard as he could. On at least one occasion, he struck Stephen Perkins with such force that the man required hospitalization. He also used a scorpion stun gun on them for his own amusement.

David Beck, his right-hand man, was the only one exempt from the abuse; in fact, he often participated in it. Together, Gerald and Beck would inflict a torture they called the "Orange Line Treatment." They would cut an orange extension cord, attach the severed end to a man's foot with duct tape, and plug the cord into an outlet wired to a light switch. Gerald would then flip the switch, sending electrical shocks through the man's body while he and Beck laughed. This "treatment" was inflicted on

Stephen Perkins so severely that his foot turned black and became badly infected.

In 1987, the twenty-five-year-old Gerald began dating sixteen-year-old Jennifer Starn. She soon moved into the Modesto home with Gerald, Stephen, and Ricky. Gerald made no effort to hide the abuse from her; he beat the men openly in front of her, and soon, he began abusing her as well. When she angered him, he would put a gun in her mouth. Jennifer quickly became pregnant twice, and the presence of two infants in the home did nothing to curb Gerald's violence. When she was two months pregnant with one of the children, he pushed her to the ground and repeatedly kicked her in the stomach, causing her to bleed. She fled barefoot to a women's shelter but stayed only four days before Gerald found her and convinced her to return.

His cruelty extended to his own children. Court documents detail the systematic abuse of his infant daughter, referred to as "Baby A." As a form of punishment, Gerald would place the six-month-old in a dark room by herself, permitting Jennifer to enter only every six hours, but not to hold or console the child. When Baby A made him angry, he would strike her on the legs with a fly swatter or a ruler. He built a contraption he called "the rack," from which he would suspend the baby in a harness. He would then attach mason jars full of water to her legs and intentionally make her cry, causing her to instinctively kick against the weights. He would also slap her hard on the side of the head, an act he called "a clapping," sometimes hitting her with enough force to cause bruising inside her ears. When she was learning to walk, he would ask her if she "wanted a clapping," and the terrified child would immediately drop to the ground and hide her head. Other members of the group participated. On one occasion, Gerald, Beck, and Vieira placed a tape recorder next to Baby A's crib, waited for her to drift off to sleep, and then screamed as loud as they could to startle her. They recorded her hysterical crying which Jennifer later played in court.

In late 1989, Gerald, Jennifer, and their children moved to the Camp, setting up in the small house on the property. Ricky Vieira came with them, moving into an adjacent trailer. Stephen Perkins, however, did not. The seventeen months he had spent with Gerald had destroyed him.

When he returned to his parents' home, he was a different person. He had lost 125 pounds (about fifty-six kilograms) and was moody and withdrawn, refusing to speak to anyone. His foot was severely infected from the Orange Line Treatments, and he had broken bones from the beatings. Gerald had warned him to tell no one, instructing him to claim he'd been in a motorcycle accident. Stephen developed severe claustrophobia and mental lapses, forgetting the day of the week. He became suicidal and eventually admitted himself to a psychiatric hospital.

With Stephen gone, Ricky Vieira became the primary target of Gerald's sadism. Gerald began using the "Will of Punishment," the wooden wheel police found during the search. He would force a member to throw the wheel in the air and catch it; whatever punishment their thumb landed on was their fate. Punishments included eating off the floor, solitary confinement, and severe beatings. The abuse also escalated to sexual assault, with Gerald forcing the men to sodomize each other in front of the group.

Soon after the move to the Camp, Jason LaMarsh and Franklin Raper arrived. Jason, who had only known the group for a few months before the murders, quickly fell in with them. Franklin Raper, however, was an outcast. No one in the group liked him. The conflict began when LaMarsh, who was sharing a trailer with Raper, woke up to find his pants pocket cut and his gun missing. He immediately blamed Raper, and from that day on, he hated him, complaining about him constantly to Gerald.

Gerald claimed he disliked Raper for being a drug user who left needles lying around. The men fought constantly, until Gerald finally told Raper to move his trailer off the property. When Raper refused, Gerald waited for him to leave, hooked the trailer to a car, and towed it off the property. He and his followers then filled Raper's car with his belongings, pushed it across the street, and set it on fire.

This act forced Franklin Raper to relocate. He moved into the house on Elm Street, a property that was already connected to the cult. The house belonged to Tanya, the sister of Jason LaMarsh's girlfriend, Michelle Evans. Even though Gerald had gotten his wish and Raper was gone, it wasn't enough. He decided that Franklin Raper needed to die.

The morning before the murders, Michelle Evans needed to retrieve some furniture from the Elm Street house. She asked Gerald, Jason, and the others to help her, knowing Franklin Raper would be there. A fight quickly broke out between LaMarsh and Raper. The group left after only forty-five minutes and returned to the Camp, but the confrontation had solidified Gerald's resolve.

That night, Gerald gathered his followers (David Beck, Ricky Vieira, Jason LaMarsh, and Ron Willey) in LaMarsh's trailer. Michelle Evans was also present. Gerald told them they were going to the house on Elm Street to kill Franklin Raper. His orders were explicit: they were to kill everyone there, leaving no witnesses. He knew Raper often let people stay with him, and he was prepared for collateral damage.

Michelle Evans's job was to draw a blueprint of the house, marking all doors and windows. She was also instructed to go in first, to gather everyone in the living room to make the attack easier. Gerald also had her call her sister, Tanya, and tell her not to go home that night.

On the night of May 20, 1990, the group held a barbecue at the Camp, doing drugs, listening to heavy metal music, and swinging bats and batons to "pump themselves up." Just after midnight, on May 21, Gerald Cruz, Jason LaMarsh, Ricky Vieira, David Beck, and Ron Willey piled into a car and headed for Franklin's house. They were armed with knives, batons, and bats. All wore camouflage clothing and masks, except for Jason LaMarsh and Michelle Evans. LaMarsh also carried his gun.

The cult members parked down the street. Michelle Evans and Jason LaMarsh got out and approached the house. Michelle went in first, likely without raising suspicion, and unlocked a window. Donna Alvarez was asleep in a bedroom when Michelle woke her, telling her she needed to get up because Tanya needed the room. Donna gathered her things and walked into the living room, where Raper was sitting in a chair. As she and Richard Ritchie headed toward another bedroom, Beck and Vieira burst in through the unlocked window, followed immediately by the rest of the men.

As the attack began, Michelle Evans walked out the front door, returned to the car, and waited. As she left, she could hear Darlene Paris screaming and pleading for her life. Amid the chaos, Donna Alvarez slipped away unnoticed and hid in the garage.

Jason LaMarsh went straight for Franklin Raper, beating him with a baton as he sat in his chair. Raper tried to shield himself with his arms, but LaMarsh struck him with such force that it broke his arm. He beat Raper relentlessly until his face was unrecognizable, then pulled out a knife and slit his throat.

While this was happening, Gerald and the other men were attacking Dennis Colwell and Richard Ritchie. Darlene Paris, watching the horror unfold, was screaming. Annoyed, Gerald looked at Ricky Vieira and ordered, "Shut her up." Vieira grabbed Darlene by the hair, pulled her head back, and began cutting at her throat. He didn't stop until he felt the blade hit bone.

One of the victims, Richard Ritchie, managed to escape the house and staggered onto the front lawn. Gerald Cruz and Ron Willey chased him down, beat him brutally, and cut his throat in full view of neighbors who were watching in shock from their homes.

When the police investigation led them back to the Camp, the arrests began. Gerald and Jennifer were taken into custody for the bomb-making materials. David Beck and Ricky Vieira were quickly located. Detectives sensed Vieira was the weak link. As a technician was hooking him up for a polygraph test, Ricky broke. "Okay," he said, "I guess I should probably tell you that I killed Darlene Paris." Jason LaMarsh had already fled the state but was arrested a week later in an Oregon motel after a friend he was traveling with, to whom he had confessed, called the police.

At trial, the full, horrific details of the murders were laid bare. The autopsies confirmed the brutality of the attack. Dennis Colwell had a skull fracture and multiple stab wounds, and his throat was cut. Franklin Raper's head was so badly beaten that his skull was fragmented, and his throat was also cut. Richard Ritchie had been stabbed in the neck, back, abdomen, liver, and heart. Darlene Paris had been beaten and stabbed, but her cause of death was the wound to her throat, which was so deep it cut down to her spine, nearly decapitating her. Her mother later said she was forced to bury her daughter in a turtleneck.

Gerald Cruz, David Beck, and Ricky Vieira were all convicted of first-degree murder and sentenced to death. They remain on death row. Jason LaMarsh was convicted of second-degree murder and sentenced to sixty-four years to life. Ron Willey's outcome was not specified in the reports. Michelle Evans, for her part in drawing the blueprint and setting the stage for the massacre, took a plea deal. In exchange for her testimony, she was found guilty of being an accessory and served only six months in prison.

Ricky Vieira continues to appeal his conviction, arguing that he was completely brainwashed by Gerald Cruz and participated only because he feared for his life. For the victims, justice was partial and complicated. Franklin Raper was a grandfather. Dennis Colwell, Richard Ritchie, and Darlene Paris were guilty of nothing more than being in the wrong place at the wrong time, their lives ended in an eruption of violence orchestrated by one man's sadistic need for absolute control.

9

ÇIFTLIK BANK SCAM

Imagine a young man born in 1991, raised in a country where graduation from top schools is supposed to be the ticket into a decent life but isn't. His peers spend years at İTÜ (İstanbul Teknik Üniversitesi), METU (Middle East Technical University), Boğaziçi — engineering, business, social sciences — only to discover that the jobs waiting for them often come with managers who can't form a clean sentence and pay offers barely above the minimum. The cycle is familiar and dispiriting. Into that landscape steps a boyish face with a grin that reads as confidence to some and condescension to others. He would, in time, be listed by Interpol. He would be called a prodigy by a few and a con man by many more.

The man's name is Mehmet Aydın. The enterprise he gave to the public imagination was Çiftlik Bank. What follows is the shape of that story as it was told to his audience and as participants later told it back — dates, names, amounts, and the reasons people offered for why they trusted him.

Aydın's family traces back to Giresun; they moved to Bursa, where he attended an imam-hatip high school (a religion focused high school) and left before completing it. He washed dishes in a café for minimum wage. On the side he tested small online hustles, including selling bet slips through a website. He loved rap, posted tracks under stage names — "Eren Çakar," "egomen" — and taught himself enough software to tinker.

None of that made him rich, but it gave him two ingredients he would use later: a feel for how to set up a website people can pay into, and a knack for telling an audience what it wants to hear.

By mid-2016 he had the framework of an idea: take the familiar pleasure loop of a farm game and couple it to real money. He could sketch the logic but not build the whole thing alone, so he pulled in a programmer he knew. The coder wasn't a star — just competent enough to make things work. Their relationship soured; in later accounts the programmer said he walked away and that even his fee had been shaved — asked for 1,000 liras (about twenty-four dollars today), got paid half. Whether that was an omen or a footnote, the pattern people later described was already visible.

On July 31, 2016, the Çiftlik Bank game went live.

It did not take long for the first test of trust. A sixteen-year-old deposited 4,000 liras (about 100 dollars today). In the following days, intake climbed to about 20,000 liras (about 500 dollars) a day. At first, the money flowed straight into his personal bank account — an amateur choice that signaled both naivety and urgency. Personal accounts draw attention when the numbers swell, and they don't look professional to someone considering an "investment." To make incoming funds look more like a business and less like a man with a bank card, he began taking payments through Papara. Within a month — September 2, 2016 — he created a company with a name designed to radiate both tech and agriculture: "Çiftlik Bilgi İşlem Bilişim Tarım ve Hayvancılık Limited Şirketi." The paid-in capital was 10,000 liras (about 250 dollars today). He was the founder.

From there, the circle widened. He brought in relatives and trusted contacts. As the operation grew more technical, he recruited "experts," in software and in agriculture, to stand beside the brand and lend it the right vocabulary. The storytelling goal was simple: a modern enterprise running on code and cows.

The internal economy was built to be simple. Deposit 10,000 liras (about 250 dollars today), receive 10,000 units of in-game "gold." This "gold" was only a name, not pegged to market precious metals, and it remained inside the system at a fixed 1:1 with the lira. A second currency — "silver"

— had a specific use: retail purchases at Çiftlik-branded delicatessens. Players were encouraged to spend time and money inside the game loop: buy animals, buy feed, buy embryos, rent storage, keep the cycle running. Animals had lifespans; inputs had prices; outputs generated revenue. New users received a free "Manisa chicken," a small gift meant to soften the first step across the threshold.

Gross income was calculated by the system; feed and other costs were deducted to produce a net. Five percent of the income was automatically converted into silver. If you made 10,000 liras (about 250 dollars today), 500 liras (about twelve dollar today) of that would appear as silver in your account, something you could spend at the company's delis. The mechanics created a rhythm: you "invest" by buying animals; you "earn" as they produce; part of that earning becomes store credit redeemable in the brand's retail network.

The deli layer mattered because it gave people something to point to. Anyone — member or not — could walk into a Çiftlik Bank delicatessen, a grocery that sells a selection of fine prepared foods, and buy cheese, honey, butter, sausage. Members, however, could settle part of the bill with silver. Franchise owners, according to people in the system, even received more for a silver transaction than a cash one — ten to twenty percent more, roughly. That detail did double work: it nudged members to shop there, and it convinced owners they were in a business with guaranteed foot traffic as the user base grew.

Some who entered as players decided the "real money" was in the storefronts and opened delis. There were conditions: standardized interiors; opening events; buses arranged from other branches to make a show of crowds. The brand took a franchise fee that rose as the network expanded. The message to the street was clear: this wasn't only an online game; it was a physical network of shops and "farms."

The more visible the network became, the more central Aydın seemed. Franchisees described WhatsApp groups where he was active, available to answer questions and to manage anxieties when rumors began to swirl. When trouble came — arguments about backdoors in the code, missing funds, managers accused of theft — he told franchise owners that internal saboteurs had hurt him too. The tone wasn't fearmongering but rather marshaling, saying: Stay in. We're solving it.

There were claims that even land purchases were padded — plots valued at one number recorded at double to skim the difference. Whether that enriched insiders or middlemen, the effect was the same: bleed the pool while the pool was full. None of it appeared to slow the expansion. The impression he needed to keep alive was that money, land, animals, and inventory were all moving in the right direction. Speed and optics mattered more than efficiency.

Three pillars of trust supported the growth. The first was liquidity — at least early on. Users could withdraw on demand. Skeptics tested the system with 1000 liras (about twenty-five dollars today), saw 1,200 liras (about thirty dollars today) a month later, and pulled it out. That receipt was convertible into persuasion: friends showed each other bank statements. The next step was intuitive — 10,000 liras (about 250 dollars today) turn into 12,000 liras (about 300 dollars today); then 100,000 liras (about 2.500 dollars today) become 120,000 liras (about 3,000 dollars today). If you didn't have that much cash, you borrowed, sold a car, sold a house. The interest cost felt irrelevant if the principal multiplied on schedule. People told themselves they'd upgrade the car next month.

The second pillar was the presence of a product. The delis existed. The shelves were stocked. People bought food. Ministry inspections of food establishments happen in Turkey; the mere fact that a deli door was open and stocked persuaded some that all of this must be under official eyes. The staged openings of "facilities" amplified the impression: if a governor, a district governor, or a mayor cuts a ribbon, how fraudulent could it be?

The third pillar was the use of recognizable faces and mass-market airtime. Celebrities fronted ads. Openings featured familiar hosts. Commercials ran across channels, including a heavily watched program, "Beyaz Show," where the promo copy promised facilities in Sakarya, Manisa, Tekirdağ, Kırklareli built to European standards. If you already liked and trusted the presenter, that confidence bled into the brand. None of this, by itself, proves a company sound; all of it, together, can quiet questions.

Behind the glass, the supply chain was more prosaic. The cheeses, honeys, butters, and sausages came from existing producers under contract and private label. A Bursa company called Feyza made kashar; other goods were filled in by different suppliers, including in İstanbul's Kağıthane. The "farms," as multiple people later described them, were built for demonstration value. One detail from a call-in segment on a daytime program captured the logic: animals purchased for a facility didn't match the stated agricultural plan, but the orders went through anyway. The priority was a look, not a yield.

That raises the questions so few asked in time: if a hundred people each bought a cow in the game, where were the hundred real cows? What ratio existed between virtual inventory and live animals? How were in-game prices set? A cow priced at a token figure on a screen bears no relation to market price. None of those mismatches derailed the story.

Faces mattered. Actor Mehmet Çevik became the front man in ads and a recurring presence at openings, later saying he had no intent to lend cover to a deception and apologizing to those who felt misled. Another recognizable figure was Cengiz Çimen — "Mülayim" from daytime TV — familiar to older audiences. "Fısfıs İsmail" (İsmail Yaşar) from "Çocuklar Duymasın" surfaced, too. The creative strategy for some commercials was almost anti-creative: so bad they stick. Lines you mock are lines you remember. As for program-integrated placement, the "Beyaz Show" promo was the apex: a trusted host's voice and platform describing the company's facilities as modern and hygienic. On paper, none of that constitutes due diligence; in practice, it looked like certification.

Layered onto the spectacle were occasional appeals to religion and public feeling — references to Jerusalem at openings, for instance — content with no material link to the business but a clear aim: align the brand with values and causes ordinary people care about.

It took time for formal complaints to catch up. In May 2017, a first tip reached the Bursa Chief Public Prosecutor. On July 31, 2017, Aydın gave a statement to police. He said the company operated three farms — Manisa, İnegöl, Tekirdağ — with roughly 100,000 live animals: 95,000 chickens and the remainder cattle, including a breed that laid "blue eggs." The blue egg hook was everywhere: a planned breeding facility, claims that the protein content was one-and-a-half times that of a normal egg, an ambition to build the world's largest blue-egg operation. He said the company had granted twenty deli distributorships, booked annual turnover of fifteen million liras (about 360,000 dollars today) on a four-million profit (about 95,000 dollars today), and was US-registered under a parent called "Fame Game." At that moment, officials didn't have documents disproving his claims; the surface still looked orderly.

In December 2017, the ownership picture shifted. Aydın transferred company shares to a Cypriot company controlled by his brother, Fatih Aydın. The Capital Markets Board filed a criminal complaint. The Ministry of Customs and Trade accused the organization of aggravated fraud. New member registrations stopped. The engine shuddered.

On January 2, Aydın tried to normalize the transfer: the virtual activities and the physical delis had been merged under the "Fame Game" umbrella, he said. He repeated points about doing in the real world what the game simulated. He noted that their work was being examined by the ministry. Twenty two days later, on January 24, 2018, he left the country without incident.

The Anadolu Chief Public Prosecutor's Office would later present the system's outline in numbers. More than half a million people joined; not all put in money. About 188,099 played only as gamers. Around 132,222 deposited funds and became victims. The flows were stark: roughly 1.12 billion liras (about twenty-four million dollars today) came in; 687 million liras (about sixteen million dollars today) went back out. Early withdrawals and ongoing liquidity explain that give-and-take. The difference offers a crude measure of loss, though it cannot capture distribution: some withdrew more than they put in, which necessarily means others bore more than their share of the deficit. Press coverage often cited 77,000 people defrauded of 511 million liras (about twelve million dollars today).

How did that money leave the country? The claims ranged from suitcase cash to structured transfers. If he converted a large share into dollars at exit, the arithmetic worked in his favor. Allegations also surfaced about networks: suggestions of ties to Gülen movement, an Islamist fraternal movement, through land purchases; reports that an Uruguayan businessman from Bursa's Kestel district, Osman Aykaç, handled construction and laundering. They remained allegations in the public telling; what mattered to victims was simpler — their money was gone.

The stories that linger come from people who thought they were stepping into a sure thing. Some tested with small amounts and stopped while others took loans, sold cars, sold houses and went in heavy. When the music stopped, a few were drawn into a second humiliation: self-styled "recovery" agents demanded 500 (about twelve dollars today) to 1,000 liras (about twenty-five dollars today) in cash from 1,650 people, promising to get their losses back. They disappeared, too.

The human need to believe ran straight through it all. A deli franchisee told a newspaper he still refused to see Aydın as a swindler, pointing to his humble background and "sparkle" when opening companies. That sentiment — "he's one of us; a modest boy" — survived footage of him living well after the collapse. It is hard to argue with grief, but it is important to see the mechanism: attachment to a person can override evidence.

What remains are lessons people claim they already knew and yet ignored: if returns are guaranteed, they are not honest. If a business must wrap itself in celebrity, spectacle, and borrowed legitimacy, it is selling confidence rather than value. If a "bank" lives only on a website and a storefront franchise, it is not a bank. And if a system begins by proving it will pay you quickly, that may not be proof of soundness — it may be bait.

10

"SHE'S FIGHTING!"

Thirty-seven-year-old Jimmy Allen, who, just eighteen minutes earlier, had discovered his wife's body hanging from the ceiling in the basement of their home in Michigan frantically called 911. He told the dispatcher he had found her and was trying to perform CPR. As instructed, he continued his efforts while emergency units raced to the scene. Officer Ben J. Horn was the first to arrive, and as he approached the residence, he was struck by an unnerving silence that stood in stark contrast to the desperation in Jimmy's voice on the call. The moment Officer Horn made his presence known, however, the silence was shattered by Jimmy's cries for help.

Inside, the officer found Jimmy in the basement, sobbing over the unresponsive body of his wife, Amy, as he continued chest compressions. He claimed she couldn't have been down for more than twenty minutes. A brief inspection of Amy's body revealed no significant injuries, only a very faint mark near her jugular. By 8:57 p.m., more officers and several Emergency Medical Technicians (EMTs) had arrived, descending into the basement to take over the life-saving efforts. Freed from the task, Jimmy's grief appeared to overwhelm him. He dramatically ripped off his shirt and collapsed onto the basement floor in a heap of emotion. Yet, just as quickly, he composed himself and watched the EMTs work on his wife.

This rapid oscillation between complete composure and theatrical emotional outbursts would become a recurring pattern throughout the night.

When an officer asked him to come upstairs, Jimmy calmly walked up the basement stairs, but upon entering the kitchen, he unleashed a sudden burst of rage on a bowl of potato chips, sending them scattering. The officers were unsure what to make of his erratic behavior as they tried to piece together the events of the evening. Jimmy provided a summary of the night, explaining that he and Amy had dropped their daughter and her friend off at a high school football game around 6:30 p.m. before heading downtown for drinks. While at a bar, an argument erupted, which resulted in Amy walking home alone while he drove. He said the arguing continued when they both got home, so he left her alone to cool off and went upstairs to watch the movie *Ace Ventura*. When it was time to pick up their daughter, he went to check on Amy and found her. He insisted that Amy had no history of anything like this and that he was completely shocked by the situation.

As the officers absorbed his story, an EMT emerged from the basement with an unexpected development. Amy was fighting; they had reestablished a faint pulse. She was still clinging to life. Instead of relief, Jimmy's reaction to this promising news appeared to be one of frustration, a response that immediately raised red flags for the officers on the scene. After momentarily leaving the room to get a new shirt, Jimmy returned and made two phone calls. The first was to his daughter, Ashley, whom he told there was an emergency and to stay put, keeping his composure to avoid panicking her. The second call was to his parents, and his demeanor shifted entirely as he spilled his heart out in a flood of emotion. Though he was crying intensely, an officer noted that there was no moisture on his face.

Shortly after, Amy was placed on a stretcher and rushed to Promedica Herrick Hospital, just two minutes away. With the basement now clear, officers began a more thorough investigation of the scene. One detail immediately stood out: the basement ceilings were unusually low, roughly seven feet high (about 2.13 meters). Given that Amy was five feet, six inches tall (about 1.67 meters), the logistics of Jimmy's implied narrative began to seem questionable.

The next morning, officers returned to the Allen home to speak with Jimmy again, hoping to get a clearer picture of the day leading up to the incident. Jimmy described a perfectly normal family day, starting with making breakfast together before he left for work and Ashley left for school. He came home from work early, around 12:30 p.m., and took a nap. Amy picked up Ashley and her friend Kayla from school, and the group had dinner together before leaving for the football game at 6:30 p.m.. From there, Jimmy and Amy went bar hopping, first to Embers Bar and Grill, and then to JR's Hometown Grill and Pub, a detail investigators later confirmed with security footage.

According to Jimmy, the trouble began at JR's when he brought up the idea of selling their house and moving back south to Florida, from where they had moved only a year prior. Amy was not receptive to the idea. She became dismissive, texting someone on her phone and responding negatively to his suggestions. He recalled her saying, "I hope that works out for you," a comment that sparked a tense argument. The tension was so thick by the time they left that Amy chose to walk home rather than ride with him. Surveillance footage confirmed this, capturing Amy walking in the direction of their house.

Jimmy stated that Amy arrived home at 7:58 p.m., grabbed an extension cord, and went to the basement. He went down to check on her at 8:05 p.m. and found her feeding one of their cats. She was angry with him, accusing him of slamming a door in her face as they left the bar, an act he insisted was an accident. They argued for another ten minutes before he went back upstairs, leaving her in the basement with the cord. At 8:40 p.m., realizing it was time to get their daughter, he went down to make peace with Amy and discovered the scene. He mentioned seeing an overturned kitty litter pail nearby when he found her. He maintained that he could never have seen this coming, describing their life as healthy and financially stable, the pinnacle of his career.

The officers' view of the Allen family began to shift dramatically when several of Amy's relatives approached them. They were concerned that Jimmy had waited fourteen hours to inform them of what had happened. They told investigators a story that painted Jimmy not as a shocked and grieving husband, but as a deeply controlling man. They explained that Amy had a son, Caleb, from a previous relationship when she was thirteen. Jimmy had initially acted as a father figure to Caleb, but the family dynamic was toxic. Amy's family claimed Jimmy monitored everything the family did, from social media to their daily diet, and that he didn't want Amy to be financially independent. His discipline of the children often went too far, and Amy's attempts to stand up to him were dismissed. Eventually, the environment became so unbearable that when Caleb was seventeen, he left to live with his grandparents. In retaliation, Jimmy forbade Amy from speaking with her family, including her son.

This portrait of an abusive and controlling husband provided a potential context for violence, but investigators still lacked a clear motive. That changed when they examined Amy's cell phone. Her text history with Jimmy confirmed his controlling behavior; he frequently texted her asking for her exact location, which he appeared to be tracking. The motive, however, was found in another conversation. Amy had been having a three-year-long affair with a married man from the East Coast named George, whom she had met online. Their messages were explicit, and they had been in constant contact on the day of the incident, texting and calling even while she was at dinner with her family. At the bar, while sitting next to her husband and arguing with him, she had been texting George. A new, powerful theory emerged: Jimmy had seen the texts, and in a fit of rage, attacked Amy in the basement.

Before investigators could follow up on this new lead, they received tragic news. On September 17, 2018, after three days on life support, Amy Allen was pronounced dead. The case was now a homicide investigation. However, when police tried to locate Jimmy for more questioning, they discovered he was gone. Just days after the incident, he had packed up his daughter, their five cats, and all their belongings and moved back to his hometown of Ocala, Florida.

The Michigan State Police took over the investigation, and one month after Amy's death, Detective Larry Rothman arranged for Jimmy to return for a formal interview. During the interview, Jimmy presented himself as a "type A personality" who valued structure and was always seeking to improve himself and his family. He framed his obsession with creating a perfect family as a strength, believing it was his role to hold them to a higher standard. He painted Amy as a socially anxious introvert who had isolated herself with a video game addiction, casting himself as the savior trying to help her break out of her shell. When Detective Rothman bluntly informed him that Amy had been having an affair, Jimmy was in complete denial. Even after being shown excerpts of her explicit conversations with George, he struggled to accept it.

Three months after Amy's death, the autopsy report was released. The cause of death was confirmed as strangulation asphyxiation, but the manner of death was listed as undetermined, pending further investigation. Detective Rothman, recalling the low basement ceiling, contacted a forensic engineering lab and asked them to recreate the scene. After months of testing, the lab concluded that, given the circumstances described, Amy's feet would have touched the ground. With this new evidence, a different forensic pathologist reviewed the case and determined the manner of death was homicide. On October 16, 2020, Jimmy Allen was charged with one felony count of open murder. He was arrested in Florida just five days before his wedding to his new fiancée and was extradited back to Michigan.

In September 2021, three years after Amy's death, Jimmy's trial began. The prosecution, led by Angie Borders, argued that Jimmy was a controlling husband who snapped after discovering his wife's affair. They called Amy's son, Caleb, who testified that Jimmy had choked him during an argument years earlier, suggesting a history of using strangulation when angry. First responders and a hospital staff member testified that Jimmy's over-the-top emotional displays seemed fake and that the lack of external injuries on Amy's body was a red flag for foul play. The prosecution's star witness was George, who took the stand to detail his three-year affair with Amy, confirming they had met in person twice, once in a hotel room, and were making plans to meet again at the end of October. Finally, Dr. Elizabeth Buck presented the results of the forensic experiment, testifying that the extension cord in question could not have suspended a 140-pound weight (about sixty-three kilograms), effectively debunking Jimmy's story.

The defense, led by attorney Daniel Garin, countered that the prosecution's case was built on speculation. They pointed to Jimmy's phone search history from that night — which included searches for Jim Carrey movies — as evidence that murder was not on his mind. Jimmy's father testified that the family had urged him to move to Florida after the tragedy, explaining his departure from the state. In a significant shift from her initial statement, Ashley testified that her mother frequently overindulged in alcohol and would become "meaner and more violent" when intoxicated. The defense argued that Amy's blood alcohol content of 0.09% was evidence of a drinking problem. They also brought in their own expert, Dr. Francisco J. Diaz, who testified that the minimal internal injuries to Amy's neck were inconsistent with a homicide. In his closing argument, Garin emphasized that Jimmy had no defensive scratches on him and portrayed Amy as a deeply troubled woman living a double life, whose isolation, drinking, and guilt over her affair ultimately led to her tragic death.

After six hours of deliberation, the jury reached a verdict. They found Jimmy Allen guilty of the lesser offense of second-degree murder. On October 21, 2021, he was sentenced to twenty to forty-five years in the Michigan Department of Corrections with an eligibility for parole in the year 2040.

On the surface, Jimmy Allen had presented himself as a grieving husband, a man caught in a tragic and unforeseeable moment. But beneath the veneer of composure and orchestrated emotion lay a history of control, manipulation, and escalating violence. The combination of forensic evidence, digital trails, and testimony from those closest to Amy ultimately unraveled the story he tried so hard to control. In the end, the tragic unraveling of a family's private life left a permanent mark on those who survived, a stark warning of the dangers that can dwell behind closed doors.

11

THE LAHORI PSYCHO

In December of 1999, a package arrived at a police office in Lahore, Pakistan. Inside, officers found a collection of photographs and a thirty-two-page diary. As they began to read, a story of unparalleled horror unfolded. The diary was a meticulous, detailed confession from a man who claimed to have raped and murdered exactly 100 boys over the course of the last eighteen months. A note included in the package provided an address, challenging the police to go there if they wanted proof. A quick check of the property records revealed the owner: a wealthy businessman named Javed Iqbal.

Javed Iqbal Mughal was born in Lahore in 1956, the 6th child in an affluent family. His father was a self-made man who worked himself to the point of exhaustion to ensure his children had every advantage. He worked punishing shifts, sometimes on as little as two hours of sleep, all to afford prestigious private schools, university fees, and trust funds for his children. Javed, like his siblings, grew up in a world of privilege, wanting for nothing. After graduating from university, he was given two large villas by his father. He chose to live in the larger one and, following his father's advice, set up a steel recasting business in the other.

As Javed entered his twenties, his parents began pressuring him to marry and start a family. He showed no interest. The pressure escalated to the point of threatening an arranged marriage, a prospect that caused Javed to break down completely. He begged for one last chance to find his own bride, even threatening to take his own life if they forced the issue. His parents relented.

Some months prior to this family drama, Javed had encountered a young homeless boy on the streets of Lahore. Moved by the child's plight, he took him into his home, clothing him and providing for him in what appeared to be an act of charity. When the pressure to marry became unbearable, Javed learned that this boy had an older sister who was also living on the streets. He asked the boy to introduce them. Ten minutes after meeting her, Javed decided this was the woman he would marry. For the young woman, who was homeless and destitute, marrying a wealthy man was a matter of survival. For Javed, it was a strategic move. By marrying the boy's sister, he was attempting to permanently bind the child to his life, making him family. The marriage was brief and produced one child before they separated. It was a union born of manipulation, not love, and it was doomed from the start.

Now single again and in his thirties, Javed's behavior grew more sinister. A family member visiting his home discovered that he was no longer housing just one boy; there were now six or seven young children living with the thirty-something-year-old man. The discovery was deeply unnerving, but it was soon overshadowed by a formal criminal accusation. Javed was charged with the rape and sodomy of one of the children living in his home.

The news of the crime ignited a firestorm of outrage in the community. A mob of townspeople, bent on revenge, descended on Javed's house. He wasn't there, but they found the other children he had been keeping. Frustrated, the mob moved on to his family's home, vandalizing it when they found it empty. Eventually, they tracked down Javed's father and brother at the family shop. The mob flooded into the store, beat both men, and then transported them to the police station in a rickshaw. It was there that the family was officially informed of the charges against Javed.

His father and brother were in denial, insisting Javed was not capable of such a thing. The police, however, claimed to have evidence. With Javed's whereabouts unknown, and uncertain of the family's involvement, the police took his father and brother into custody. Javed's father seemed more devastated by the damage to the family's reputation than by the suffering of his son's victim. His mother, however, was disgusted by her son's actions and resolved to help the police find him. She went to Javed's house and found a thirteen-year-old boy who claimed to have lived there for months. Believing it would lure her son out of hiding, she took the boy to the police station. The gambit worked. When Javed learned what his mother had done, he emerged to confront her, and the waiting police arrested him. For the rape and sodomy of a child, he was sentenced to just six months in jail.

While he was incarcerated, the stress of the situation caused Javed's father to suffer a serious heart attack. Though ashamed of the disgrace his son had brought upon the family, his father's loyalty never wavered. He spent a great deal of money trying to secure Javed's early release from prison. Upon his release, the family, aware of his predilections, pushed him into another marriage, hoping to steer him away from young boys. Like the first, this marriage was short-lived.

In 1992, Javed's father suffered another, fatal heart attack, an event precipitated by years of stress over his son's crimes. He was the last family member who maintained regular contact with Javed. With his father gone, the rest of the family, led by his disgusted mother, cut him off completely. From his father's estate, Javed inherited three million rupees (about 34,000 dollars). With this money, he purchased a large house in Lahore and set up a new business: a video game arcade. It was the first of its kind in the town, and it was strategically designed to attract his preferred victims. He would stand for hours, creepily watching the young boys who flocked to his establishment, singling out his favorites for free gifts and discount tokens.

He developed a particularly insidious tactic for luring his victims. He would slyly drop a 100-rupee note (about one dollar) on the floor, wait for a boy to pick it up, and then loudly announce that he had lost the money. When the boy who had taken the note remained silent, Javed would take him next door to his house and force him into a strip search, an act that frequently escalated into sexual assault.

This pattern of abuse continued for years. Shockingly, it was something of an open secret. The boys who frequented the arcade knew what the owner was like; they shared stories of his assaults among themselves, yet they kept coming back. Some parents and members of the community were also aware of what was happening behind the closed doors of the arcade, but nothing was ever done. Some of the parents who knew their children were being abused had been paid by Javed to keep silent. Others were too terrified of the notoriously corrupt Pakistani police to report the crimes, fearing that they could end up worse off for being seen as a nuisance.

In his mid-thirties, Javed's life took another dramatic turn when his arcade was robbed. He and an employee were beaten so severely they were nearly killed. The injuries left Javed bedridden for a long time, and he was forced to sell his house, his car, and what remained of his business to cover his hospital bills. During this period of convalescence, he was unable to care for his aging mother, who subsequently passed away. It is believed that this confluence of events — the violent assault, the loss of his wealth, and the death of his mother — was the catalyst that transformed Javed Iqbal from a serial child abuser into a serial killer.

Between 1998 and 1999, Javed began his killing spree. The streets of Lahore were home to as many as 5,000 homeless children, a vast and vulnerable population from which to choose his victims. He would lure them with the promise of food, shelter, and fresh clothing — the basic necessities they so desperately needed for survival. Once he had them in his home, he would photograph them, sometimes clothed, sometimes not, keeping a meticulous record of his crimes. He had set a goal for himself: he would kill exactly 100 boys and then he would stop. After sexually assaulting and strangling his victims, he would dismember their bodies and dissolve them in vats of acid.

When police, guided by the confessional diary, entered Javed's small, one-bedroom apartment, they found a house of horrors. Though the bodies were gone, the evidence was overwhelming. They collected fifty-eight pieces of children's clothing, along with the photographs he had taken of his victims. The news of the discovery sent shockwaves through the country. People were horrified that such atrocities could have been happening under their noses. The police put out a public announcement, asking parents of missing children to come to the station to try and identify the clothing. Hundreds of families came forward, revealing a hidden epidemic of missing children that had gone largely unreported due to the public's deep distrust of the police.

While the country reeled from the revelations, Javed Iqbal was nowhere to be found. The police launched one of the largest manhunts in Pakistan's history, focusing their search on the Ravi River, where Javed had mentioned in his diary he might go to drown himself. The manhunt came to a dramatic end on December 30, 1999. That morning, a disheveled-looking man burst into the offices of the Daily Jang newspaper. "I am Javed Iqbal, killer of a 100 boys," he announced to the stunned journal-ists. "I hate this world. I am not ashamed of my actions and I am ready to die. I have no regrets."

He had turned himself in to the media because he was convinced the police would kill him. The newspaper staff immediately called the author-ities, and within minutes, the building was surrounded by 100 armed soldiers. Javed Iqbal was arrested, and later that evening, four fourteen-year-old boys — his accomplices — were taken into custody at his home. These boys, however, were not willing participants; they had been trauma-tized and forced to help him dismember the bodies of his victims. One of the boys would later die in police custody. The official cause of death was suicide — he had allegedly jumped from a high window — but it is widely believed that he was beaten to death by the police.

During his interrogation, Javed Iqbal was unrepentant. He said he could have killed 500 boys but stopped at 100 because that was his predeter-mined goal. His motives were twofold: a sick, sexual attraction to young boys, and a burning hatred for the police, whom he blamed for a brutal beating during a previous arrest that had left him crippled. In his diary, he wrote, "My mother cried for me. I want 100 mothers to cry for their children."

At his trial, Javed, along with his three surviving accomplices, changed his story completely. He denied everything, claiming the entire affair was an elaborate "social experiment" designed to raise awareness for the plight of runaway children. The court saw through his charade. He and his main accomplice were found guilty. The judge, in a move that reflected the public's outrage, delivered a shocking sentence: "You will be strangled to death in front of the parents whose children you killed. Your body will be cut into 100 pieces and put in acid, the same way you killed those children." The sentence was later revised to a standard execution after intervention from human rights officials.

In the aftermath, a strange and unsettling theory emerged, propagated by Javed's own brother. He claimed that Javed had been framed by the police, who needed a scapegoat to account for the hundreds of unsolved cases of missing boys in Lahore. He raised several compelling points. How could Javed have murdered and dismembered 100 boys in a small apartment with paper-thin walls without any of his neighbors hearing or seeing anything? Furthermore, how was it that several of the boys Javed had supposedly murdered had since turned up alive, reunited with their families?

On October 8, 2001, before any execution could be carried out, Javed Iqbal and his main accomplice were found dead in their prison cells. The official report stated that they had hanged themselves with their bedsheets in a suicide pact. An autopsy, however, told a different story. Both men had been savagely beaten just before their deaths. Javed's body was covered in injuries inflicted by a heavy, blunt weapon. In the end, it seemed, he had met the violent fate he feared at the hands of the very institution he so despised. None of his family members came to claim his body. A statement from the family declared, "We have nothing to do with him. He died for us on the day that he confessed to killing 100 children."

12

THE SUMMERFIELD SIX

The call to the authorities came after a confession, but not the kind made in the sterile confines of an interrogation room. This one was born of panic and guilt in a family home, when a news report about a missing teenager flashed across the television screen. At that moment, Kyle Hooper, a sixteen-year-old boy, broke down in front of his mother. He told her he knew what had happened to eighteen-year-old Seth Jackson, who had vanished the night of Sunday, April 17, 2011. The story he unburdened was so appalling that his mother immediately contacted the police. She pointed them toward a ramshackle house in Summerfield, Florida, indicating that this unassuming location was the site of a dark and gruesome secret.

When investigators arrived at the house, owned by eighteen-year-old Charlie Ely, they rounded up the young people present and began to unravel a story far more horrifying than they could have anticipated. One by one, they were brought to the station: Charlie Ely; Amber Wright, the fifteen-year-old ex-girlfriend of the missing boy; Kyle Hooper, Amber's half-brother; and Justin Soto, a twenty-year-old known to his friends as "Roach." All were residents or frequent guests at the house. The only person missing was another eighteen-year-old, Mike Bargo, a man who would soon be identified as the plot's central figure.

Seth Jackson was a typical teenager living in Summerfield with his parents, Scott and Sonia, and his two older brothers. He had a love for animals and harbored aspirations of one day competing in the Ultimate Fighting Championship, a dream his parents had agreed to support with training courses once he turned eighteen. He had been in a relationship with fifteen-year-old Amber Wright, and while it may have started happily, it soured after about a year. The situation was complicated further when Amber grew close to Mike Bargo, who was not just any rival but also Seth's best friend. The breakup, fueled by speculation that Amber had been cheating on him with Mike, left Seth traumatized.

On the night he disappeared, Sunday, April 17th, Seth was with his friend, Will Samalot. After visiting another friend, they began walking home shortly after 9:00 p.m. Will noticed that Seth seemed distracted, constantly texting on his phone. When the friends parted ways, it was the last time anyone other than his killers would see Seth Jackson alive. The next day, when he failed to return home, his mother, Sonia, filed a missing person's report.

The text messages recovered from Seth's phone told the story of his final hours. They were from Amber, who was proposing they meet to talk about "working things out." She told him she was bringing her friend Charlie Ely for support and instructed him where to wait. Seth's reply was laced with a chilling prescience. He warned her that if he got jumped, she could "say goodbye." Amber reassured him, claiming she could never do that and that she just wanted them to be back together. His last text message confirmed he was walking to their meeting spot, a corner where they had once fought.

At the sheriff's office, the interrogations began. Twenty-year-old Justin Soto was evasive from the start. He claimed to know nothing about a kid named Seth, other than that he was a "little white boy" who used to date Amber. When questioned about the fresh, deep scratches on his legs, he offered a flimsy excuse about walking through the woods and getting tangled in vines. The detectives were not convinced. The scratches looked more like the result of running through the dark woods, not a casual walk. His answers were vague, and he repeatedly used phrases like "pretty much," a verbal tic that often signals a person is withholding the full truth.

In separate rooms, Amber Wright and Charlie Ely presented a coordinated version of events. They admitted that Amber had lured Seth to the house under the pretense of a reconciliation. They claimed that after they talked for a while, Seth showed up at Charlie's house unannounced about an hour later. According to their initial story, Seth was sitting in a chair when, without any warning, Kyle Hooper emerged and struck him. In this telling, they were innocent bystanders who, frightened by the sudden violence, fled to a bedroom and hid. They said they heard Mike Bargo's door fly open, followed by a series of gunshots. They claimed they remained in the room until the next morning, emerging to a house that smelled strongly of bleach. They both insisted that Justin Soto was not even there that night.

The entire narrative constructed by Justin, Amber, and Charlie collapsed when detectives confronted them with the confession of Kyle Hooper. After being separated from his mother, the sixteen-year-old finally unburdened himself of the complete, horrific truth. His story began not with the murder, but with the turmoil in his own life. He explained that he had been fighting with his parents and, feeling alienated, had moved into Charlie's house. His anger and frustration were simmering on the night of the murder.

Kyle told detectives that the group, including Justin Soto, was at the house when Mike Bargo, high on an unknown quantity of white pills he had been snorting, became agitated and violent. When Seth's name came up, Mike declared his intention to kill him that night and asked the others if they were "down." The motive was a potent mix of jealousy and wounded pride. Mike was with Amber, but the animosity with Seth ran deeper. The two had recently gotten into a physical fight, which Seth had apparently won, deeply humiliating Mike.

Kyle admitted that he, too, hated Seth, claiming he had found Seth in bed with his ex-girlfriend. But the driving force, he insisted, was Mike. He recounted how Mike had volunteered to take all the blame, assuring the others he had nothing to lose. With that assurance, the plan was solidified. Kyle stated unequivocally that everyone present agreed to the murder: Amber, Charlie, Justin Soto, himself, and Mike Bargo. Amber's role was to be the bait. She was to call Seth and lure him to the house.

Faced with Kyle's detailed confession, the other stories crumbled. The detectives now had the leverage they needed. One by one, they confronted Justin, Amber, and Charlie with the truth, pointing out the inconsistencies in their fabricated tales. The pressure mounted until each of them broke. Charlie was the first of the girls to admit she knew something violent was planned. Amber, confronted with her brother's account, finally confessed her role in knowingly luring Seth to his death. Justin, told that everyone else was blaming him, abandoned his pretense of ignorance and began to recount his part in the events of that night.

With the confessions aligned, a single, horrifying narrative of Seth Jackson's murder emerged. When Seth arrived at the house, he was led into a trap. As he sat in a chair, Kyle Hooper approached from behind and struck him over the head with a wooden stick, hitting him so hard the stick broke into pieces. Justin Soto then joined the assault, also hitting Seth with a stick. Wounded, Seth tried to flee toward the kitchen, but Mike Bargo appeared and shot him in the back with a .22 caliber revolver.

As Seth fell, Justin grabbed him in a chokehold while Mike continued to shoot him, firing approximately five rounds into his body. Kyle recounted the harrowing moments that followed, describing how he was ordered to drag Seth's body, which was still partially alive, up the stairs and into a bathroom. Inside the bathroom, the brutality escalated. With Seth lying in the bathtub, Mike continued his frenzied attack, punching him repeatedly. Kyle described having to physically pull Mike away from the body. It was then, with Seth either dying or already dead, that Mike began to break his kneecaps with a hard object, a final act of desecration.

After the murder, the group's focus shifted to disposing of the evidence. They wrapped Seth's body in a blue sleeping bag and carried it out to a fire pit in the backyard. Justin admitted it was his job to tend the fire, for which he had been collecting firewood. To mask the smell of the burning body, they threw two old car tires onto the pyre. As the body burned through the night, Mike Bargo continued to display a depraved and psychopathic demeanor. Kyle described how, even after Seth was dead, Mike struck the body with a shovel as it lay in the fire pit.

The following morning, the grizzly task continued. Kyle recalled watching Mike sift through the ashes in the fire pit, picking out teeth and fragments of Seth's skull and casually playing with the victim's tongue before placing the remains into paint containers. The final step of the disposal involved Amber and Kyle's stepfather, James Havens III. According to multiple accounts, Amber texted Havens and asked him to come to the house. Once there, Havens helped Mike and Justin load the paint cans filled with Seth's remains, along with cinder blocks, into the back of his truck. Mike directed them to a remote, water-filled quarry, a place he knew from a past swimming trip. There, they tied the cinder blocks to the buckets with a dog leash and threw them into the water, hoping to conceal their crime forever.

While the four suspects were confessing at the station, Mike Bargo was still at large. He had fled to the town of Starke, Florida, seeking refuge at the home of his new girlfriend's father, James Williams Sr. Unaware of the true reason for his visit, Williams offered him a place to stay. However, Mike's conscience, or perhaps his ego, wouldn't allow him to stay silent. He confessed to Williams, fabricating a story that he had killed a man who had assaulted his sister. He then told Williams's girlfriend, Crystal Anderson, the entire story of Seth's murder, claiming he had done it because Seth had allegedly assaulted Amber. After Williams convinced him to surrender, the police, who had already tracked him to the location, surrounded the house and took him into custody. Brought to an interrogation room, Mike Bargo was read his rights. Before any meaningful questioning could begin, he invoked his right to an attorney, and the interview was promptly terminated.

The so-called "Summerfield Six" — Mike Bargo, Amber Wright, Kyle Hooper, Charlie Ely, Justin Soto, and James Havens III — were all charged for their roles in the murder of Seth Jackson. James Havens III pleaded guilty to being an accessory after the fact for his role in disposing of the body. The others went to trial. Amber Wright, Kyle Hooper, and Justin Soto were all convicted of first-degree murder and sentenced to life in prison. Charlie Ely was also convicted of first-degree murder and received a life sentence, but in 2020, after serving nearly a decade, she was granted a retrial. She accepted a plea deal for second-degree murder and was freed at the age of 27.

As the mastermind and triggerman, Mike Bargo faced the stiffest penalty. He was convicted of first-degree murder and sentenced to death. He currently awaits his fate on Florida's death row. As he was led from the courtroom after his sentencing, his final reported words were, "May God have mercy on my soul."

13

THE PRINCE OF FRAUD

After purchasing two Rolex watches, a gold bracelet, and a massive diamond pinky ring, the man known as Prince Khalid of Saudi Arabia boarded a private jet bound for New York. Upon landing, his limousine delivered him to the Four Seasons Hotel, where he had rented out the entire top floor. As he settled in to enjoy a meal from room service, a loud, insistent knock shattered the opulent tranquility. Before he could react, two men burst through the door. They beat him, forced him into a car, and drove him back to the airport. During a moment of inattention, the prince managed to slip away, frantically alerting police that he had been kidnapped by two armed men.

However, when officers arrived, they did not arrest the alleged kidnappers. Instead, the man they put in handcuffs was the prince himself. It turned out that he was not Prince Khalid, nor was he even Arab. He was a con man from Michigan named Anthony Gignac, and for the better part of 30 years, he had been successfully posing as a member of the Saudi royal family, swindling millions of dollars from his victims. The two men who had taken him were not kidnappers but bounty hunters, tasked with returning him to Miami to face justice for his long list of crimes.

The story of Anthony Gignac began in 1970, far from the gilded palaces he would one day claim as his own. He was born, not Anthony Gignac, but Jose Moreno in the slums of Bogota, Colombia. According to Gignac's own account — a narrative that requires a healthy dose of skepticism — his early life was a relentless trauma. He claimed that he and his brother, Daniel, ran away from home after their father murdered their younger brother, unable to afford to feed all three children. For the next two years, the boys lived on the streets, with Jose resorting to selling his body just to ensure his brother had food. All of this, he alleged, happened before he was six years old.

After two years on the streets, the Moreno brothers were adopted by Nancy and Jim Gignac and brought to the suburbs of Michigan, where Jose was renamed Anthony. Life in America was an improvement, but it was not easy. Anthony was bullied at school for his appearance and had few friends. He found his escape in television, specifically in a show called *Lifestyles of the Rich and Famous*, which ignited a lifelong obsession with wealth, power, and fame that would ultimately consume him.

His career as a grifter began in the 6th grade. His adopted mother received a call from a local car dealership, informing her that the "prince's" Mercedes was ready for pickup. twelve-year-old Tony had convinced the dealership that he was a Saudi prince and that his father, the king, would settle the bill later. They had even allowed him to test drive the vehicle. This incident convinced his parents that he had serious mental health issues, and he spent much of his adolescence in mental institutions. At seventeen, he ran away from home for good. He soon found lodging with an Arab family by threatening them, claiming to be Saudi royalty and warning that his father's secret police would come after them if they refused him shelter. His stay was brief, however, as he was soon arrested for impersonating Adnan Khashoggi, a Saudi arms dealer who was, at the time, the richest man in the world.

After this arrest, Gignac fled Michigan for California, believing that if he could deceive actual Arab people, scamming others would be even easier. He was correct. For the next several years, he perfected his craft, grifting his way across the United States. He wore designer clothes, rode in limousines, and dined on fine food, living out the fantasy he had seen on television. His method was simple and repeatable: he would convince people he was a Saudi prince, they would provide him with free goods and services, and eventually, when the scheme was discovered, he would go to jail. Upon release, he would simply move to a new city and begin the cycle anew.

His exploits earned him the nickname "The Prince of Fraud." In 1991, while posing as Prince Khalid Al-Saud, he ran up a $10,000 bill on limousines and luxury hotels and conned Rodeo Drive shopkeepers out of Louis Vuitton luggage and a rare coin collection. After that four-day spree, he was arrested. From there, he went to San Francisco, where he stayed at the Ritz-Carlton for two months under the prince's name before being sent back to prison. His most audacious early scam occurred in 1993, when he checked into a premier Hawaiian resort and racked up a $20,000 bill, which he managed to pay off by selling an imaginary oil field to another hotel guest. This pattern of audacious fraud and subsequent arrest continued for years until a scam in Chicago involving $50,000 worth of clothing from Saks Fifth Avenue landed him in more serious trouble.

Facing his 27th offense, Gignac knew he needed a top-tier lawyer. He even managed to get a meeting with Johnnie Cochran, of O.J. Simpson trial fame, but Cochran refused the case due to "questions about authenticity." Gignac then found a lawyer named Oscar Rodriguez, whom he success-fully convinced that he was, in fact, the prince. He promised Rodriguez that if he took the case, he would be made the personal attorney for the entire Saudi royal family in the United States. Though skeptical, Rodriguez was swayed by the small chance that the story was true and posted Gignac's $50,000 bail, with the understanding that the royal family would reimburse him within twenty-four hours.

When the money never arrived, Rodriguez had to return his client to jail. It was then that Gignac hatched another brilliant idea. He told Rodriguez to take him to an American Express office. Thirty minutes later, in an era of less stringent financial security, Gignac walked out with a credit card that had a $200 million line of credit. He immediately paid Rodriguez back and embarked on one of the most unhinged shopping sprees in history, buying Rolexes, jewelry, and fine art. Any doubts Rodriguez had were erased, until a frantic call from American Express confirmed that Gignac was a fraud and that he needed to be stopped before he spent the entire $200 million. By then, Gignac was already on a plane to New York. Panicked, Rodriguez sent two bounty hunters to capture him, which led to the chaotic scene at the Four Seasons and LaGuardia Airport.

The genius behind Gignac's long-running scam was revealed during the legal proceedings. He had been able to gain access to accounts and secure lines of credit because he had legally changed his name to Khalid bin Al-Saud. His Social Security number, immigration records, and college transcripts were all under that name. On paper, he was the prince, and he had the documents to prove it. Despite this cleverness, he was sentenced to four years in prison, with another three added after a failed escape attempt involving a fire and shampoo-covered floors.

Upon his next release, Gignac decided he needed to be a "better criminal." He was tired of short-lived scams and wanted to enjoy the princely lifestyle for longer stretches. He recognized his weakness was on the business side of his cons, so he sought a partner who could provide legitimacy and business acumen. He found that partner in Carl Williamson, a London-born banker with extensive connections to the wealthy. Together, they launched a new venture called Martin Williamson International.

Their primary scheme revolved around the highly anticipated initial public offering (IPO) of Saudi Aramco, the sixth largest company in the world. Williamson, claiming to have known Gignac for twenty years, told potential investors they could get in on the IPO before it went public. He showed them fraudulent documents proving Gignac had over $2 billion in assets. The pitch worked, and they collected $8 million from twenty-six different investors.

For Gignac, however, it was never just about the money; it was about the image. He flaunted his wealth on Instagram with a constant stream of posts featuring luxury cars, piles of cash, and Rolexes. His dog even wore a diamond collar. This social media presence wasn't just for show; it added a layer of credibility to his persona. Between photos of his lavish lifestyle, he would post pictures of actual Saudi royals, which he claimed to have taken himself.

Their success with the IPO scheme emboldened them, and they set their sights on a much larger target: billionaire real estate heir Jeff Soffer, whose family owned the famed Fontainebleau Hotel in Miami. The hotel had been in debt for years, so Soffer was receptive when a supposed Saudi prince called with a massive investment offer. Gignac and Soffer began spending time together, even flying on a private plane to Aspen to discuss business.

This trip, however, marked the beginning of the end for the Prince of Fraud. Soffer had been secretly running a background check on Gignac. When Gignac got word of this, he feigned outrage and threatened to call off the deal. A panicked Soffer, on the advice of Carl Williamson, gave Gignac a lavish Cartier bracelet as a peace offering. The gesture seemed to work, and to smooth things over, Soffer invited Gignac to a fancy dinner. It was there that Gignac made his fatal mistake: he ordered an appetizer containing prosciutto, a pork product forbidden in Islam.

The detail clicked in Soffer's mind. He started reviewing Gignac's Instagram feed through a new lens, noticing all the other non-Islamic behaviors: his ownership of dogs, his consumption of alcohol, his gambling — all proudly advertised to the world. While true Arab royals might indulge in such activities privately, they would never be so brazenly public about them. Soffer knew he had been duped. He had his private investigator confirm his suspicions, which took only five minutes, and then alerted the State Department and the Federal Bureau of Investigation (FBI).

By then, Gignac was traveling the world, living lavishly off his ill-gotten gains. While he was away, federal agents built their case, raiding his Miami penthouse and seizing half a million dollars' worth of jewelry, cash, and art. When Gignac finally returned to the United States, federal agents swarmed him before he could even get off the plane, swapping his diamond bracelets for a pair made of stainless steel. He was charged with wire fraud, conspiracy, and aggravated identity theft. His partner, Carl Williamson, was also charged as a co-conspirator. Facing the prospect of a long prison sentence, Williamson hanged himself in his home.

Anthony Gignac was found guilty on all charges and sentenced to eighteen years in federal prison. In a twisted way, after a lifetime of deception, he finally achieved the one thing he had always craved above all else: he might not have the riches, but he was finally, undeniably famous.

14

THE CELEBRITY CANNIBAL

In the summer of 1981, a small man living in a quiet apartment in the Latin Quarter of Paris prepared for dinner. His name was Issei Sagawa, a Japanese doctoral student in comparative literature at the Sorbonne. He was unassuming in appearance—thin, frail, and barely over five feet (about 152 centimeters) tall. To his neighbors, he was polite and soft-spoken, the kind of man who seemed perpetually lost in his books. But that evening, he was waiting for a woman named Renée Hartevelt, a fellow student he admired deeply. She had agreed to come by and help him with a German poem he wanted to record for study. When she arrived, she had no reason to suspect that the man she considered a harmless friend had spent years imagining the moment he might kill and eat another human being.

Issei Sagawa was born on April 26, 1949, in Kobe, Japan. He came from wealth and privilege. His father was a powerful businessman — president of Kurita Water Industries—while his grandfather had been the editor of one of Japan's largest newspapers. His mother stayed home to care for the family, and by all accounts, the Sagawa household was loving, traditional, and financially secure. There was no history of neglect or violence, no trauma that might foreshadow the horrors their eldest son would later commit. Yet, from the moment he entered the world, something about Issei seemed offbeat, fragile, and uncertain.

He was born prematurely, so small that his father could hold him in the palm of one hand. As a baby, he suffered from enteritis, an inflammation of the intestines that nearly killed him. The doctors' treatments saved his life but left him sickly and frail. Throughout childhood, his delicate health kept him apart from other children. He was quiet, shy, and often lost in his imagination. Books became his refuge. He read constantly — fairy tales, folklore, and literature that transported him away from the weak, awkward body he despised. In the stories he loved, heroes triumphed over monsters. Yet somewhere in his mind, those monsters began to fascinate him more than the heroes did.

He later described a memory from his early years, a moment that stayed with him for life. His uncle had once played a game with him and his younger brother, pretending to be a man-eating giant who chased them around the house. Their father would "rescue" them in the end, and everyone would laugh. For most children, it was harmless fun, but Issei recalled an emotion he didn't understand — a strange mix of fear and excitement, something deeper than play. He would later say that this was his first awakening, the moment he became fascinated by stories of cannibalism. Tales like *Hansel and Gretel* — where children are nearly eaten by a witch — stirred something in him. They frightened him, but they also thrilled him. He didn't know why.

The Sagawa household was affectionate but reserved. Sex was a topic no one ever mentioned. As a result, when Issei reached adolescence and his body began to change, he didn't understand what was happening. The first time he experienced sexual arousal, he thought he was ill. Without any guidance or discussion, his curiosity took dark turns. He began to act out secret experiments — things that left him ashamed but also confusedly exhilarated. His understanding of desire became warped, tangled up with guilt and secrecy. By the time he was a teenager, his fantasies had already begun to merge with violence.

When he was around six years old, he experienced another memory that haunted him. He looked at the bare thighs of a classmate and thought to himself that he wanted to bite them. He was just a child, but the thought felt instinctive. As he grew older, the urge didn't fade. Instead, it became more specific: he imagined consuming women — especially those he found beautiful, strong, and healthy, everything he believed he was not.

By the time he reached high school, Issei understood that these thoughts were not normal. At fifteen, he tried to seek psychiatric help, contacting a psychologist, but he never went through with it. He couldn't bring himself to confess such fantasies to anyone, especially his parents. From the outside, he remained the quiet, bookish son of a respectable family, but internally, his mind was already turning toward something monstrous.

After earning his master's degree in English literature in Japan, Sagawa enrolled at Wako University in Tokyo. He was intelligent and deeply interested in Western culture, particularly European literature. Yet even as he read the classics, his dark fascination persisted. In 1972, when he was 24, he saw a tall, blonde German woman walking along a Tokyo street. To most men, she might have been simply beautiful. To Issei, she was prey. That summer, he followed her home. Late one night, he crept through her unlocked window, clutching an umbrella as a makeshift weapon. She was asleep and naked. He later claimed that he didn't intend to kill her — he just wanted to take a bite of her flesh. Before he could act, she woke, screamed, and overpowered him easily.

The police arrived quickly and arrested him, charging him with attempted rape. The true intention behind his intrusion was never revealed to authorities. His wealthy father intervened, paid a settlement to the victim, and ensured that the charges were dropped. Issei walked free. Nothing in his life changed, except that his fantasies grew more powerful. He had come close to realizing them, and now he knew they were not impossible.

Nine years later, in 1981, Issei Sagawa was living in Paris. He had moved there to pursue a PhD in comparative literature at the Sorbonne, one of Europe's most prestigious universities. His new life seemed cosmopolitan, even romantic — a young Japanese scholar in the heart of France, surrounded by art and intellectuals. But inside his small apartment in the city's Latin Quarter, he lived a double life. By day he attended lectures and read poetry; by night he visited sex workers, bringing them back to his apartment with a gun hidden in his bag. He never followed through, always freezing at the last moment. But every attempt brought him closer to the reality of what he wanted to do.

It was during this time that he met Renée Hartevelt. She was 25, Dutch, and brilliant. A fellow PhD student studying French literature, she was tall, elegant, and fluent in three languages. To Issei, she embodied everything he admired and envied. He saw in her a kind of perfection — intellectual, physical, and moral. They met in class, and he quickly found a way to spend time with her. Claiming that he needed help improving his German, he offered to pay her for tutoring sessions, supported, he said, by his father's wealth. Renée agreed. She considered him an odd but kind friend, someone who seemed lonely and harmless.

Over the following weeks, they met regularly. They talked about literature, music, and art. Renée enjoyed his company but to Issei, these meetings became unbearable. He wanted more than friendship. He wanted to consume her — to literally take her into himself. In his own words, he felt small, weak, and ugly, while she was tall and beautiful. He believed that by eating her, he could somehow absorb her vitality. It was a delusion, but one that had obsessed him for decades.

One evening, he invited her to his apartment for dinner, asking her to read aloud from a German poem he admired. She sat at his desk, her back to him, unaware that a rifle was hidden in a drawer nearby. He raised the gun to shoot, but it jammed. She didn't notice. He laughed nervously, pretended nothing had happened, and saw her off as though the night had been ordinary. But the failure only deepened his obsession.

A few days later, on June 11, 1981, he invited her again under the same pretext. This time, he offered her tea, secretly mixed with whiskey. When she seemed relaxed, he confessed that he loved her. Renée, polite but firm, told him she valued his friendship but did not feel the same way. She tried to let him down gently and Issei said he understood. Then he handed her the book of poems and asked her to read. She sat down, facing the window, and began. Behind her, he raised the rifle. The shot entered her neck. For a moment, she kept reading before collapsing to the floor.

The sound of the gun had been muffled by the apartment's thick walls. No one came. Issei fainted briefly, overcome by shock. When he woke, the reality of what he had done began to settle. He had killed her. And now, his fantasy could finally be realized.

He laid a towel beneath her head, undressed her, and began to prepare her body. His obsession had always focused on one part of the body—the thighs and buttocks. He attempted to bite into the flesh but found his teeth too weak. He fetched a fruit knife, then a sharper one, but neither worked. Finally, he left the apartment and went to a store, purchasing a meat knife. With it, he began cutting. Later, he described the taste and texture in grotesque detail, comparing the fat to corn-colored butter and the flesh to raw tuna. He cooked some portions, ate others raw, experimenting with sauces and seasonings. He took photographs of each stage, documenting the process as if it were a ritual or a study.

For two days, he continued, storing pieces of her in plastic bags and the refrigerator. When the body began to decay and flies appeared, he realized he had to dispose of it. He dismembered the remains, placed them in two large suitcases, and called a taxi. The driver helped him load the heavy bags and joked, "What's in here, a body?" Issei smiled weakly and said they were full of books.

He asked to be taken to the Bois de Boulogne, a large park west of Paris. It was evening, around eight p.m., and the park was still busy. As he struggled to drag the suitcases toward a secluded lake, passersby watched him curiously. The small man sweating and dragging two bulky cases drew attention. Feeling overwhelmed, he left the bags near the water's edge and walked a few steps away to catch his breath. At that moment, an older man nearby called out, asking if the bags were his. Issei replied that they were not and walked away quickly.

The man, suspicious, opened one of the cases. Inside, wrapped in a blood-soaked sheet, was a human torso. He screamed for help. Police arrived within minutes, cordoned off the area, and began their investigation. Witnesses described a small Japanese man as the one who had left the suitcases. It did not take long for detectives to connect him to the address of a local student — Issei Sagawa.

When police entered his apartment, they found the evidence unmistakable. The refrigerator contained human remains. Photographs, tools, and books lay scattered around the room. Issei did not resist. When asked why he had done it, he replied calmly that he had killed her to eat her flesh.

Despite the confession and overwhelming evidence, the legal process that followed was a failure of justice. The French court deemed him mentally unfit to stand trial, diagnosing him as legally insane. He was sent to a psychiatric institution rather than prison, where he remained for only two years. His father hired prominent lawyers and paid for his care. In 1984, after negotiations between France and Japan, he was deported to his home country, officially transferred to a hospital in Tokyo.

Upon arrival, Japanese doctors examined him and declared him sane—but evil. They believed his crime had been driven not by psychosis but by perversion and desire. Yet because the French authorities refused to release the case documents, Japan had no legal evidence to prosecute him. Without those files, there could be no trial. After fifteen months of observation, the hospital released him on August 12, 1986. He walked out a free man.

The reaction in Japan was unlike anything the French could have imagined. Instead of disgust or fear, the media treated Issei Sagawa as a morbid celebrity. His crime became a national curiosity. Newspapers published interviews, magazines offered him columns, and publishers commissioned books. He wrote essays describing the murder in chilling detail, later collected in a best-selling volume that sold over 200,000 copies. Photographs from the crime scene — leaked illegally — circulated in print, turning the tragedy of Renée Hartevelt into spectacle.

Sagawa became a frequent guest on talk shows, where he spoke openly about cannibalism. He drew cartoons and wrote novels that mixed fantasy and confession. He acted in low-budget films and even appeared in pornography, often cast as himself — a man whose notoriety was his only appeal. In one adult film, he lived for a day with a co-star, and after they had sex, he revealed who he was, showing her photographs of his crime. The woman burst into tears. Yet, strangely, they remained friends afterward.

For years, Sagawa lived off the income from these appearances and from royalties. He published a comic book featuring graphic illustrations of the murder. He painted nude women, selling the artworks to collectors. He was both reviled and fascinated by the attention, calling himself cursed by his own freedom. "Not being able to live as a normal person," he told *Vice* in 2009, "is my punishment." But his statements lacked remorse. In that same interview, he admitted that his desires had never disappeared. Even as an aging man, he said, he still fantasized about consuming human flesh. On his way to the interview, he confessed, he had seen a woman on the street and imagined eating her legs.

By that point, his life had deteriorated into quiet decay. He lived alone in a small apartment outside Tokyo, supported occasionally by his younger brother. In 2013, he suffered a cerebral hemorrhage that left him paralyzed and confined to a wheelchair. He could no longer eat solid food and was fed through a tube. Yet even then, he spoke publicly about his wish to die at the hands of a beautiful woman, slowly and painfully, as if to complete some twisted cycle of desire and death.

Renée Hartevelt's family never spoke publicly about her murder. They avoided interviews, refusing to turn their daughter's tragedy into spectacle. Their silence stands in stark contrast to the noise that surrounded her killer. For them, there was only grief and disbelief: a young woman full of promise, her life taken and desecrated, while the man who killed her became infamous and free.

Issei Sagawa's story is one of failure — not just personal but systemic. The legal loopholes that allowed his release exposed the fragility of justice when nations fail to cooperate. His transformation from murderer to media figure revealed society's own morbid fascination with evil. Over time, his fame faded, but he never expressed true guilt. Instead, he lived out his remaining years as a symbol of horror — an aging man trapped inside a body that once longed to consume others, reduced now to one that could barely feed itself.

15

THE HOLY ROLLERS CULT

In 1903, the small farming community of Corvallis, Oregon, was the epitome of a town where time moved at a slower, more predictable pace. It was a place where everyone knew everyone else's business, where secrets were impossible to keep, and where the local newspaper reported on the mundane triumphs of its citizens, such as a man's swift bicycle journey to a neighboring town or the comical terror of a store employee who mistook a large rat for a panther. Life was simple, quiet, and largely uneventful. That all changed the day a stranger strolled into town with a fierce knowledge of scripture, a disarming charm, and a bold, world-altering declaration: he had a direct line to God. The man's name was Franz Edmund Creffield, and his arrival would unleash a torrent of religious fanaticism that would rapidly devolve into a bizarre and dangerous cult, plunging the once-peaceful community into a constant state of chaos filled with rumors of strange rituals, orgies, and ultimately, a string of violent deaths that would leave families shattered for decades to come.

Little is known about Franz Creffield's life before he appeared in Oregon. It is believed he was born in Germany sometime in the 1870s, and based on his later obsession with scripture, it's thought he came from a deeply religious background, perhaps even having formally studied theology. By the time he was in his twenties, he had made his way to the United States, and records place him as a member of the Salvation Army, Protestant Christian church and an international charitable organisation, in Oregon by 1899. For a time, the organization, with its military-style ranks and focus on evangelical charity work, seemed a perfect fit for the intensely devout young man. He excelled, and the higher-ups, seeing his potential as a future leader, even selected him for officer training school.

But something inside Creffield began to shift. He grew even more fanatical in his beliefs, and a rift formed between him and the other members. He started to openly criticize the Salvation Army's focus on fundraising, believing they were placing too much emphasis on money and not enough on pure spirituality. The conflict festered until, in 1901, Creffield claimed to have been visited by the Holy Spirit, who delivered a divine message: the Salvation Army was not entirely of God, and he was to leave its ranks immediately. He obeyed, traveling to Salem, Oregon, where he enrolled in a training school for aspiring preachers run by a Pentecostal minister named Martin L. Ryan.

For a while, he seemed to thrive under Ryan's teachings, but soon, the Holy Spirit allegedly appeared to him again, this time with a far grander pronouncement. The spirit told Creffield that he was God's chosen one. This anointing filled him with a new sense of purpose and arrogance. Believing he no longer needed anyone's guidance, he decided he was ready to set out on his own and establish a new church with himself as its one true prophet. In 1903, he left Salem and traveled forty miles (about sixty-five kilometers) south, arriving in the unsuspecting town of Corvallis.

Creffield knew that if he simply walked into town and announced his divine status, he would be dismissed as a lunatic. He had to ease people into his radical theology, so he began by preaching conventional sermons about being a good person and helping one's neighbors, singing familiar hymns, and hosting services that felt no different from any other church in the area. This approach allowed him to slowly build a small but loyal following. Once he had gained their trust, he began to subtly introduce his own unique doctrines. He spoke of how God had communicated with him directly, and he promised his followers that if they gave themselves over to God completely, they too could one day hear His voice. He introduced the concept of a "holy roll" in heaven, a sacred list upon which their names could be written, guaranteeing their salvation. But, he also said space on this roll was limited, forcing them to commit to his teachings fully and immediately or risk eternal damnation.

This tactic worked. While some were skeptical and left his services, a significant number of people, many of them disillusioned former members of the Salvation Army, were captivated by his message and became his most devoted followers. With his core group secured, Creffield began to introduce stranger and more intense practices. He focused heavily on hell and repentance, and he instilled in his flock a sense of superiority, claiming that because they were led by a true prophet, they were inherently better than all other religious groups. He also claimed to possess divine healing powers, waving his hands over his followers and praying until they believed they had been cured of their ailments.

The centerpiece of his new church was the ritual of repentance. These sessions were anything but peaceful. Creffield would have his followers pray over each other for hours on end, their prayers escalating into convulsive screams and chants. He then instructed them to roll around on the ground, praying to heaven, sometimes for as long as twenty-four hours straight. The effect of this practice was profound. Mentally and physically exhausted, sleep-deprived, and disoriented from the endless rolling, his followers would begin to experience auditory and visual hallucinations, which they interpreted as the divine messages Creffield had promised. This shared delusion sealed their faith. They were utterly convinced that Creffield was a true prophet who had given them the secret to communicating directly with God.

These loud and chaotic meetings quickly drew the ire of the other townspeople. The all-night screaming and chanting made sleep impossible, and the behavior of Creffield's female followers became a source of local scandal. The constant rolling left their hair undone and disheveled, and they often walked around barefoot, actions considered immodest for women of that era. Words like "sect" and "cult" began to circulate, and the townspeople mockingly dubbed the group the "Holy Rollers" for their bizarre rituals. After months of escalating tension, the community had had enough and city officials formally banned Creffield from holding his services within the Corvallis city limits. The town hoped this would be the end of the matter, but for Creffield's followers, their faith was unshakable.

Creffield, ever the opportunist, claimed that God had once again visited him, conveniently instructing him to move his flock to Smith Island, a small, uninhabited piece of land just three miles (about five kilometers) outside of town. In the summer of 1903, approximately twenty of his most loyal followers abandoned their jobs, their homes, and in some cases, their spouses and children, to join him.

Among those who followed him to the island were several key figures whose lives would become tragically intertwined with the cult's fate. There was the Hurt family, led by the patriarch O.V. Hurt and his wife, Sarah. Their twenty-three-year-old daughter, Maud, a woman described as both beautiful and intensely intelligent, had been a religious prodigy since childhood and became one of Creffield's most ardent disciples. She convinced her mother, Sarah, her sister May, and her brother Frank to join her on the island, terrified that their souls would be lost if they didn't get their names on the holy roll. Frank's fiancée, Molly Sandell, also joined the exodus. Then there were Donna and Esther Mitchell, two sisters from a family of seven children who had been abandoned by their father after their mother's death. Donna was married to a man named Burgess Starr, while fifteen-year-old Esther had left the Salvation Army to follow Creffield. The group also included Cora Hartley and her daughter Sophie, the wife and child of Lewis Hartley, by far the wealthiest man in the region, who despised Creffield and the hold he had on his family.

On Smith Island, away from the prying eyes of society, Creffield's control intensified. They lived in tents and spent their days in a state of constant religious frenzy, with multi-day "roll-a-thons" becoming a regular occurrence. Creffield's talk of the apocalypse ramped up, and he proclaimed himself "Joshua the Holy Prophet," a name his followers dutifully adopted. He ordered them to shed their worldly possessions, forcing them to wear thin, simple dresses or sometimes nothing at all.

The first sign of his manipulative nature came when he targeted Maud Hurt's wealthy fiancé, James Barry, who had provided the seed money for

Creffield's church. When Creffield demanded Barry fund the construction of a tabernacle, Barry not only refused but asked when Creffield planned to repay the initial loan. Enraged, Creffield claimed God had canceled the debt and ordered a stunned Maud to immediately break off their engagement, which she did without hesitation. After this, he systematically broke up all the other unmarried couples in the group.

He then implemented a deeply disturbing ceremony he called being "endowed with the grace of love." He would summon the women and girls of the cult, one by one, into his private tent for hours of supposed "prayer." While what happened inside was never definitively proven, it's widely believed he manipulated them into performing sexual acts under the guise of religious purification. At the end of each session, he would order the woman, regardless of her age or marital status, to kiss him. Any refusal was met with accusations of demonic possession, followed by brutal beatings to "drive the devil out." When some of the men in the group began to express doubts about his methods, Creffield swiftly kicked them out, consolidating his power and leaving himself with a flock of mostly compliant women. One of the men kicked out, Burgess Starr, later told reporters that Creffield had his followers so completely in his power that they would have jumped into a river if he had commanded it.

At the end of the summer, with the weather turning cold, the group needed a new place to stay. Maud Hurt offered up her family's home, which was conveniently located just outside the Corvallis city limits where Creffield's ban was not in effect. Her father, O.V. Hurt had been waiting all summer for his family to return, and though he despised Creffield, he tolerated the cult's presence in his home just to be reunited with his wife and children. His reward for this devotion was constant torment. The cult members, including his own family, refused to call him by his name, referring to him only as the "black devil" and constantly warning him that God would smite him for his lack of faith. After months of this psychological abuse, the beleaguered O.V. Hurt finally broke and joined the group himself.

With the entire Hurt family now under his control, Creffield's behavior grew even more erratic. During a traditional spring cleaning, he ordered his followers not to clean the house, but to burn it. They dragged all of the Hurt family's possessions outside and threw them onto a giant bonfire, along with items brought from their own former homes in Corvallis. They also sacrificed a dog, and rumors began to swirl that they had sacrificed Hurt's adopted toddler, Martha, as well. The rumor, though false, prompted a police visit. The officers who entered the Hurt home walked into a scene of pure madness. The cult members were scattered around a room in a trance-like state, some kneeling, some rolling on the floor, all looking pale and haggard with hollowed eyes. In the center of the room, a young girl with a cloth over her head was channeling a message from God while others wrote down her words.

The visit from the police did little to slow Creffield's descent. After O.V. was briefly convinced to leave the cult and kicked the group out of his house, they moved into the nearby home of Frank and Molly Hurt. It was there that Creffield had his most audacious revelation yet: God had commanded him to find a woman who would become the next Virgin Mary and bear the second Christ. He claimed he could "purify" the women of their past sins, making even mothers eligible for this holy duty. This was the origin of the group's other name, the "Brides of Christ," and it served as Creffield's justification for having sex with all the women and underage girls in the cult, often in group orgies, under the pretext of purification. He first chose sixteen-year-old Esther Mitchell to be his bride, but her older sister had her committed to an orphanage to protect her. His next choice was Maud Hurt.

But before he could marry Maud, a vigilante group of twenty local men calling themselves the "White Caps" stormed the house in the middle of the night. They kidnapped Creffield and the other male members, marched them naked through the center of Corvallis, and publicly tarred and feathered them as a warning to leave town for good. Undeterred, Creffield married Maud Hurt the very next day before fleeing to Portland. The law finally caught up with him when Donna Starr, Burgess's wife, officially filed a complaint of adultery against him, which was a crime at the time. After a manhunt, Creffield was found hiding in a shallow hole dug beneath the Hurt family's house, naked and emaciated. It was later revealed that while O.V. Hurt was at work, Creffield had been crawling out from under the house to conduct orgies with his female followers, who had been sneaking him food. He was finally tried, found guilty of adultery, and sentenced to two years in prison.

Creffield was released from prison after serving only seventeen months, and he immediately set out to reassemble his flock. His followers, who had been released from the state insane asylum where their families had committed them, remained as devoted as ever. He gathered them once more, this time with the goal of establishing a "New Eden" on the Oregon coast. After a failed murder attempt by the enraged Lewis Hartley, whose gun misfired five times — an event Creffield touted as proof of his divine protection — he abandoned the majority of his followers in a remote cave at Cummins Creek, telling them to wait for his return while he and Maud went to Seattle.

But Creffield's day of reckoning was at hand. George Mitchell, the brother of Donna and Esther, had been consumed with rage for months over the abuse his sisters had endured, tracked Creffield to Seattle. On May 7, 1906, as Creffield and Maud walked down the sidewalk, George stepped out from the shadows, raised his pistol, and fired a single bullet into the back of the prophet's head, killing him instantly. George Mitchell sat calmly on the curb, smoked a cigar, and waited for the police. The public, believing the murder to be entirely justified, rallied behind him, raising thousands for his defense. At his trial, after O.V. Hurt gave a heart-wrenching testimony about the destruction of his family, the jury returned a verdict of not guilty.

The saga, however, was far from over. The followers who had been left in the cave were discovered nearly a month later, starving and delusional, still waiting for their leader to return. When they learned of his death, they were devastated, but none took it harder than Esther Mitchell. A few days after her brother's acquittal, as George prepared to board a train, Esther approached him at the station. After a brief farewell, she pulled out a gun and shot her brother in the head, killing him in the exact same manner he had killed Creffield. During the investigation, it was discovered that Maud Hurt had conspired with Esther to commit the murder. Before she could be tried, Maud committed suicide in her jail cell by swallowing strychnine. Esther was found to be insane and was sent to a psychiatric hospital. A few years after her release, still haunted by her past, she took her own life in the same way, poisoning herself with strychnine at the age of twenty-six. And so, the reign of the Holy Rollers ended not with a divine resurrection, but with a trail of broken lives and a series of tragic, violent deaths, a testament to how one charismatic stranger could walk into a quiet town and tear it apart from the inside out.

16

THE GHOST IN THE SKY

The day before Thanksgiving, 1971, was a time of hurried motion across the United States, a great annual convergence of families preparing for the holiday. Airports were filled with the low hum of routine travel, a backdrop of gate announcements, rolling luggage, and brief farewells. At the airport in Portland, Oregon, the rhythm was no different. Travelers checked in, milled about the gates, and waited for their calls to board Northwest Orient Flight 305, a short, thirty-minute commuter hop to Seattle, Washington. Among the anonymous faces in the terminal was a man who approached the ticket counter and gave the name Dan Cooper. He was described as being in his mid-forties, with a slim build, and he was dressed in the unremarkable attire of a traveling businessman: a dark suit, a white shirt, a narrow black tie, and a pair of mirrored sunglasses that concealed his eyes. He paid twenty dollars in cash for his one-way ticket, a transaction so ordinary that it would have been forgotten by the end of the day.

In an era before the stringent security protocols that would later define air travel, boarding a domestic flight was a simple, almost casual act. There were no metal detectors to walk through, no baggage X-rays, no mandatory identification checks, no nothing. It was entirely possible to walk onto a commercial airliner carrying anything one could conceal in a briefcase or coat pocket, just as Dan Cooper did. He found his assigned seat, 18C, at the very back of the Boeing 727, lit a Raleigh cigarette, and flagged down a flight attendant named Florence Schaffner to order a drink: a bourbon and Seven Up on the rocks. He settled into his seat, a quiet and solitary figure, just another passenger on a short flight home for the holidays.

The plane took off on schedule, climbing into the gray, overcast sky of the Pacific Northwest. As it ascended, Cooper leaned forward slightly and handed the folded note to Florence Schaffner. She initially dismissed the gesture, assuming it was the clumsy, unsolicited advance of a lonely businessman — a phone number, perhaps, or a forward invitation. She slipped the note into her purse without a glance. But Cooper leaned closer, his voice low but firm. "Miss," he said, "you'd better look at that note. I have a bomb." The quiet insistence in his tone, a stark contrast to the casual atmosphere of the cabin, cut through her professional composure. She retrieved the note and read the neatly printed words. They were stark and direct, stating that he had a bomb in his briefcase and that he wanted her to sit beside him.

Schaffner felt a surge of cold disbelief, but one look at the man's impassive face told her this was not a joke. She asked to see the device, and Cooper obliged, cracking open his attaché case just enough for her to glimpse a terrifying arrangement of wires, red-colored sticks that resembled dynamite, and a large battery. It was undeniably a bomb. He calmly closed the case and laid out his terms. He held the bare ends of two wires, making it clear that all he needed to do was touch them together to detonate the device and tear the plane from the sky. The hijacking of Flight 305 had begun.

Following Cooper's instructions, Schaffner walked to the front of the plane and discreetly informed the captain. The message was relayed from the cockpit to the control tower in Seattle, a calm but urgent transmission that set in motion a massive, multi-agency response. Northwest Orient, the FBI, and local law enforcement were all alerted. On the ground, officials scrambled to react, but inside the pressurized cabin, Dan Cooper remained a picture of composure. He sipped his bourbon, smoked his cigarettes, and politely but firmly reiterated his demands to the flight crew.

He wanted $200,000 (about $1.6 million today), delivered in a knapsack. And he wanted four parachutes: two primary back chutes and two reserve front chutes. The flight attendants, now including a second stewardess named Tina Mucklow who had become the primary liaison with Cooper, carried his handwritten demands to the captain. Cooper, ever meticulous, would later ask for these notes to be returned to him, ensuring he left as little evidence as possible.

Northwest Orient's president, Donald Nyrop, immediately authorized full cooperation. There would be no attempt to challenge the hijacker; the lives of the passengers and crew were the only priority. In Seattle, FBI agents rushed to Seafirst Bank to procure the ransom money. They gathered 10,000 individual twenty-dollar bills, meticulously photographing each one to create a record of their pre-recorded serial numbers. The cash was stuffed into a bank bag and placed inside a knapsack as instructed. Meanwhile, authorities at McChord Air Force Base were tasked with providing the parachutes.

While the complex logistics unfolded on the ground, Flight 305 circled Puget Sound for two hours, burning fuel to ensure a safe landing weight. During this time, Cooper's demeanor never wavered. He was calm, even gentlemanly, engaging in polite conversation with Tina Mucklow. He paid for his drink and even offered to tip her. His apparent lack of agitation was unnerving. He seemed entirely in control of the situation, a man executing a well-rehearsed plan.

Finally, the plane landed at Seattle-Tacoma Airport. Cooper directed the pilots to taxi to a remote, isolated section of the runway, far from the main terminal and shrouded in darkness and rain. There, a single airline employee drove out to the aircraft with the knapsack of money and the parachutes. The exchange was tense but smooth. The items were handed over through the plane's galley door, and once Cooper had confirmed the contents, he made good on his word. He allowed all thirty-six passengers and two of the flight attendants, including a visibly relieved Florence Schaffner, to get off the plane. The passengers, who had remained entirely oblivious to the life-threatening drama unfolding just a few rows behind them, walked off into the rainy Seattle night, believing they had been delayed by a simple mechanical issue.

The flight crew — the pilot, co-pilot, flight engineer, and Tina Mucklow — remained as hostages. Once the plane was refueled, Cooper gave his new, highly specific flight plan. He instructed the pilots to fly towards Mexico City, a destination the captain immediately explained was impossible. They did not have enough fuel for such a long journey. The captain suggested Reno or Phoenix as alternatives. "Reno's nice," Cooper replied casually. "Let's go to Reno."

He then issued a precise set of flight instructions that were both bizarre and dangerous. The plane was to fly at a low altitude of 10,000 feet (about 3,000 meters high), with the landing gear and wing flaps extended down, a configuration that would limit its speed to a sluggish 200 miles per hour (about 322 kilometers per hour). The cabin was to remain unpressurized. The autopilot was set to a low-altitude flight path known as Victor 23. This unusual setup suggested to the crew that Cooper knew exactly what he was doing; he was creating the ideal conditions for a low-speed, low-altitude parachute jump. To enforce these conditions, two Air Force F-106 fighter jets were scrambled to shadow the airliner, but they struggled to maintain the slow speed and were forced to repeatedly circle the hijacked plane rather than follow it closely.

With the flight underway, Cooper ordered Tina Mucklow to go to the cockpit and remain there with the rest of the crew, ensuring he would be alone in the main cabin. As she left, she saw him tying something around his waist; she assumed he was securing the heavy bag of money to his body. A short time later, at approximately 8:13 p.m., a warning light illuminated in the cockpit, indicating that the aft stairway door at the rear of the plane had been opened. The Boeing 727 was one of the only commercial aircraft with such a feature, and in 1971, there was no mechanism — known as a Cooper Vane — to prevent it from being deployed in mid-air. The crew felt a sudden, distinct change in the cabin pressure. The pilot got on the intercom. There was no answer. The man who called himself Dan Cooper had jumped from the plane, disappearing with his money and parachutes into the raging, black storm of the Pacific Northwest night. He was never seen or heard from again.

When the plane landed safely in Reno, it was met by a swarm of FBI agents and law enforcement, who were stunned to find the hijacker gone.

An immediate and thorough search of the aircraft yielded what little evidence Cooper had left behind: the black clip-on tie and mother-of-pearl tie pin, eight Raleigh cigarette butts, and two of the four parachutes he had requested — one primary chute and one reserve chute that had been partially opened, perhaps for him to inspect its components. The bomb, the briefcase, and the ransom notes had all vanished with him.

Working with the crew's detailed statements, the FBI quickly produced a composite sketch of the suspect. Aviation experts at Boeing, using the plane's known flight path and the precise moment the cabin pressure changed, calculated a probable drop zone. Factoring in the severe weather and strong westerly winds, they designated a vast, twenty-eight square mile (about seventy-two square kilometers) search area of dense, rugged wilderness near Ariel, Washington. On Thanksgiving morning, one of the largest and most intensive manhunts in American history began. For weeks, hundreds of FBI agents, National Guardsmen, and military personnel, assisted by helicopters and spotter planes, combed the dense forests and remote farmland. They found nothing — no parachute, no money, no knapsack, and no body. It was as if Dan Cooper had been swallowed whole by the wilderness.

The story of the audacious crime captured the public's imagination, and the media quickly elevated the hijacker to the status of a living legend. In an early wire report, a journalist mistakenly referred to him as "D.B. Cooper," and despite immediate corrections, the catchier, more alliterative name stuck, forever cementing his place in American folklore. In the turbulent context of the early 1970s, an era defined by the Vietnam War, civil rights protests, and a deep-seated distrust of authority, many people saw Cooper not as a violent criminal, but as a modern-day pirate, a cool and clever gentleman thief who had executed a daring plan and gotten away with it.

For nearly a decade, the case remained a frustrating cold file for the FBI. Then, in February 1980, what seemed like a major breakthrough occurred. An eight-year old boy named Brian Ingram was digging a fire pit in the sand while on a family picnic on the banks of the Columbia River, at a spot called Tena Bar. His hands uncovered three decaying, tightly bound bundles of cash, the rubber bands still clinging to the moldy bills. His family turned the money over to the FBI, where the serial numbers were checked against the ransom list. It was a definitive match. The discovery of $5,800 of Cooper's money, however, only deepened the mystery. The location was more than twenty miles (about thirty-two kilometers) from the originally designated drop zone, and in the opposite direction of the prevailing winds on the night of the jump. Geologists added another layer of confusion, determining that the money was found above a layer of sand that had been dredged from the riverbed in 1974, meaning the cash must have arrived on the riverbank at least three years after the hijacking. This led many to speculate that Cooper himself, alive and well, had returned to bury it, but an extensive excavation of the area yielded no further clues.

Years turned into decades, and the case file swelled with over a thousand suspects, but none could ever be definitively linked to the crime. The legend of D.B. Cooper only grew, celebrated annually in Ariel, Washington, with a party in his honor. In July 2016, after forty-five years of fruitless investigation, the FBI officially announced it was closing its active investigation into the Cooper case, citing a need to redirect resources to other priorities. The case was now officially cold, left to a dedicated subculture of citizen sleuths, amateur detectives, and independent researchers who refused to let the mystery die.

It was one of these groups, led by scientist Tom Kaye, that began to apply modern forensic technology to the old evidence, a process that systematically dismantled the myth of the expert hijacker. Using a powerful electron microscope, Kaye's team analyzed the clip-on tie Cooper left behind. They discovered thousands of particles of rare elements, including pure titanium, cerium, and strontium sulfide. In 1971, this specific combination was exceptionally rare, strongly suggesting that Cooper may have been an engineer, a manager, or a chemist at a high-tech manufacturing firm, possibly in the then-booming aerospace industry. Boeing, in fact, was a major user of these materials at the time.

This new scientific lens also reframed Cooper's actions on the plane. The long-held assumption that he was an experienced parachutist was challenged. A true professional, investigators now argued, would have made very different choices. He would have specified large-denomination bills to reduce the weight and bulk of the ransom; instead, the twenty-dollar bills made the money bag a cumbersome twenty-three pounds (about ten kilograms). He chose the inferior of the two primary parachutes provided, an older military-style chute known as an NB-8, which was uncomfortable, difficult to deploy, and non-maneuverable. He also jumped on a stormy night, into freezing, 200-mile-per-hour (about 322 kilometers per hours) winds, wearing a business suit and loafers with no helmet, goggles, or gloves. His claim that he didn't need instructions for the parachutes, once seen as a sign of expertise, was reinterpreted as the bluff and bravado of a desperate amateur.

The most crucial piece of the puzzle remained the recovered money. Tom Kaye and his team revisited the discovery site and, using modern GPS and archival photographs, made a pivotal discovery: the 1974 dredging had stopped 150 feet (about forty-five meters) short of where the money was found. This meant the original FBI conclusion was wrong; the money had not been buried after 1974 but had likely been deposited on the riverbank naturally, within months of the jump. With this new timeline, the only logical way for the money to have traveled over twenty miles (about thirty-two kilometers) from the drop zone was by water.

Kaye's team constructed the first truly comprehensive theory of Cooper's final moments. Reviewing the flight path, they determined that at the moment of the jump, the plane was directly over the Lewis River. Given the non-maneuverable NB-8 parachute, the powerful westerly winds would have carried Cooper directly into the frigid, turbulent waters of either the Lewis River or the vast Lake Merwin. Hitting the near-freezing water, laden with a twenty-three-pound (about ten kilograms) bag of money and likely entangled in his parachute harness, his chances of survival would have been almost zero. Hypothermia would have set in within minutes. His body, along with the money, would have been carried down the fast-running river toward its confluence with the Columbia. This explained how the money got into the river system, but not how it ended up upstream on a sandbar. Kaye proposed a final, grim possibility. At the time, the Columbia River was a busy shipping lane. It's plausible that Cooper's body and the money bag became snagged on a ship's propeller and were carried upstream. The violent motion could have ripped the bag open, spilling some of the contents, which then washed ashore before being covered by sand. As for Cooper's body, the powerful currents of the Columbia would have likely pulled it out into the Pacific Ocean within days, where it would be lost forever.

This scientific account suggests the legendary outlaw did not survive to enjoy his spoils on a beach in Mexico, but instead died a cold and lonely death that very night. Yet, while evidence points to his death, the mystery of his identity remains. Over the decades, a number of compelling suspects have been proposed. There was Robert Rackstraw, a Vietnam veteran with extensive paratrooper and explosives training, championed by a team of private investigators but long-cleared by the FBI. There was L.D. Cooper, whose niece came forward claiming he was the hijacker. And there was Walter R. Peca, another military veteran identified through linguistic analysis of a potential hijacker letter. Each suspect came with a tantalizing narrative, but never any definitive proof. The scientific evidence strongly suggests a tragic and solitary end, but without a body, without a confession, the case remains suspended in uncertainty. The official file may be closed, but the legend of the man who hijacked an airplane and leaped into history endures, a ghost in the American sky.

17

THE COMMANDO KILLER

He sat calmly on the minibus, a man on the run who had evaded capture for three years. But his distinctive features, the kind that are impossible to disguise, had given him away. Another passenger, glancing from the news on his phone to the man's face, had made the connection. The man, a brilliant and methodical killer, understood immediately that the chase was over. He stopped the vehicle, crossed the road, and boarded another bus heading in the opposite direction, a final, desperate gambit, but it was too late. The witness had seen it all, noting the new license plate and alerting the authorities. When the police pulled the minibus over and boarded, the man offered no resistance. He simply stood and surrendered. "I won't run anymore. I'm very tired," he said. "Okay, I am Atalay Filiz."

The capture of Atalay Filiz marked the end of a manhunt that had gripped Turkey, a story involving international disappearances, meticulously planned executions, and a killer who possessed a chilling combination of high intelligence and profound social detachment. He was a classic organized killer, a type more commonly associated with European or American case files, a rarity in the annals of Turkish crime. Unlike many killers who emerged from the margins of society, Filiz was a product of privilege and promise, a man whose intellectual gifts made his descent into brutal violence all the more terrifying.

Atalay Filiz was born in 1986 in Balıkesir, Bandırma, the son of a staff colonel and military pilot who later became a captain for Turkish Airlines. From a young age, it was clear that Atalay was exceptionally intelligent, but this brilliance was coupled with a deeply asocial and cold personality. His teachers would later describe him as a student who was remarkably successful yet unsettlingly unpredictable, a boy from whom you could "never know what he would do or what would become of him." He harbored a persistent dream of living abroad, of escaping the confines of his own culture for something different.

His academic prowess was undeniable. He gained admission to Istanbul's Galatasaray High School, one of the most prestigious and difficult-to-enter schools in the country, and graduated with honors. He finished third in his class. Yet, when it came time for the university entrance exams in 2005, he made a deliberate choice that baffled those who knew his capabilities. He intentionally answered questions incorrectly, sabotaging his own results. His goal was not a Turkish university; it was France. With his father's financial support, he enrolled in a biology program at the University of Paris-Sud.

It was in France that Atalay's life took the first of its dark turns. His father, through his military connections, arranged for him to connect with Göktuğ Demirarslan, the son of a close army friend who was also studying in Paris. The young men became roommates, sharing a house. It was during this period that Atalay, who had reportedly never had a girlfriend in high school, experienced his first real romance. He met a Russian exchange student named Olga Seregina and quickly became infatuated, his affection spiraling into a powerful obsession. The social circle was completed when Olga's friend, another Russian student named Elena Radchikova, began dating Göktuğ. For a time, the couples lived a seemingly normal student life.

As time passed, Atalay's obsession with Olga intensified. They even vacationed together with his family in Fethiye, Turkey, in August 2011. But the relationship was fraught with conflict, and Olga told her friends that she wanted to end it but couldn't. Soon after, Olga vanished. On December 16, 2011, she was working as a babysitter for a family in Paris. She had asked her employers for permission to leave, explaining that a friend of her boyfriend, Atalay, had arrived and she needed to meet him. She walked out of the house and was never seen again. Open-source records later confirmed that Atalay Filiz was in France on a ten-day military leave at the time of her disappearance. For investigators and those who knew the depths of his obsession, the conclusion was inescapable: Olga was his first victim, a trial run for the murders that would follow.

With Olga gone, Atalay returned to Turkey, but his focus had shifted with a predatory intensity. His obsession transferred directly onto Elena. He began to relentlessly pursue her, bombarding her with messages and emails. His advances were firmly rejected; Elena was in a committed relationship with his roommate and friend, Göktuğ. He even tried to sabotage their relationship, falsely telling Elena he had a video of Göktuğ cheating on her. For a man with Atalay's narcissistic and controlling personality, this rejection was an intolerable wound. His infatuation curdled into a lethal combination of jealousy and rage. The primary motive for the double murder was now clear: if he could not have Elena, then no one could, especially not his friend. This motive was compounded by a growing paranoia. He became convinced that Göktuğ and Elena not only suspected him of murdering Olga but were also sharing their suspicions with others, threatening to expose him.

His response was not one of panic, but of cold, methodical planning. He purchased an old, inconspicuous beige Fiat 131 car with a Kütahya license plate and drove to Ankara, where the couple now lived. In a move that demonstrated both his technical foresight and his fatal arrogance, he planted a tracking device in Göktuğ's car. It was a simple old-school mobile phone rigged to a charger and hidden in the gasoline vent pipe, but the SIM card inside was registered in his own name — a crucial mistake that would later unravel his entire scheme.

His initial plan to ambush them was thwarted when the couple left for a fifteen-day vacation in Antalya. Atalay waited patiently. When the tracking device signaled that their car was finally on the move, he put his plan back into motion. On the evening of September 16, 2013, in a housing complex in Ankara's Eryaman district, he prepared his disguise.

He put on women's clothes and a headscarf, and used a makeup kit to alter his appearance, transforming himself to avoid recognition. Armed with a hunting rifle he had legally purchased after obtaining a license by feigning mental health issues, he set up an ambush among the trees. As Göktuğ Demirarslan and Elena Radchikova approached their home, he opened fire at close range, shooting them both. As they lay wounded on the ground, he approached and fired a single, final shot into each of their heads, splattering skull fragments as far as ten feet (about three meters) away.

The double murder initially stumped the police. There were few eyewitnesses, and the killer had vanished. The investigation dragged on for months until relatives of Demirarslan took his car for maintenance and workers discovered the hidden tracking device. The SIM card provided the police with their first solid lead: the name Atalay Filiz. They cross-referenced this with security footage from the area, which showed a beige Fiat 131 car repeatedly circling the neighborhood in the days leading up to the murders, a car that was conspicuously absent after the killings. The vehicle was eventually found abandoned in Istanbul a month later. Inside, police discovered the makeup kits and hair dye alongside a grim collection of tools that could be used for dismemberment: an excavator, a shovel, various saws, screwdrivers, ropes, and surgical materials. An arrest warrant was issued on October 31, 2013, but Atalay was already gone.

For the next three years, from 2013 to 2016, Atalay Filiz was a ghost. Evidence suggested he had spent time in Portugal in January 2014, where his mother and sister were also staying in a different hotel. Throughout his time as a fugitive, he demonstrated remarkable adaptability and foresight. He used a series of false identities, most notably Furkan Altın, and relied on his intelligence and language skills to survive. He worked odd, low-profile jobs that paid in cash — as a waiter, a porter in a cafe, and in a kebab shop — allowing him to avoid creating a digital or financial footprint. He was known to carry large amounts of cash, including Euros, to facilitate quick movements. During this period, he also dedicated himself to honing his survival skills, meticulously studying commando training manuals and reading everything he could find about how to live off the land. In a warehouse he had rented, police later found murder novels, films, and CDs of the show *Dexter*. This was not the behavior of a man simply hiding; it was the preparation of a man who intended to remain a fugitive indefinitely.

In 2016, he surfaced in Tuzla, a district of Istanbul. Using his alias, he got a job as a waiter at a tea garden owned by a history teacher, Fatma Kayıkçı, and her husband. They even rented him a nearby apartment. He lived a quiet, unassuming life, though his behavior was odd; he avoided cameras, used back roads, and didn't respond to his fake name unless it was shouted. For a time, it seemed he had successfully buried his past.

But Fatma Kayıkçı was an observant and intelligent woman. She began to grow suspicious of her quiet tenant. She had a sense that he was entering her home and going through her belongings. A meticulous person by nature, she began to measure the exact placement of objects on her desk, noting their positions millimetrically. When she returned, she found that they had been moved, confirming that her tenant had been searching through her personal information.

One evening, while watching a television news program, a segment re-airing the story of the 2013 Ankara murders came on. As the fugitive's face was shown on the screen, Fatma froze. She recognized the man wanted for a brutal double homicide as her tenant, "Furkan." On May 27, 2016, as he was leaving his apartment, she confronted him at the door. "What's up, Atalay?" she asked. That simple question, born of courage and recognition, was a death sentence.

Realizing his cover was blown, Atalay's survival instincts took over. He began stalking his landlady. The next day, he ambushed her, stabbing her eleven times. In a final act of brutality designed to conceal his crime, he dismembered her body, packed the remains into a large suitcase, and abandoned it in a nearby wooded area.

With the discovery of Fatma's body, Atalay was once again a fugitive, now the subject of a nationwide manhunt. He fled to a place where he believed he was most equipped to survive: the forest. Putting his years of self-study into practice, he spent about a week living in a national park near Izmir, surviving by eating frogs and insects and using gels to ward off flies. But eventually, he grew tired of hiding and decided to make another escape, likely planning to flee the country for good.

It was this final escape attempt that led to his downfall. He made his way to Izmir, where he boarded a minibus. It was there that a fellow passenger, scrolling through the news on his phone, recognized the most wanted man in Turkey sitting just a few feet away. The chase that followed was brief, ending with his calm and almost resigned surrender. When he was captured, he was carrying a survival kit of his own making: two hunting knives, pepper spray, four fake IDs, three fake driver's licenses, fourteen credit cards, a fake French citizenship certificate, and a large amount of cash in both Turkish Lira and Euros. He also had a bizarre list of pornographic film actresses, mostly from France, with their addresses written on a kebab order slip.

The aftermath of his capture was as sensational as the manhunt itself. While in custody, a police officer took a "selfie" with a smiling Atalay Filiz. The photograph was leaked to the media and caused a national outcry. Citizens were disgusted that an officer would pose cheerfully with a notorious triple murderer, and the incident led to an internal investigation, becoming an infamous footnote in the case's history.

In custody, Atalay Filiz remained a chilling enigma. He denied any involvement in the disappearance of Olga. For the murders of Göktuğ Demirarslan, Elena Radchikova, and Fatma Kayıkçı, he was tried and received three separate aggravated life sentences. He was found to be mentally sound and fully culpable for his crimes. He expressed no remorse for his actions. He was the classic organized killer: highly intelligent, meticulous in his planning, and able to maintain a facade of normalcy while harboring a profoundly violent nature. He displayed all the hallmarks of a narcissistic personality, with a complete lack of empathy and an unshakeable belief in his own superiority.

He did, however, offer a twisted justification for the murder of Göktuğ Demirarslan. He claimed that Göktuğ was a member of the FETÖ terrorist organization, an entity widely reviled in Turkey. In his warped logic, he was not a murderer but a patriot carrying out the will of the people. "By killing him," he stated, "I actually fulfilled something the Turkish citizens wanted." He offered no such rationale for the murder of

Elena, whose only crime was rejecting him, or for Fatma Kayıkçı, whose only crime was discovering the truth. His was a mind that operated on a logic entirely its own, a cold and calculating intelligence devoid of humanity, forever marked by the chilling contradictions of a brilliant student and a brutal killer.

18

A CHILD'S DEATH SENTENCE

The words from the judge were a formal declaration, a procedural stamp on a life already derailed. But for the fifteen-year-old boy at the center of it, the reality of the sentence took time to land. It was in the sterile, echoing corridors of the classification unit that the abstract legal term — *life without parole* — began to take on a terrifying, concrete shape. A deputy called out to his colleagues, his voice a mixture of bureaucratic process and disbelief. "Man, we got a juvenile down here and he was just sentenced to life."

Suddenly, Kenneth Young was no longer just another young offender in the juvenile wing. His sentence made him an anomaly, a liability. He was abruptly pulled from the juvenile section and thrown into confinement, the isolation a direct consequence of the legal weight now attached to his name. "You can't come out of confinement because of your sentencing," they told him.

He was still a child, trying to grasp a concept that confounds many adults: a life sentence. The words did not register; they felt detached from his reality. Officials delivered the decision with blunt finality, informing him that he would not be going home and that his life would end behind bars. The idea seemed impossible, and he pushed it away. Everything had happened too quickly — one day he was a fifteen-year-old moving through society, the next he was removed from it and told he would never return. He had been condemned to die in a Florida prison for crimes committed at fourteen even though across the four robberies that led to his sentences, no one had been killed.

Before the robberies, before the courtroom and the life sentence, there was a boy trying to navigate a world that had offered him very little stability. Kenneth Young grew up in a low-income area of Tampa, Florida, an environment where the lines between survival and crime were often blurred. His father passed away when he was too young to form lasting memories, leaving a void that was never filled. The dominant force in his young life was his mother, Stephanie, a woman he loved deeply but who was locked in a decades-long battle with crack cocaine addiction.

His childhood was a chaotic rotation of neglect and fleeting moments of care. There were times when his mother would lock him and his sister in a room and disappear for days on end. As a young boy, Kenneth would get on his bicycle and ride through the neighborhood, pedaling toward the known drug houses, trying to find his mother and pull her away. He would plead with her to come home, to take a shower, to eat. On other occasions, when her addiction overwhelmed her ability to parent, his grandparents would step in, taking the children into their home and providing a semblance of order.

At school, teachers saw a kid who wasn't aggressive or foul-mouthed, but who was clearly struggling. He would show up late, tell jokes, and flash wads of cash that a twelve-year-old had no business possessing. The money and the beeper were constant problems, symbols of a street life that was pulling him away from the classroom. One teacher recalled the only time she wrote a disciplinary referral for him. His beeper went off in class, and when she asked for it, he swore at her — an act so out of character that it signaled a deeper turmoil. When the school sent him home and called his mother, she answered and said, "He's with me." He had not gone to the mall or a friend's house; when he was in trouble, he ran to the one person who was both the source of and the solution to his pain.

By the time he was fourteen, he was enmeshed in a world shaped by his mother's addiction. One of her dealers was a twenty-four-year-old man named Jacques Bethea. It was this connection that would irrevocably alter the course of Kenneth's life. According to Kenneth, his mother had stolen drugs from Bethea, and the older man came to collect the debt. He didn't demand it from Stephanie; he turned to her fourteen-year-old son. Bethea threatened to kill his mother if Kenneth didn't help him commit a series of robberies. For a boy who had spent his childhood trying to protect his mother, there was no choice at all.

In the summer of 2000, over a thirty-day period, Kenneth Young and Jacques Bethea embarked on a robbery spree across the Tampa Bay area. The crimes were violent, brazen, and terrifying for the victims. Bethea was the clear leader. He was the one with the gun, a .38 Colt special revolver, and the one who did most of the talking, his voice loud and aggressive as he shoved the weapon in people's faces and forced them to the ground.

At a Comfort Inn, two clerks were working when the pair entered. One clerk, Sandra Christopher, recalled the moment vividly. Two men came through the door, and she knew instantly that something was wrong. One asked for the restroom, and as he walked down the hall, he ran into her coworker, Rosa, who began to scream. Bethea grabbed Rosa, holding her while pointing the gun at Christopher. When Rosa managed to break free and run for help, the men fled.

At another hotel, the scene was even more harrowing. Bethea vaulted over the counter, grabbed a female clerk by her ponytail, and pressed the gun to her head. "Give me the money," he yelled. After she emptied the register, he demanded she open the safe. She told him she couldn't. "If you don't open the safe, I'm going to blow your head off," he screamed. The clerk later testified that Kenneth was not behind the counter with them; he remained in the lobby. At a critical moment, as Bethea's threats escalated, Kenneth appeared at the doorway. "You can't do that," he said. "We have to leave." Enraged, Bethea threw the clerk to the floor, kicked her in the back, and then both he and Kenneth fled.

Kenneth's role, as he later described it, was to act as a scout, to check for surveillance cameras, and to grab the money or valuables once Bethea had control of the scene. He was an active participant, a fact he would later take full responsibility for, but the dynamic was clear: a twenty-four-year-old with a gun and a criminal history was calling the shots, and a fourteen-year-old boy was following his lead. The spree came to an end after a deputy spotted their vehicle, a green Chrysler Sebring. A short chase ended on a dead-end dirt road, where Bethea and Young were arrested. Inside the car, police found the revolver, cash, stolen jewelry, and a VCR containing a tape from one of the robberies.

The trials that followed produced a staggering and deeply unequal outcome. Jacques Bethea, the twenty-four-year-old armed adult who had held a gun to people's heads and threatened to kill them, was given a single life sentence. Kenneth Young, his fourteen-year-old accomplice, was tried and convicted for his role in four separate robberies. The judge handed him four consecutive life sentences without the possibility of parole. For all practical and theoretical purposes, he was condemned to die in prison.

Kenneth Young entered the adult prison system as a "jitterbug," a term used for the youngest, most vulnerable inmates who often feel they have to prove themselves to survive. Yet, in the face of a hopeless sentence, he did something remarkable. Over the next eleven years, in some of Florida's most violent institutions, he maintained a nearly spotless record. He accumulated only one disciplinary report — for not making his bed on a Saturday morning. Because his life sentence made him ineligible for educational or vocational programs — the system saw no point in investing in someone who would never be released — he pursued self-improvement on his own. He earned sixteen certificates, took care of elderly and mentally ill inmates, and worked to become a better person.

While Kenneth was quietly surviving in prison, a legal battle was raging across the country over the constitutionality of sentencing children to die in prison. In 2010, the U.S. Supreme Court delivered a landmark ruling in the case of *Graham v. Florida*. The Court declared that sentencing a juvenile to life without parole for a non-homicide crime was a violation of the Eighth Amendment's ban on "cruel and unusual punishments." The justices argued that "kids are different" — their brains are not fully developed, they are more susceptible to persuasion, and they possess a greater capacity for rehabilitation than adults. The ruling didn't guarantee release, but it mandated that individuals like Kenneth Young be given a "meaningful opportunity to obtain release based on demonstrated maturity and rehabilitation." After exhausting all his appeals, this Supreme Court decision gave Kenneth his first glimmer of hope. He was granted a resentencing hearing.

The hearing became a battleground over the very soul of juvenile justice. The prosecution sought to retry the original case, focusing on the terror the victims had experienced. Sandra Christopher, one of the hotel clerks, testified for the first time, recounting the trauma of having a gun held to her head. "When they say your life flashes before your eyes, it does," she told the court. While she acknowledged Kenneth's desire for release, she added, "I'm not ready to have him walking around where I live, and I'm not moving."

The defense, led by attorney Paolo Annino, argued that the hearing was not about relitigating the past but about assessing the man Kenneth had become. They presented evidence of his exemplary prison record and called a psychologist who testified about the impulsivity and poor judgment inherent in the adolescent brain. Kenneth's mother, Stephanie, took the stand, tearfully reading a letter in which she begged for forgiveness for the role her addiction played in her son's life. "Please, your honor," she pleaded, "help me put my family back together."

Kenneth himself addressed the court, his voice steady and filled with remorse. "First and foremost, your honor, I want to take the time out and say I take full responsibility for my actions and my role in these crimes," he began. "I have lived with regret every day... I am no longer the same person I used to be." He apologized directly to his victims, concluding his statement by quoting the Bible: "When I was a child, I thought as a child, but when I became a man, I put away all childish things."

The prosecution asked the judge for a forty-year sentence, a term that would keep Kenneth in prison until he was around 50 years old. The defense argued for his release, based on the eleven years he had already served and his profound transformation. The decision rested with the judge.

His ruling was a stunning rebuke of the spirit of the *Graham* decision. He acknowledged the many certificates Kenneth had earned but framed them not as evidence of rehabilitation but as proof that "the Department of Corrections and your particular incarceration was appropriate and effective." He dismissed the defense's plea for release with scorn. "If I follow your attorney's request to release you today, I might as well just give you the key to the city, a parade, and dinner at Bern's," he said. "That would be an award, a gift that you will not get from this court. You will not get it, sir, because you do not deserve it."

He acknowledged Kenneth's remorse and rehabilitation but then explicitly stated he would not rely on it. The judge insisted on "personal responsibility and accountability," stating there was no legal basis to blame Jacques Bethea for his conduct. He then sentenced Kenneth Young to 30 years in prison.

The sentence was a crushing blow. It was not life, but it felt like a rejection of everything he had worked for. "I thought that he would probably see that I had shown from the time I was fourteen years old all the way till I'm twenty-six that I have matured," Kenneth said afterward. "I thought that that'll mean something to him. But he just basically told me that it doesn't mean anything."

His legal team immediately saw the flaw in the judge's reasoning. The Supreme Court had mandated that resentencing must provide a "meaningful opportunity" for release based on "demonstrated maturity and rehabilitation." The judge had found that Kenneth was rehabilitated but then explicitly refused to give that finding any weight in his decision. This became the basis for a new appeal. The fight was not over.

By 2019, Kenneth Young had been incarcerated for more than fifteen years. The frightened fourteen-year-old boy handed a life sentence had grown into a man, and his case had become a focal point for a growing number of advocates, lawyers, and law students who viewed his sentence as a stark example of the justice system's capacity for cruelty toward children. The Supreme Court's *Graham v. Florida* decision had cracked open the door to his prison cell, but the path to actually walking through it remained long and fraught with legal obstacles.

Early that year, he was once again brought before a Florida court for a second resentencing hearing. The setting was familiar, but the stakes felt different. This hearing was less about the crimes of the past and more about the man of the present. The central question was whether the child who had made catastrophic mistakes under duress had truly been redeemed by the man he had become.

His defense team laid out the story of his transformation. They presented his immaculate disciplinary record and called witnesses — psychologists and prison staff — who testified to his maturity, his deep remorse, and his role as a mentor to younger inmates. In response, the prosecution re-emphasized the violence of the original robberies and the lasting trauma inflicted upon the victims, arguing that a significant punishment was still warranted. For hours, the courtroom was a theater where the concepts of justice and mercy were weighed against each other.

At the conclusion of the hearing, Kenneth Young was not granted his freedom. The judge handed down a new sentence, one that still stretched for decades into the future. It was not the outcome Kenneth and his supporters had prayed for, but it contained a crucial element of progress: the sentence explicitly acknowledged his youth at the time of the crimes and his proven capacity for change. He was escorted back to prison, not defeated, but determined to hold on to the hope he had fought so hard to reclaim.

For the next two years, his legal team continued their relentless fight. They filed appeals and petitions, pushing the courts to deliver a ruling that would finally give Kenneth a real chance to re-enter the world he had been forced to leave as a boy.

That chance finally came in the summer of 2021. After years of sustained legal pressure and litigation, the Florida courts approved his release. On July 1, 2021, more than two decades after he was first arrested, Kenneth Young walked out of prison, a free man.

Confronted with what many considered an ongoing injustice, Kenneth found a renewed sense of purpose. He had endured years inside some of Florida's harshest prisons and had weathered the devastation of being resentenced. He was no longer the frightened fifteen-year-old who once denied his fate, but a man who recognized a faint, distant light ahead. Once resigned to die behind bars, he now clung to the possibility of something more. He resolved to nurture that glimmer of hope, turning it into strength to keep pushing forward with his case. The boy was gone, but what remained was a man who refused to surrender the one thing the system could never fully take — hope.

19

THE COLT CLAN

In 2012, in a small village in New South Wales, Australia, the ordinary sounds of a school playground — the laughter of children, the rhythmic creak of swings, the scuff of shoes on dirt — were pierced by a comment so disturbing it would unravel a history of secrets buried for nearly half a century. A young girl, playing amongst her friends, casually mentioned that her twelve-year-old sister was pregnant. As if this were not shocking enough, she added a chilling detail: the family did not know which of her brothers was the baby's father. The statement, delivered with a child's unfiltered innocence, betrayed a reality so far outside the bounds of normal society that it was almost incomprehensible. This was not a single, isolated incident of abuse. It was the first loose thread that, when pulled, would unravel the darkest and most deeply entrenched case of generational incest and inbreeding Australia had ever seen, exposing a family clan of nearly 40 people living in a world of their own making, governed by a doctrine of abuse that had been passed down for five generations.

The family was known to the public only by the pseudonym given to them by the courts: the Colt family. It was not their real name, a measure taken to protect the identities of the many children who were victims, and even, controversially, the perpetrators themselves. To the locals in the area around the town of Boroa, the Colts were a mystery. They lived on a large, isolated farm deep in the woods, a property few outsiders were ever permitted to enter. They were known to be standoffish and strange, a reclusive clan that kept to itself. While some of the adults would occasionally leave the property to work odd jobs, for the most part, the family was a self-contained unit, deliberately cut off from the outside world. The community knew there were children on the farm, but they had no idea of the true number, no idea of the squalor they lived in.

The children were the most isolated members of the clan. They were not enrolled in public school until government child services, having noted the family was receiving benefits for a number of children, discovered they were receiving no formal education. Even after they were forced to enroll some of the children, their attendance was extremely spotty. On the rare days they did show up, their appearance was a cause for alarm. They were consistently dirty, their clothes were ragged, and it was clear they were not receiving adequate medical or dental care. They were intellectually and socially far behind their peers, struggling to keep up in the classroom and to interact with other children. Teachers had a strange and unsettling feeling about the family, a sense that something was deeply wrong. Between 2010 and 2012, a concerned individual or group of individuals filed a total of seven "risk of significant harm" reports with the authorities, but for reasons that remain unclear, little was done. It took the unfiltered words of a child on a playground to finally force the hand of the authorities. On July 18, 2012, police and child services officers drove down the long, unpaved road to the Colt farm, prepared to investigate a claim of abuse.

The roots of this nightmare stretched back decades, to a time before the family had even set foot in Australia. The original matriarch and patriarch were given the pseudonyms June and Tim Colt. June was born in 1948, and Tim in 1943. The pattern of inbreeding that would come to define their family had already begun in the generation before them; June's own parents were brother and sister. June and Tim married in 1966 and went on to have seven children of their own: Rhonda, Betty, Sher, Frank, Charlie, Paula, and Martha. Sometime in the 1970s, the entire family left their home in New Zealand and moved to Australia, beginning a nomadic lifestyle that would become a key component of their survival. They moved constantly, from state to state, never staying in one place for too long. This perpetual motion was a defense mechanism, a way to evade the scrutiny of their growing family and peculiar habits.

During this time, Tim Colt cultivated a chillingly effective public facade. He formed a family band, featuring himself, his son Charlie, and his daughter Martha, along with one of his other daughters. They played guitar and mandolin and sang wholesome country love songs, performing at festivals and music halls all across Australia. They gained a small but dedicated following, recorded albums, and even released a collection of love songs. To the outside world, they were a charming, musical, and tight-knit family. This wholesome image was a carefully constructed lie. Behind the scenes, Tim Colt was not just a father and a bandleader; he was the architect of an incestuous cult, and his family was his captive flock.

He had begun sexually abusing his own daughters when they were as young as twelve years old. But his depravity did not stop there. He actively encouraged and normalized sexual activity between his children, brain-washing them from a young age to believe that incest was not only accept-able but expected. He was the unquestioned leader, the patriarch who controlled every aspect of his family's lives, and his doctrine was one of complete sexual freedom within the family, with no boundaries of age or relation. The oldest daughter, Rhonda, went on to have five children; four of them were fathered by her own father, Tim. The youngest daughter, Martha, had six children, most of whom were fathered by her brother, Charlie, though it is believed Tim may have fathered some of them as well. Martha and Charlie eventually began living as a couple, sharing a bed and raising their children — who were also their nieces and nephews — together.

But it was Betty, Tim's second daughter, who was said to be his favorite. She embraced her father's twisted ideology most completely and was groomed to be his successor, the next matriarch of the Colt clan. She went on to have thirteen children, the majority of whom were believed to have been fathered by Tim himself. The cycle was relentless. When one of the girls became pregnant, they were forbidden from seeking prenatal medical care. If a birth in a hospital was unavoidable, they would lie about the identity of the father. The moment they felt the locals in any given town were becoming suspicious, they would pack up their lives and move on, the family band providing the perfect cover for their transient existence.

In 2001, the matriarch, June Colt, died. She was only in her early fifties. Following her death, the family moved again, this time to a very remote area of Western Australia, seeking even greater isolation as their numbers swelled. When Tim Colt, the patriarch and the catalyst for decades of abuse, died in 2009, the cycle did not end. Instead, his children, now adults, worked to perpetuate it. Betty, as planned, ascended to the role of leader. The family purchased the large, secluded plot of land outside of Boroa, a property that was perfect for their needs. It was nestled in a back-woods area, far from the rest of society, a place where no one would even notice they were there. Here, the abuse and inbreeding continued unabated, now entering its fourth and fifth generations. The adult members of the family, themselves victims of their father's horrifying indoctrination, now became the perpetrators, brainwashing their own children to believe that sexual relationships with their parents, siblings, aunts, uncles, and cousins were normal, encouraged, and expected. The youngest members of the clan, many of whom were the products of multiple generations of inbreeding and suffered from severe cognitive delays, were the easiest to manipulate. They were born into a world where they were surrounded by sexual predators, completely cut off from any outside influence that might have told them that their reality was a living nightmare.

When the authorities arrived at the Colt farm that day in July 2012, the first thing that struck them was the sheer squalor of the living conditions. The property housed two travel trailers, a small garden shed, and a larger shed that had been converted into a makeshift dormitory with tents set up inside. Everything was coated in a thick layer of filth. The trailers were filled with dirt, mud, and hazardous materials. Cigarette butts littered the floors, and trash was piled in every corner. In one of the children's beds, officers found a live kangaroo sleeping. The tiny kitchen area was completely unsanitary, with dirt caked onto the cooking surfaces. Windows were broken, and exposed electrical wires snaked across the walls. There was no running water, no toilets, no shower, and no bathtub. The family had been relieving themselves in the woods, and without access to toilet paper, the state of their personal hygiene was unimaginable. A small tub of murky water found in one of the rooms served as the communal hand-washing station. The stench of stale urine and feces was so overpowering that it was almost too much for the case workers to handle.

It was immediately clear that these people had been living in abhorrent, subhuman conditions for years. The decision was made on the spot to remove all the underage children from the farm. A total of twelve children, ranging in age from five to fifteen, were taken into protective custody and placed in foster care while the investigation proceeded. Their physical and mental condition was catastrophic. Nearly all of them had severe, untreated fungal infections and rampant dental decay. They were all underweight and malnourished. They couldn't read or write, and some of them could barely speak coherently. They had never been taught the most basic life skills; they couldn't hold utensils, eating with their hands instead, and some of them didn't even know what toilet paper was. Several of the children walked with a noticeable limp, and one of the boys suffered from severe, untreated psoriasis that covered his skin. Many of them had distinct physical abnormalities, described as low-slung ears and misaligned facial features, the tragic and visible markers of generations of inbreeding. Even the teenagers would soil themselves, having never been properly toilet-trained. The fifteen-year-old, Bobby, was found to be functioning at the level of a kindergartener.

Once in the safety of foster care, the children began to exhibit deeply disturbing behaviors that spoke to the profound sexual trauma they had endured. Even the youngest children were hypersexualized. Cindy, the five-year-old, was caught by her foster parents engaging in sexual acts with herself on multiple occasions, telling them that her older siblings had taught her how. One of the young girls repeatedly tried to kiss her foster father in a sexually inappropriate manner, becoming upset and confused when he stopped her. Two of the boys, nine-year-old Dwayne and twelve-year-old Brian, were caught tying up their eighteen-year-old foster sister, their intentions chillingly unclear. Some of the boys casually told their foster parents that they used to mutilate the genitals of the farm animals for fun, simply because they were bored. During supervised visitations, the siblings would be openly inappropriate with each other, with no sense of shame or understanding that their behavior was wrong.

Slowly, as they began to trust the therapists and caseworkers, the children started to talk. Their stories painted a picture of a world of unrelenting abuse. Seven-year-old Nadia described watching her mother, Martha, and her uncle, Charlie — who was also her biological father — having sex in the tent right next to her. Dwayne explained the family's primary rule for secrecy: they were told to never tell anyone that his father was, in fact, his grandfather, because his mother, Betty, would go to jail if anyone found out. The threat of their mothers being taken away was the tool used to ensure their silence. Thirteen-year-old Kimberly described being forced to perform oral sex on her nine-year-old brother while her eight-year-old cousin watched, and when she told her mother about it, nothing was done. The girls told stories of being tied to trees while they were assaulted by their brothers, cousins, and uncles, sometimes with sticks and other objects. They spoke of running and hiding in the woods in a desperate attempt to escape the constant threat of abuse.

To confirm the children's harrowing testimonies, the court ordered genetic testing on all twelve of the minors who had been removed from the farm. The results were a stark, scientific confirmation of the family's dark secret. Eleven of the twelve children were the products of incest. Some were the children of half-siblings, cousins, or uncles, while others were the product of closely related parents, such as full siblings or a parent and their child. The one child who did not have related parents was five-year-old Cindy, the youngest daughter of Rhonda. Rhonda claimed that Cindy's father was a man she had a brief affair with while working as a fruit picker. It was a telling detail that Cindy, the only child in the group with a diverse genetic background, was also the only one who was well-spoken, developmentally on track, and had no learning disabilities.

The genetic consequences of the Colt family's practices were not just developmental; they were fatal. A two-month-old baby girl named Sally, the daughter of siblings Tammy and Derek, had died from a rare genetic disorder called Zellweger syndrome just before the case broke. This disorder, which is almost always fatal, is autosomal recessive, meaning both parents must carry the same mutated gene for it to occur in their child. The likelihood of this happening increases exponentially in inbred families, where relatives are far more likely to share the same harmful mutations. Sally's death was a direct and tragic result of the generations of inbreeding that had concentrated these lethal genes within the family.

After everything the children had revealed, after the horrifying conditions of the farm had been documented, and after the DNA tests had provided irrefutable proof of years of incest, one would expect the full weight of the justice system to come down on the adult perpetrators. But what followed was a shocking failure of justice. In court, all of the mothers steadfastly denied that even a single case of incest had ever occurred. They concocted elaborate stories, claiming all the children had been conceived by unrelated outsiders — drifters, and in one fanciful tale, a Scandinavian tourist named Sven. They simply could not, or would not, accept the DNA evidence, insisting the court should believe their word over scientific proof.

Because of their complete refusal to acknowledge the truth, the court ruled that the children would be permanently removed from their care. But the criminal consequences were astonishingly light. Of a total of eighty charges — including incest, child sexual abuse, and perjury — brought against eight of the adults in the clan, most were inexplicably dropped. Charlie, one of the worst offenders, who was facing twenty-seven counts, was ultimately acquitted of two counts of raping a minor after a judge cited "inconsistencies" in the young girl's testimony. The women served only brief sentences of one to two years for perjury. The only significant prison time was served by Betty's brother Rodri, who was sentenced to four years for the violent rape of his seventeen-year-old niece, and Betty herself, who was sentenced to twelve months in 2013 after police, using a phone tap, uncovered her plot to kidnap two of her sons from foster care. The same phone tap also recorded her making disturbingly flirtatious and sexual comments to her fifteen-year-old son.

Today, the children who were removed from that farm are protected by a veil of secrecy, their true identities and whereabouts unknown. Many of them are now adults, facing the lifelong task of healing from a childhood of unimaginable trauma. Disturbingly, it seems that some of them have re-established contact with their mothers. Betty Colt's social media accounts show that she is still surrounded by her family, the clan still tightly knit. In one sickeningly ironic post, she shared a photo of herself with two of her relatives, captioned with the words: "Love makes a family." The adults in this case all began as victims of their father, Tim, a man who unfortunately died before he could ever face justice. But at some point, they made a choice not to break the cycle of abuse, but to embrace it, to perpetuate it, and to inflict upon their own children the same horrors they had endured. They knew what they were doing was wrong — the constant moving, the lies about paternity, the threats used to silence the children, all prove it. And for that, the justice system, in its baffling leniency, failed to hold them truly responsible.

20

THE CALL FROM 3:45 AM

Manchester, New Hampshire, holds the title of the state's most bustling city, a place locals have sometimes dubbed "Queen City" or even "Manch Vegas," a nod to illicit gambling operations that dotted its businesses in the 1980s and 90s. It was here, on April 3, 1966, that Lauren Rahn was born. Her early life was shaped by her parents' divorce when she was just an infant, leaving her to be raised by her mother, Judith. Her father remained largely absent from her life. When Lauren was 4, she and Judith relocated to Miami, Florida, but they returned to Manchester six years later. In 1980, they settled into a third floor apartment at 289 Merrimack Street, in the heart of the city. Within months, during her spring break from school, the fourteen-year-old girl would vanish from that apartment, leaving behind a case that remains one of New Hampshire's most curious and tragic unsolved mysteries.

As a student at Parkside Junior High, Lauren was known as a good student and had a fine relationship with her mother. She was drawn to the arts, passionate about singing and dancing, and held a dream of one day becoming an actress in Hollywood. This ambition was fueled by a dissatisfaction with small-town life; she wanted to see what else the world had to offer and seemed to be in a hurry to grow up so she could get out. She spent a significant amount of time with her friends, wandering the streets, and was not against drinking alcohol or smoking marijuana. On occasion, she even spoke of running away to jumpstart her career.

There was a persistent rumor in town about a man who worked at a local corner store, a man who was reportedly interested in young girls and had no issue selling alcohol to minors. In 1980, the legal drinking age was eighteen while Lauren was fourteen. Her aunt, Diane Penal, later summarized the situation, stating that Lauren was not a bad kid or in a dark place; she was an angel who simply "hung around with the wrong people for a while." With Lauren's father out of the picture, Judith was actively involved in the dating scene, navigating several short-lived relationships. Lauren often joined her mother and these men on outings, but Judith always made it clear that her daughter was the most important person in her life. She assured Lauren that she would not hesitate to end any relationship that made her feel uncomfortable.

The day Lauren disappeared was during her April vacation from school. At the time, her mother, Judith, was seeing a professional tennis player who frequently traveled for tournaments. Normally, Lauren would have tagged along, and they would spend the day at the event. On this particular day, however, Lauren asked if she could stay home instead. Judith was reluctant at first, but she recognized her daughter was growing up fast and ultimately allowed it. On April 26, 1980, Judith said goodbye to her daughter, telling her she loved her and to behave before heading out to the tennis match. She planned to be home later that night, having no idea it would be the last time she would ever see Lauren.

With the apartment to herself, Lauren spent part of the day at her favorite convenience store, where she reportedly restocked shelves, possibly in exchange for alcohol. As evening rolled around, she invited two friends over: One male and one female. Their names have never been publicly released, but they can be referred to as Mark and Sarah. The teenagers spent the night hanging out, drinking a six-pack of beer and some wine while watching television. The night seemed to be winding down normally until the early hours of the next morning.

At approximately 12:30 a.m. on April 27, Lauren and Mark were sitting in the living room when they heard voices in the apartment building's hallway. Worried that Judith was returning home and they would be in trouble for drinking, Mark decided to leave. He exited through the apartment's back door, and he later recalled hearing Lauren lock the door behind him as he left. This account was supported by a neighbor, who also reported hearing voices near the apartment around that same time. After Mark was gone, Lauren and Sarah decided to head to bed.

About forty-five minutes later, around 1:15 a.m., Judith returned home with her boyfriend. She immediately sensed that something was wrong. The first unsettling detail was the darkness. All the lights in the hallways of the three floor apartment building were off, which was not normal. When she reached her apartment, she found the second anomaly: the door was unlocked. This was unusual, as she always reminded her daughter to lock it, but she reasoned that Lauren might have forgotten.

Judith checked her daughter's bedroom and saw a figure sleeping in the bed. Assuming it was Lauren, she quietly left the room. Moments later, her boyfriend noticed the third and most bizarre detail: the back door was unlocked and slightly ajar. Judith found this very strange, as they rarely used that door. She decided to wake Lauren to ask why the door had been left open. As she approached the bed, she discovered it was not her daughter at all; it was Lauren's friend, Sarah.

Sarah explained that Lauren had initially been in bed with her, but after a while, she had taken her pillow and blanket to sleep on the couch in the living room. Judith had seen the pillow and blanket on the couch when she first arrived but had assumed Lauren had just been watching a movie and fallen asleep there. When questioned, Sarah, who was intoxicated, could not remember any further details about the night and had no idea where Lauren could be. A frantic inspection of the apartment revealed Lauren's purse, her brand-new sneakers, and a recent birthday gift all still in the living room. None of her other belongings, including her money or clothing, were missing. There were absolutely no signs of a struggle.

Judith's first calls were to family members who lived in town, hoping Lauren might be with them. When those calls led nowhere, she and her boyfriend began to search the neighborhood frantically. With no sign of the girl anywhere, Judith called 911 at 3:45 a.m. to report her daughter missing. When officers responded, there was not an immediate sense of urgency. As is often the case with missing teenagers, police initially suspected Lauren had run away and would return when she was ready. They noted that she had left behind items a runaway would normally take, but at the moment, there was no evidence that any foul play had occurred.

Police did take a statement from Sarah, who informed them of the night's events: she, Lauren, and Mark had been drinking, Mark left, and the girls went to bed. She reiterated that Lauren got up at some point to sleep on the couch, though she offered no explanation for why Lauren might have done this. Investigators also tracked down Mark, whose statement matched Sarah's account. He explained that he left to avoid being caught drinking with underage girls, which suggested he was at least eighteen years old. He was never considered a suspect in the disappearance.

As days passed with no word from Lauren, the police began to revise their runaway theory. They came to believe she had likely left the apartment on her own, perhaps to get more to drink or something to eat, and encountered some form of trouble outside. This theory, however, did not account for the most disturbing discovery of the investigation. Police found that there had been no power outage or blown fuse in the apartment building that night. Someone had physically twisted the light bulbs in every single fixture, on every floor and in every hallway, just enough to extinguish the lights and plunge the building into darkness.

With word of the girl's disappearance hitting the media, a potential lead emerged from a bus company employee who reported selling a ticket to a girl matching Lauren's description on the day she vanished. This was followed by a statement from a bus driver from the same company, who identified Lauren from an old photograph and claimed to have dropped her off in Park Square in Boston. Hope for this lead faded, however, when the driver was shown a more recent photo of Lauren. He expressed doubt, stating he was no longer certain the girl he dropped off was her.

One of the most baffling aspects of the case involved a series of strange phone calls that began right after Lauren vanished. For about a year following the disappearance, Judith began to receive mysterious calls at her home. They always came at the same time: around 3:45 a.m., the exact time she had first called the police to report Lauren missing. The calls were chillingly silent. Each time Judith answered, there was no voice on the other end, only an unsettling silence, as if someone were listening. The calls also increased in frequency during the holiday seasons.

Then, in October 1980, less than six months after Lauren disappeared, Judith discovered strange charges on her phone bill. The records showed calls made from her account, originating from a motel in Santa Monica, California. In that era, calls could be charged to a home phone number by calling the phone company and entering a PIN, a method cheaper than placing a collect call. Someone had a hold of Judith's PIN. Two of the calls had been made to a motel in Santa Ana, California, and one was made to a teen assistance hotline. All three calls were placed in July 1980, approximately three months after Lauren vanished.

Judith had no connections to anyone in California, which made her believe the calls might have been from Lauren. Further investigation into the teen hotline led to a physician in California who ran it, but he claimed to have no knowledge of Lauren or the call. In a strange turn, when contacted by the Center for Missing and Exploited Children five years later, the man's story changed. He was more open about the hotline and admitted that his wife frequently had runaway girls stop by their house for guidance. He allowed for the possibility that one of them may have been from New Hampshire and around Lauren's age, but there was no proof linking Lauren to him.

Frustrated by the stalled investigation, Judith hired a private investigator in 1986. The detective traveled to California to follow up on the phone calls. He reportedly found that the Santa Monica motel from which the calls originated may have been at the center of an adult film industry ring at the time, with an individual supposedly using the location for filming. Despite this, investigators were unable to link this activity to Lauren in any way.

That same year, another odd call was received by a childhood friend of Lauren's named Roger Murcer. Roger was not home, so his mother answered the phone. The woman on the other end identified herself as either "Lori" or "Loren" and claimed to be Roger's ex-girlfriend. The call was brief, and the caller terminated the conversation without providing any more information. The silent calls to Judith's home eventually stopped after she remarried, moved to Florida, and changed her phone number.

Judith has remained firm in her belief that the three calls from California were made by Lauren. She also suspects that one of Lauren's friends knows more than they have said, and perhaps that there was even another person in the apartment that night who Sarah and Mark have chosen to remain silent about.

Over the years, numerous sightings of Lauren were reported, but none were ever confirmed. In 1981, a year after her disappearance, a family member thought they spotted her at a bus station in Boston, but the woman was gone before authorities could follow up. On October 5, 1980, a body was found in Henderson, Nevada, and authorities initially considered it might be Lauren due to a strong resemblance; however, further investigation confirmed it was not a match. The last reported sighting occurred in 1988, in Anchorage, Alaska. The witness claimed to have seen a woman they believed was Lauren, who would have been twenty-two years old, working as a prostitute. Authorities were unable to track down the woman, and the sighting was never confirmed.

In 1985, an unusual turn of events added another layer of unresolved questions to the case: Mark, the male friend who was in the apartment that night, died by suicide. Although he had not been considered a suspect, investigators noted it was a piece of information that could not be ignored, leaving open the possibility that he knew something about what happened to Lauren or was involved and feeling overwhelmed with guilt.

Desperate for a breakthrough, authorities began to examine other similar disappearances in the area. The first name that emerged was Rachel Garden, a fifteen-year-old who disappeared on March 22, 1980, just a month before Lauren, from Newton, New Hampshire, only twenty-five miles away (about forty kilometers). She had been walking home when she vanished, and her case also remains unsolved. An even more striking case occurred on June 8, 1980, just six weeks after Lauren vanished. A twenty-five-year-old woman named Denise Daneault went missing from a bar in Manchester. Denise, who had brown hair and hazel eyes, bore a close resemblance to Lauren. She was a divorced mother of two and lived in an apartment just two blocks away from Lauren and Judith. Like Lauren and Rachel, Denise has never been found.

Decades later, investigators discovered a deeply concerning connection: a suspected serial killer, Terry Rasmussen, who used the alias Bob Evans, had been residing in the Manchester area during that time. Rasmussen, nicknamed the "Chameleon Killer," was eventually linked to the chilling Bear Brook murders, a case involving four female victims found in Bear Brook State Park, just fifteen miles (about twenty-five kilometers) north of Manchester. One of those victims was identified as Rasmussen's own biological daughter. Authorities suspect he may have been involved in up to six other murders or disappearances. However, Terry Rasmussen died in prison in 2010, taking any information he might have had about Lauren Rahn's disappearance to the grave.

In the absence of evidence, police have settled on the simplest theory as the most prevailing one: that Lauren stepped outside her apartment to meet someone, fully intending to return, but was met with foul play. The detail of the loosened lightbulbs, which seems to suggest a planned abduction, is explained away by authorities as an unconnected coincidence — perhaps a prank by another tenant. They argue that an abductor would not go through the trouble of unscrewing all the bulbs, as it would take time and increase the risk of being caught. Others argue it would have the opposite effect, concealing an identity in the darkness.

More than forty-four years later, Lauren Rahn remains missing. The case has grown cold, frozen in the moment a fourteen-year-old girl left her belongings on the floor and vanished from an apartment with an unlocked door. Someone out there undoubtedly holds the information needed to uncover what happened, but as so much time has passed, the silence that began in a darkened hallway continues.

21

THE BONES ON MIDDLE MOUNTAIN

The 911 call came in from Elaine Redwine, her voice tight with a fear that was just beginning to take shape. Her thirteen-year-old son, Dylan Redwine, was visiting his father, Mark Redwine, in Durango, Colorado, for a court-ordered Thanksgiving visit. Dylan had not even been there for a full twenty-four hours, and now his father was texting Elaine to say he couldn't find him. For Elaine, who lived six hours away, that was an impossible scenario. She got in her car and drove, an agonizing journey into a mystery that would consume the state and unravel a dark family secret.

When the first searchers, including Elaine's stepfather, arrived at Mark Redwine's house, the scene was unsettling. The terrain was some of the most rugged in North America, and the temperature that night was predicted to drop below freezing. A missing boy in that environment was a dire emergency. Yet, as searchers scoured the area until 1:00 a.m., Mark Redwine never came outside to help. Instead, at a reasonable hour, he turned off all the lights in his house as if he were going to bed, leaving the search party in the dark.

In the following days, as hundreds of volunteers joined the search, Mark pushed the effort to center on a mountain lake dam about seven miles (about eleven kilometers) from his home. He told everyone that Dylan was a "big fisherman" and that his fishing pole was missing from the house, suggesting his son had wandered off to the dam. Volunteers, including a grieving Elaine, walked the steep, treacherous banks of the lake, finding nothing. Dylan's friends knew the story didn't add up. One friend, Ryan, had been texting with Dylan the night he vanished. Dylan had been excited to see his friends and had made plans to meet Ryan at 6:30 the next morning. He never showed up.

The visit to his father itself had been contentious. Dylan had not wanted to go. It was part of a court-ordered visitation stemming from his parents' bitter divorce. Elaine's mother was sick with cancer, and the family knew it would likely be her last Thanksgiving; Dylan had pleaded to stay with her but the court order was inflexible. Surveillance video from the airport showed a cold reunion, with no hugs or smiles exchanged between father and son. Their first stop was a Walmart, where video showed Dylan and Mark shopping separately. Dylan was seen texting, already making plans to be away from his father.

After stopping for a hamburger, they arrived at Mark's home. Mark would later tell investigators that they had "rough housed" a bit but that no one was hurt. At 9:46 p.m. that night, Dylan Redwine's cell phone stopped working. He was never seen or heard from again.

Suspicion quickly fell on Mark, whose behavior grew increasingly bizarre. He spoke of his son in the past tense at a prayer vigil, saying how much he "loved" and "cared" about the boy, before immediately pivoting to blame Elaine. In his first interview with police, he suggested Elaine was responsible for Dylan's disappearance, claiming his son had run away because of problems with his mother. This theory was flatly rejected by both Elaine and Dylan's older brother, Cory, who insisted Dylan would never run away without contacting one of them.

Two months after Dylan vanished, Elaine and Cory organized a protest outside Mark's house, demanding answers from the last person to see the boy alive. Mark's public response was to accuse his ex-wife of being involved. But investigators were already focused on what was inside Mark's home. During an FBI-assisted search, cadaver dogs alerted to the scent of human remains inside the living room and in the bed of Mark's pickup truck.

Investigators brought Mark in for a polygraph test. Elaine had already taken one and passed; Mark failed miserably. He was found to be deceptive on the key question: "Do you know where Dylan Redwine is?" In the interrogation room, investigators tried to offer him a way out, suggesting it was an accident, that maybe the "rough housing" had gone wrong. They guaranteed they would not arrest him that day if he just led them to Dylan's body. Mark refused, stone-faced, insisting he had no idea where his son was.

Mark Redwine, investigators would learn, had a lot to hide. The true motive, the spark that likely ignited the fatal confrontation, was revealed by Cory. He recounted a trip he and Dylan had taken with Mark years earlier. In a hotel room, the boys had borrowed their father's laptop and discovered a deleted file. What they saw horrified them: pictures of their father, Mark, dressed in women's clothing and a diaper, relieving himself and then cleaning it with his mouth. Cory, sickened, snapped a few photos of the laptop screen with his cell phone.

Cory told Dylan to keep the pictures a secret, but thirteen-year-old Dylan was honest and confrontational. He didn't like to be quieted. In a later argument, Dylan demanded Cory send him the "poop pics," as he called them, to use as a weapon against his father. Cory sent them, an act he would forever regret. Investigators believed this confrontation was the flashpoint. On that last night, Dylan, trapped in a court-ordered visit with a father he despised, had confronted Mark with the one thing that could destroy him.

With Dylan still missing, that secret was about to become public. The family agreed to appear on the *Dr. Phil*, where Elaine and Cory confronted Mark on national television. When Dr. Phil asked Mark if the photos were genuine, Mark launched into a nonsensical, fabricated story. He admitted his face was in the photos but claimed he had fabricated the images himself as part of an outrageous "scheme" to catch Elaine and Cory, whom he *believed* were breaking into his house. He claimed he planted the photos, never intending for them to be seen. For Elaine, watching his convoluted lies and his cold body language, any last shred of hope she had was extinguished. She knew then that Dylan was no longer alive.

The search for Dylan was stalled by the harsh Colorado winter, which closed off the high country around Mark's home. But when the snow melted in the spring of 2013, search teams were finally able to access a rugged area called Middle Mountain Road. The area became a focus after Elaine's stepfather spotted Mark driving down from the mountain early one morning. During a massive, four-day search involving dog handlers, ATVs, and repelling teams, a searcher found a single Nike Air Jordan shoe, a size seven youth, matching the one Dylan was seen wearing in the Walmart surveillance video. The next day, human-remain dogs alerted in the same area, and searchers found two small bones. Then, another searcher looked down and found a long bone. They were Dylan's.

When investigators called Mark to inform him that his son's remains had been found, his response was cold and belligerent. He mockingly told her to pull her head out of a "sociopath ass" and that finding 2% of Dylan's remains does not constitute him being found. He later told her that with only 2% of the body recovered, they could never prove he was murdered. The fishing pole he had insisted was missing — the one that sent hundreds of volunteers on a wild goose chase to the dam — mysteriously reappeared in his garage.

For two more years, the case stalled, as the most critical piece of evidence — the skull — was still missing. Then, in 2015, hikers found a human skull about a mile and a half away from where the other bones had been located. Elaine knew in her heart it was Dylan. With a new, more aggressive district attorney in office, the case was finally brought before a grand jury. The jury returned an indictment for second-degree murder and child abuse resulting in death. Prosecutors did not pursue first-degree murder because they did not have evidence that Mark had planned or premeditated the killing.

Mark Redwine, then working as a trucker in Washington state, was arrested. Video of his arrest showed him looking utterly shocked, telling officers he had "no idea" what the warrant was about. He thought he had gotten away with it.

The trial, nearly nine years after Dylan's disappearance, began in 2021. The prosecution laid out its simple and tragic case: a damaged relationship that turned deadly. To help the jury visualize the crime, prosecutors recreated Mark Redwine's living room in a separate courtroom, allowing them to see the layout and the actual evidence, including the blood found on the couches, floor, and coffee table that was a 100% match to Dylan Redwine.

Elaine testified about her son and her final, unanswered texts to him, including the last one she ever sent: "Dylan please be safe mom is here to come get you." The defense's cross-examination focused heavily on her public accusations, grilling her about comments she'd made on Facebook pages like "Arrest Mark Redwine."

Cory Redwine also testified, describing the horrifying discovery of the photos and the effect it had on his younger brother. In a moment of raw emotion, when asked how he felt about his father, Cory admitted, "I still love him."

The defense argued that the case was thin and built on emotion. They claimed the marks on the skull were consistent with animal damage and that Dylan had likely been attacked by a bear or mountain lion. The prosecution countered, pointing out that predators do not typically move their prey more than a quarter-mile; Dylan's skull was found over a mile from his other remains. Furthermore, it made no sense that a thirteen-year-old boy would be on that remote mountainside in shorts and a t-shirt in the middle of November.

Throughout the graphic testimony, Mark Redwine sat stone-faced, never shedding a tear, never reacting at all, even as witnesses described his son's remains. He opted not to testify. After five weeks, the jury returned its verdict in just six hours: guilty on all counts.

At the sentencing, Dylan's family finally came face to face with the man who had taken his life. His mother, Elaine, spoke through tears, her words filled with grief and disbelief as she imagined her son's final moments — looking up at his father and realizing the truth. Dylan's older brother, Cory, called his little brother a hero, describing him as a brave thirteen-year-old who confronted their father with the honesty and courage Cory wished he himself had shown. When given a chance to speak, Mark Redwine declined, offering no apology or acknowledgment. The judge, condemning his complete lack of remorse and his dismissal of the trial as a "sham," imposed the maximum sentence: forty-eight years in prison.

22

A DEPUTY'S DAUGHTER

In the early hours of May 26, 2012, a young man named Seth Techel was talking to the 911 dispatcher, telling that his wife had been shot. Deputies rushed to the couple's rural trailer home in Agency, Iowa, a small community where everyone knew one another. The first officer on the scene, like most who would arrive that morning, knew the Techels personally. He found Seth outside, visibly distressed, striking a truck and sobbing next to a fence line. Inside, paramedics found twenty-three-year-old Lisa Techel, five months pregnant, dead in her bed from a single gunshot wound.

Seth claimed he was in the shower when the shot rang out. He said he ran to the bedroom to find his wife mortally wounded and then heard a noise in the living room, where he discovered the front door wide open. He saw no one. By his account, an intruder had entered their home, murdered his wife, and vanished without a trace. From the moment the first responders arrived, a primary suspect was identified, but it was not Seth. It was the Techels' mentally unstable neighbor, a man with whom they had been locked in an escalating feud.

To the outside world, Seth and Lisa Techel were the picture of a perfect young couple. They had met as teenagers at a local bowling alley where they both worked, fallen in love, and married in the autumn of 2011. They lived in a small trailer home in Agency, a village of fewer than 1,000 people, and were excitedly awaiting the birth of their baby girl, whom they planned to name Zoe. Their lives were deeply enmeshed in the local law enforcement community. Lisa worked as a jailer in a neighboring county and was a reserve deputy in Wapello County, serving alongside her father, Deputy Todd Caldwell. Seth, who worked a security job, had just been offered a position as a jailer in Wapello and had aspirations of one day joining the sheriff's department himself. On the surface, their future looked bright.

But hidden from the view of their close-knit community was a deeply troubled marriage. In January, just a few months after their wedding, Lisa had discovered text messages between Seth and his co-worker, Rachel McFarland. They had met in late 2011 and quickly began a secret affair. While they were not sleeping together, they had been exchanging sexually charged messages and photos for months. When Lisa confronted him, Seth swore he would end all contact with Rachel. Instead, he purchased a second phone, registered it under the alias "Rick Jones," and continued the illicit correspondence.

On May 25th, the day before the murder, Seth and Lisa were seen around town running errands. They chatted with a worker at their credit union about the pregnancy and had lunch at a local restaurant where a waitress noted their apparent ease and normalcy. All the while, Seth was texting Rachel on his secret phone. The last messages he sent her, after 11:00 p.m. that night, confirmed what Rachel wanted to hear: Seth had told Lisa he wanted a divorce, and she would be packing her things the next day.

According to Seth, the alarm clock in their bedroom went off at 4:30 a.m. on May 26th. He got up to let their dog, Remington, outside while Lisa stayed in bed. He claimed the dog acted as if something was "fishy" outside, though it did not bark. He went back inside, reset the alarm for 5:00 a.m., and lay back down. When the alarm sounded again, he got in the shower. He said he was in there for no more than five minutes when he heard a loud bang from the bedroom. He grabbed a towel, ran into the bedroom, and turned on the light. The dog was cowering in the closet, and Lisa was lying in bed. When he shook her, she moaned faintly. After that he noticed a hole in the covers. He pulled the covers back, and saw a hole in her bra. Just then, he heard a thud from the living room. He grabbed his pistol from the nightstand, ran down the hallway, and found the front door wide open. He ran onto the porch but saw and heard nothing. When he returned to the bedroom, he said Lisa was unresponsive and no longer breathing. That is when he called 911.

The crime scene quickly became chaotic. In addition to the first responders, numerous members of the Wapello County Sheriff's Department arrived, many of whom were friends and colleagues. Within minutes, Lisa's father, Deputy Todd Caldwell, was contacted. He and Lisa's stepmother arrived and were allowed into the trailer to view the tragic scene. Upon seeing his daughter, Deputy Caldwell instantly believed he knew who was responsible, and it was not his son-in-law. Dashcam footage captured him yelling at his colleagues to "go get him now," and the other officers knew exactly who he meant: their neighbor, Brian Tate.

Tate was a disabled veteran diagnosed with paranoid schizophrenia. In the weeks leading up to the murder, the Techels and Tate had been engaged in a bizarre and escalating feud. It began when Seth moved a dead deer from the road into a ditch, and Lisa later saw the deer hide hanging in a tree on Tate's property. The hide was then mysteriously thrown back and forth between the properties. The conflict intensified when Seth encouraged some of his younger friends to vandalize Tate's property, dumping buckets of dog feces on his porch and throwing rocks at his shed. Tate had called the sheriff's department to complain about what he called "acts of terrorism," and the responding officer was none other than Deputy Todd Caldwell. Unaware he was speaking to Lisa's father, Tate told the deputy that the Techels were terrorists. The week of the murder, Lisa had found a deer hide in their driveway, and Seth had later found footprints near his fence line and had to rush their dog to the vet for suspected poisoning.

Prompted by Deputy Caldwell's urgency, officers descended on Brian Tate's home, fully armed and prepared for a violent confrontation. Instead, they found him enjoying a quiet morning with his mother, who insisted he had been sleeping all night. Tate was calm, on his medication, and invited the officers to sit on his porch for a chat.

The investigation at the Techel home proceeded. The Division of Criminal Investigation (DCI) was called in to assist. Deputies confirmed the shower was still wet and dripping. Two cell phones belonging to Seth — his regular one and the "Rick Jones" burner phone — were collected. There were no signs of forced entry or a struggle, and nothing of value had been taken. Seth was not swabbed for gunshot residue, nor was Brian Tate.

That afternoon, Seth agreed to a five-hour interview with DCI agent Chris Thomas. For the first four hours, the interview was non-confrontational, with a local deputy who knew Seth sitting in, likely to put him at ease. Seth repeated his story about the intruder and pointed the finger directly at Brian Tate. However, while the interview was ongoing, other investigators were speaking to Seth's friends. A close friend, Colton Millard, told them that Seth had confided in him about the affair with Rachel McFarland and had even shown him some of the photos she had sent. This information was immediately relayed to Agent Thomas, and the tone of the interrogation shifted. The interview ended abruptly when Seth's father secured him a lawyer, but the damage was done. The DCI was now convinced that Seth Techel had a lot to hide.

The murder weapon was found the next day. A Mossberg model 500 shotgun was lying in plain view in some tall grass about 90 feet (about 30 meters) from the trailer's front door. The gun belonged to Seth's former roommate, who had left it in the trailer when he moved out. Crucially, Seth had omitted this specific shotgun from the list of firearms he had provided to the DCI. The gun was found with one fired round jammed in the chamber, something friends of Seth said had never happened when they had fired it, suggesting it may have been last used by someone unfamiliar with the weapon.

The evidence against Seth was now overwhelming. He had a powerful motive: he wanted out of his marriage to be with Rachel McFarland but feared a divorce would alienate his influential father-in-law and destroy his burgeoning law enforcement career. His texts to Rachel, particularly the "just give me two more weeks" message and the lie about telling Lisa he wanted a divorce, were damning. Six weeks after the murder, Seth Techel was arrested and charged with first-degree murder and the non-consensual termination of a human pregnancy.

Seth's first trial began in February 2013. The prosecution laid out what they saw as a simple motive of love and lust. Rachel McFarland testified about the affair, and a co-worker testified that after a heated phone call with Lisa, Seth had remarked that "it would be easier if she was in Iraq and died." The defense argued that Brian Tate, who had passed away in the months prior to the trial, was the real killer. They criticized the police for their "tunnel vision" and for overlooking potential evidence at the scene. After four agonizing days of deliberation, the jury came back deadlocked, split ten to two in favor of a guilty verdict. A mistrial was declared.

A second trial was held two months later in a different county. No new evidence or arguments were presented. The result was the same: another hung jury, this time split nine to three for guilty. Again, a mistrial was declared.

Days before a third trial was set to begin, the defense made a bombshell discovery. Lisa's cell phone, which had been collected at the scene, had never been properly examined by investigators. When its contents were finally accessed in May 2014, they revealed a stunning secret: Lisa had also been having an affair. Text messages between her and a co-worker, Jason Tennis, showed an affair that had begun before her marriage to Seth and had apparently continued after. Tennis, when questioned, initially lied about the affair but later admitted to it, claiming their sexual relationship had ended a couple of months before the murder.

The third trial commenced just three days later, with the defense's request for a continuance denied. They now argued there were three potential suspects besides Seth: Brian Tate, Rachel's spurned ex-boyfriend, and now Jason Tennis. Tennis denied any involvement in the murder, and his wife provided an alibi. A rushed DNA analysis showed he was not the father of Lisa's unborn child and did not match the DNA found on a cigarette butt in the Techels' driveway. This time, the new evidence was not enough to sway the jury. After three trials, they were finally able to reach a unanimous decision: Seth Techel was found guilty on both counts.

In September 2014, after years of legal battles, Lisa's family was given the opportunity to deliver their victim impact statements. Her father, Todd Caldwell, once a staunch supporter of his son-in-law, now faced him as his daughter's killer. He recounted how Seth had told his wife that he had looked into Lisa's eyes as she took her last breath. "I have nightmares about that," he told the court. "And in my nightmares, I always wake up and wonder if Lisa was thinking, 'I need my dad.'" Seth Techel received the maximum sentence: life in prison without the possibility of parole, plus an additional twenty-five years. His subsequent appeals were all unsuccessful, bringing the tragic case to a final, definitive close.

23

THE CIPHER THAT FBI COULDN'T SOLVE

On June 30, 1999, the St. Charles County Sheriff's Department in Missouri received a call just before 1:00 p.m. A woman driving near Route 367, close to the town of West Alton about twenty miles (about thirty-two kilometers) outside St. Louis had spotted something unusual in a cornfield — a dark mound lying among the crops. As she got closer, the shape resolved into a human body, already in an advanced state of decomposition under the sweltering summer heat.

Investigators heading to the scene had a grim sense of foreboding. This particular stretch of road was remote, isolated, and had a history. Just four years earlier, in 1995, the body of an alleged sex worker had been found nearby, riddled with bullets. It was known locally as a dumping ground, a place where inconvenient problems could be quietly disposed of. This new discovery was likely another homicide.

They found the body lying face down: a slim, 5'6" (about 167 centimeters) African-American man, dressed in filthy Lee blue jeans and a stained white t-shirt. The scene offered few immediate clues. There was no murder weapon, no signs of a struggle, and given the location, no witnesses. The state of decomposition suggested the body had been lying there for weeks, exposed to the elements. It was sheer luck, investigators realized, that he had been found at all before nature reclaimed him entirely.

A search of the body yielded no identification, only an emergency room ticket and two crumbled pieces of paper tucked into a front pocket. These papers would become the central, enduring mystery of the case. They were covered in what initially looked like random scribbles — a chaotic jumble of letters and numbers spread across more than 30 lines of text. At first glance, it seemed like meaningless gibberish.

But closer inspection revealed a deliberate structure. Certain combinations of letters repeated consistently. Some sections were circled, almost like items checked off a list. Numbers — 74, 75, 194 — appeared sporadically. Parentheses grouped specific letter combinations. It wasn't random; it was structured, complex, and seemingly coded. Someone, investigators believed, had invested considerable time and thought into creating these notes. The question was, who? And more importantly, what did they mean?

With no other leads, the body was sent for forensic identification. The advanced decomposition made identification difficult, but miraculously, the fingertips were preserved well enough to yield a match in the police database. The victim was Ricky McCormick, a forty-one-year-old local gas station employee. To the investigators' surprise, no one had reported him missing.

Armed with a name, detectives began trying to piece together Ricky's final days, hoping to understand how he ended up dead in a remote cornfield so far from his St. Louis home. They spoke to his girlfriend, Sandra. She confirmed Ricky didn't own a car and relied on hitchhiking or public transport. This squared with the lack of any vehicle at the scene or registered in his name. But the cornfield was twenty miles (about thirty-two kilometers) from his home, in an area with no public transportation routes. How had he gotten there?

Ricky's family painted a picture of a man plagued by chronic health problems — heart and lung issues, severe asthma, persistent chest pain — exacerbated by heavy smoking and an alarming consumption of caffeinated drinks, sometimes up to twenty a day. Could he have walked?

Given his poor health, a six hour plus trek through the Missouri heat seemed improbable. Yet, his family insisted it wasn't impossible, suggesting he might have collapsed and died from the strain. The more likely scenario, however, was homicide: someone had brought him there, dumped his body, and disappeared.

The emergency room ticket found in his pocket provided a starting point for a timeline. Hospital records showed Ricky had walked into Barnes-Jewish Hospital on June 22nd, complaining of chest pains and shortness of breath. He was admitted for observation and released two days later, on June 24th. After leaving the hospital, he visited his favorite aunt, Gloria. She told police their conversation was unusually brief and guarded. He revealed little about what was going on in his life and declined her offer of a ride, leaving after only an hour.

The very next day, June 25th, Ricky went to another emergency room, this time complaining of breathing difficulties after mowing grass. Doctors diagnosed an asthma flare-up and released him the same evening. But according to Aunt Gloria, he apparently didn't go home, instead spending the night in the hospital waiting room. Was it his health, or was something else going on? Gloria began to suspect he might have known his life was in danger and didn't want to involve her.

On June 26th, Ricky called Sandra, telling her he was heading to the gas station for food. It was the last time she ever spoke to him. The last confirmed sighting of Ricky McCormick alive was on June 27th, seen by an employee at the gas station where he worked. His body was found three days later, on June 30th.

The autopsy initially offered little clarity. The advanced state of decomposition, far beyond what would be expected for just three days, confounded the pathologist. The cause of death was officially listed as undetermined. The decomposition mystery, however, had a plausible explanation: a severe heatwave had gripped St. Louis during those exact days. Temperatures soared to 90°F (32°C) with 85% humidity. Forensic experts explained that such extreme heat could drastically accelerate decomposition, altering tissue, obscuring wounds, and allowing insects to rapidly consume evidence. The body could easily look weeks old after only three days under those conditions.

For years, the undetermined cause of death was the official story. However, documents released in 2025 revealed a crucial detail withheld from the public: investigators *had* found a possible cause of death back in 2001. A letter from a detective stated they found a cut to Ricky's throat and believed it was the fatal injury. This shifted the narrative definitively towards homicide. Someone wanted Ricky dead.

Sandra, his girlfriend, provided a potential motive. She told investigators Ricky had been acting strangely, scared and anxious, in the weeks before his death. While he worked at an Amoco gas station, he had also taken on a side job delivering packages, often requiring him to travel out of state via Greyhound bus. Sandra confirmed it was drug trafficking; Ricky would return with large Ziploc bags of marijuana, the size of baseballs. He had made two trips to Florida in 1999. After his last trip to Orlando on June 15th, his fear intensified. When Sandra asked who the drugs belonged to, Ricky told her he was holding them for "Baha," one of the two brothers who ran the gas station. Sandra's immediate thought upon learning of Ricky's death pointed directly at this man: Baha Hamdullah.

The Amoco gas station and the Hamdullah family had a violent history. The original owner, Fawaz Hamdan, was imprisoned in 1994 for murdering his neighbor with a butcher knife. Jumah Hamdullah took over, operating under the alias "David Ratigan," and hired his brother, Baha "Bob" Hamdullah, to help run it. Baha was known to police as a loud, dangerous figure. In 1997, he attempted a drive-by shooting. Nine months later, he opened fire on his other brother, Bajett, who lied to protect him. Later that same month, Baha was arrested for assault after beating a homeless man, Elroy Carr, with a rusty hammer for refusing to leave the gas station property. Two weeks before Baha's trial for that assault, Elroy Carr was mysteriously gunned down. The case against Baha collapsed. Though never proven, police sources were certain Baha had ordered the hit. Detectives knew Baha Hamdullah — with his gang connections, drug use, reported weapon ownership, and history of violence — was a prime suspect in Ricky McCormick's murder.

Investigators identified a second credible suspect: Gregory Lamar Knox, a well-known drug dealer operating in Ricky and Sandra's apartment complex. Knox also had a violent reputation and had been named a suspect in multiple homicides, including murder-for-hire schemes. Crucially, a separate, unrelated investigation had already linked Knox to the Hamdullah brothers. During that investigation, a confidential informant told police Knox was responsible for the murder of a Black man who worked at a gas station on Shaw Avenue, whose body was dumped near West Alton — details that perfectly matched Ricky McCormick's case.

With two strong suspects tied to drug trafficking and violence, investigators set up surveillance. For weeks, they watched the gas station, the Hamdullah brothers' homes, and Gregory Knox's apartment complex. They needed something concrete, anything to link them to Ricky's death or confirm the drug operation. But the surveillance yielded nothing. Without evidence, the suspects were effectively cleared, and the homicide investigation went cold.

The only remaining avenue was the mysterious notes. Digging deeper into Ricky's past, detectives uncovered a complicated history. Family members, excluding his mother Frankie who spoke dismissively of his mental capacity, described him fondly, though they acknowledged he was different. Teachers recalled him telling odd stories and being isolated. He struggled academically, shuffled from grade to grade despite being unable to read or write, and eventually dropped out of high school, functionally illiterate. The only thing he could reliably write was his own name.

However, some family members offered a stunning revelation: as a child, Ricky used to write in code. They described it as meaningless "scribbles" or "chicken scratch" that none of them could ever understand. Could the notes found in his pocket be a continuation, a more developed version, of this childhood habit? It seemed plausible, especially given his illiteracy. This personal code might have been the only way he could write things down.

The St. Charles County Sheriff's Department knew deciphering the notes was beyond their capabilities. In late 2001, the notes landed on the desk of Dan Olsen at the FBI's Cryptanalysis and Racketeering Records Unit (CRRU), the elite cod-breaking division that had tackled everything from Nazi spy codes to the Zodiac Killer's ciphers. Olsen and his team quickly confirmed the notes weren't random; the structure, repeated patterns, and circled sections indicated intent. It was a cipher. The problem was, it was unlike anything they had ever encountered.

The CRRU team tried everything. Manual analysis with graph paper and pencil revealed patterns — the letter 'E' seemed to act as a spacer, certain letter combinations repeated — but no clear system emerged. State-of-the-art cipher-breaking software, updated repeatedly over the years, also failed. Experts from around the world were consulted, but the code remained opaque. Even the American Cryptogram Association, a group of amateur enthusiasts known for cracking codes that stumped professionals, were baffled when presented with the notes at their annual convention. Ricky's cipher operated by unknown rules.

After a decade of fruitless effort, the CRRU faced a choice: give up or go public. In a rare admission of defeat, the FBI released the notes online on March 29, 2011, appealing to the general public for help. "We are really good at what we do," Dan Olsen stated, "but we could use some help with this one." They hoped for a breakthrough similar to the Zodiac case, where a schoolteacher and his wife cracked the first cipher.

The public response was overwhelming. The FBI website crashed under the traffic. Online communities on Reddit, WebSleuths, and Google Groups exploded with theories and attempted solutions. Some speculated it was a simple substitution or transposition cipher. Others proposed more complex systems like the Vigenère or Nihilist ciphers. Frequency analysis showed 'N', 'S', and especially 'E' were common, supporting the 'E' as a spacer theory but contradicting typical cipher patterns where common English letters should be disguised.

Some claimed to have solved it, like one Redditor who used "ACSM" (letters found in the corner of a note) as a keyword, producing a message allegedly from Ricky asking for the notes to be decrypted to explain his death. However, these solutions often lacked methodological rigor, changing systems mid-decryption or removing letters arbitrarily to make them fit, and couldn't be replicated.

The release of more case details in 2012 by the *Riverfront Times*, including Ricky's drug ties and illiteracy, shifted speculation towards shorthand or personalized code. Theories emerged that the notes detailed drug deals, listing dealers, quantities, and money. One plausible theory suggested they were bus routes, as many number combinations (71, 74, 75, etc.) matched actual Metro bus routes in North St. Louis County, and the recurring "NCBE" could stand for North County Bus End/Exchange, a major hub. If true, this could potentially trace Ricky's final journey.

Despite thousands of attempts, no proposed solution has ever been verified by the FBI. The code remains unbroken, joining the mere 1% of ciphers the CRRU examines annually that go unsolved. The most likely explanation is that Ricky, hampered by illiteracy but needing to record information, developed a deeply idiosyncratic system known only to him.

This possibility raises ethical questions. If these are Ricky's private thoughts, should they be publicly dissected, even in pursuit of justice? As Nick Pelling of Cipher Mysteries wrote, reading them might only reveal the struggles of "a poor, illiterate guy," leaving a feeling of "deep sadness."

Ricky McCormick's life was undeniably complex. He faced mental health challenges and lived in difficult circumstances, yet he was also involved in criminal activity and had a conviction for statutory rape. Whether he was a victim exploited by dangerous men like Baha Hamdullah or a willing participant remains unclear. Both Hamdullah and Gregory Knox eventually faced justice for other crimes but were never charged in connection with Ricky's death. Baha Hamdullah was convicted for a separate murder in 2002, had it overturned, was acquitted on retrial, and reportedly moved to Ohio. Gregory Knox served time for drug distribution.

Over twenty-five years after his body was found, the death of Ricky McCormick is still officially unsolved. The two pages of intricate code found in his pocket, perhaps holding the key to his whereabouts, his killer, or simply his private thoughts, remain an impenetrable enigma, a silent testament to a life and death shrouded in mystery.

24

JAZZ MURDERS

The man who has come to be known as "Axeman" moved through New Orleans homes in 1918 and 1919, striking families in their beds, leaving doors chiseled open and household tools abandoned in yards. He was never identified. The city recorded a pattern, not a name: an intruder who preferred night, entered by removing a door panel or taking advantage of a gap, used the victim's own axe or any object at hand, and departed without taking valuables. Some targets survived long enough to describe a dark, looming form. Others were found by relatives or neighbors in rooms where blood had coated walls and floors. The record that remains is a series of scenes — addresses, bodies, instruments close by — that ties the murders together but stops short of proof about the person who carried them out.

The first killing ascribed to the Axeman occurred on May 23, 1918. Joseph and Katherine Maggio, an Italian couple who ran a grocery and lived in the apartment above it, were attacked in their sleep. Entry to the home was forced by chiseling away a lower panel of the door. Their throats were slit; Katherine's wound was so deep that her head was nearly severed. The attacker then used an axe from the couple's own home to inflict additional blows. Evidence was left in plain view. Outside the residence, police recovered the axe, still bloody. A few doors down, they found a razor with blood on it — the likely instrument used to cut the victims' throats. Inside, they noted a pile of blood-soaked clothing the killer had apparently discarded in favor of clean garments before leaving.

Joseph's brothers, Jake and Andrew, lived next door. They did not report hearing the attack. About two hours later, they heard groans and entered their brother's home. Katherine was already dead. Joseph lay beside her, alive but mortally wounded; he died within minutes of their arrival. The proximity of the brothers and the late discovery drew suspicion in the first wave of investigative questions, and attention turned especially to Andrew, who owned a nearby barber shop and had access to razors. An employee recalled Andrew taking a particular razor home days earlier to sharpen it. Police confronted him about the coincidence and about the failure to hear a prolonged assault in the next apartment. Andrew said he had been out celebrating acceptance into the Navy, returned home intoxicated, and slept in a way that masked any noise. He said he woke at 4:30 a.m. for a drink and then heard the groans. With no direct evidence tying him to the crime and plausible explanations for the razor and the missed sounds, he was not charged. Nothing in the apartment suggested theft; drawers were not rifled, and money or goods were not missing. The scene looked like an entry for a single purpose.

A month later, on June 27, 1918, another residence above a business became a crime scene. Louis Bessemer, who owned a bakery, and his mistress, Harriet Lou, slept in the apartment above the shop. A deliveryman arrived in the morning and found the bakery closed when it should have been open. Circling to a back entrance, he noticed a door panel had been chiseled out. Inside the living quarters, he saw blood on walls, floors, and even the ceiling. In the bedroom, Bessemer and Harriet lay in pools of blood, both still alive but severely injured from single axe blows to the head. Police recovered Bessemer's own axe, bloodied, in the bathroom. At the hospital, Bessemer regained enough stability to talk but could only report that he had awakened to a figure leaving the room, too quickly to identify. Harriet's condition was worse. She was in and out of consciousness with extensive trauma and required weeks of treatment.

A worker at Bessemer's bakery, a forty-one-year-old Black man, was arrested without supporting evidence. The timing and his employment status seemed to be the basis for suspicion. No physical link emerged; he was eventually released. While Harriet remained hospitalized, her statements shifted. At one point she described the attacker as a mixed-race man in racist terms. Later she accused Bessemer himself, calling him a German spy and suggesting he had attacked her, then injured himself to cover it. Police searched and found multilingual correspondence in his rooms, which they interpreted as suspicious. He was arrested on that theory, briefly convicted, and then acquitted. Officers who had pursued the espionage angle were demoted. Harriet died after seven weeks of treatment, and Bessemer was again arrested — this time for her murder — held for many months, and finally acquitted. Once more, no one remained in custody for the attack itself.

On August 5, 1918, the pattern reached a new kind of target. Anna Schnieder, eight months pregnant, was found by her husband on their bed, face smashed and scalp lacerated, teeth missing, blood saturating linens. The assault weapon appeared to be her bedside lamp. She had been attacked while sleeping and could recall only a shape leaving the room when she came to. Despite the trauma, she survived, and two days later, she delivered a healthy baby girl. As in earlier attacks, nothing suggested robbery; the intruder had come and gone with no sign of searching or theft.

Five days after Anna's assault, on August 10, Pauline and Mary Brunner woke to sounds from their uncle's room. They found their uncle, Joseph Ramana, bleeding on the floor from head wounds caused by an axe. Some accounts note that the nieces glimpsed a man fleeing — described as dark-skinned, heavyset, dressed in a dark suit with a slouched hat — though the certainty of that description varies among tellings. In the yard, officers recovered an axe. A lower panel of the door had again been chiseled out to gain entry. Ramana, 80 years old, died two days later.

By then, the similarities were clear enough that investigators publicly linked the crimes and increased night patrols. The combination of door panels removed, householder axes used, and the absence of theft suggested one offender or a set of offenders using the same method. The city reacted first with alarm and then with routines designed to make entry harder. Reports of suspicious men with axes spiked and led to false leads. The Axeman waited out the extra police presence for nine months.

The next attack came on March 10, 1919. A neighbor heard screams from the home of the Cortemiglia family and ran inside. Rose Cortemiglia, the mother, staggered into the hall, wounded and clutching her two-year-old daughter, Mary, who had been struck once in the neck and killed. Rose had been struck in the head with an axe. Her husband, Charles, lay collapsed on the floor with similar wounds. Both adults survived after hospital treatment. The child did not. In the aftermath, Rose accused the neighbor who had entered the home that night. He was sixty-nine, ill, and frail. When police dismissed that possibility, she accused his son, Frank, an eighteen-year-old about six feet tall (about 182 centimeters) and 200 pounds (about ninety kilograms). Entry to the house — by removing a small door panel — seemed to rule out a large attacker forcing himself through that gap. Charles denied his wife's story. Nevertheless, police arrested both neighbors. The older man received a life sentence for attempted murder; the younger, accused as the principal assailant, was sentenced to death by hanging. About a year into the proceedings, Charles divorced Rose. Her accusations then collapsed. She recanted, saying neither neighbor had attacked them. The men were released.

Three days after the Cortemiglia assault, a local newspaper received the letter that would define the case in the city's imagination. The author called himself the Axeman, described himself as a spirit and a demon, taunted police, and made a demand: at 12:15 a.m. on an upcoming Tuesday, every home should have jazz music playing. Those who did not "jazz it out," the letter said, would "get the ax." The threat, theatrical as it sounded, had an effect. That night, homes put on records, clubs were packed, bands played continuously, and no attack occurred.

Months passed without a new case. In August 1919, the Axeman reappeared in the record. Steve Barker awoke to a figure standing over his bed and was struck immediately with an axe. He later stumbled to a neighbor's house and collapsed. He could not recall the attack after regaining consciousness. The injuries were severe; accounts say his skull was split. The house showed familiar signs: careful entry, a chiseled door panel, and no theft. Three weeks later, in early September, nineteen-year-old Sarah

Lawmen was assaulted in her sleep by an intruder who entered through an open window rather than a door. Neighbors found her hours later, gravely injured. Teeth were missing; head wounds were extensive. She survived but could not provide a description. An axe lay on the lawn. Because the entry method differed from the door-panel pattern, some considered this event a possible copycat.

The last killing commonly attributed to the Axeman took place on October 27, 1919. Esther Pepitone awoke to noises from the bedroom and, from the doorway, saw two men fleeing. Her husband, Mike, had been struck in the head eighteen times with an axe. He died before police arrived. The scene diverges from the earlier pattern. The number of blows far exceeded previous counts in cases linked to the Axeman, and the presence of two men contrasted with earlier reports of a single shadowed figure. Some sources noted a different tool found at the scene, something used to erect circus tents and a circus was in town at the time. Those details fed the idea that this was not the same offender but an opportunistic killing concealed behind the Axeman's well-known method. Police took note of Esther's composure, which they considered unusually calm.

The Axeman's identity was never established by evidence produced in court. In place of a name, the case accumulated explanations. One centered on motive. Many of the victims were Italian immigrants or Italian Americans, often small business owners — a demographic that had become visible and successful in the city. Police and commentators considered whether the targeting reflected racial or ethnic animus, jealousy, or reprisals disguised as random attacks. Others saw points of overlap with organized crime. The Pepitone case in particular attracted a mafia theory on the logic that two men, a flurry of blows, and an emphatic killing looked like a directed vendetta rather than a serial offender's pattern. The lack of theft across scenes continued to suggest that money or goods were not the goal.

The suspect most often discussed in conversations is Joseph Mumphrey. Two years after Mike Pepitone's death, Esther moved to Los Angeles and remarried a man named Angelo. On the second anniversary of Mike's murder, her second husband disappeared. A man who had done business with Angelo — Mumphrey — came to Esther's door and demanded 500 dollars and her jewelry. Esther retrieved a revolver instead and shot him dead. She told police she believed he had killed her first husband. Background details about Mumphrey made him a plausible focus. He had a long criminal record, was linked to a blackmailing gang that targeted Italians, and had been in and out of prison. The timing of his prison terms lined up in a general way with the period when attacks attributed to the Axeman occurred and when, earlier, Italian business owners were assaulted or murdered in 1910–1912. There were some beatings, some shootings, some undetermined circumstances, all clustered around Italian proprietors during a period of community growth and friction. Mumphrey was free during some of those years and incarcerated from 1912 to 1918, a span that ended just as the Axeman attacks began. However, none of that amounts to proof. It is a timeline and a set of affinities. Esther's identification was never tested in court because the man she pointed to was dead. The Los Angeles shooting removed the possibility of a confession or a trial that could have drawn lines between incidents in two cities.

Another suspect is Jake Bird, arrested in 1947 for a double murder committed with an axe, who then claimed responsibility for many killings across the United States. He had lived in New Orleans as a teenager in 1918–1919. The script notes the practical question raised by the door panels: an adult man of large build would have trouble slipping through the small openings the Axeman created. A teenager might not. That is an observation about size, not about evidence. Bird did not confess to the New Orleans crimes, and no link beyond timing and weapon exists in the account provided.

The question of copycats recurs at the outer edges of the case. Some see the last two events — a window entry in early September and the two men in the Pepitone bedroom in late October — as inconsistent with the core pattern. Others consider whether a single offender could have varied his method when opportunity presented itself. The same kind of debate appears around the 1910–1912 cluster of assaults and killings of Italian business owners. In a city with active organized crime, a period of massive demographic change, and rising resentment toward successful immigrant shopkeepers, some of those attacks could be reprisals, some robberies, some personal disputes, and some the work of a single offender.

The Axeman's presence in the city's history rests on these facts and on the way the case interacted with public fear. The letter promising death to any home that did not play jazz at a specified time may have been a hoax, but it captured the city's attention and produced a measurable response. The open windows shut; door panels were reinforced. Patrols increased and then receded when nothing happened for months. The killings began again and then stopped. Explanations gathered around the gaps, and each explanation reflected a different part of the city's life at the time: ethnic tension, organized crime, opportunistic violence, media theater. Without a confession or physical evidence that could be tied to a suspect, the chapter ends where it began: scenes linked by method and time, a letter that might have been from the offender or might not, arrests that did not hold, and a name — Axeman — that the city gave to an absence.

CONCLUSION

As we close these files, the silence that follows is often the heaviest part of the journey. We have traveled from the deceptive quiet of rural Australia to the crowded streets of Lahore, uncovering the scars left by murder, mystery, and madness. What remains is not just a collection of facts, but a sobering reminder of how easily the thin line between order and chaos can be erased.

The cases we've explored—the unsolved ciphers, the blood-signed contracts, and the shattered trust of global scams—leave us with more than just chills. They force us to confront the reality that the "monsters" of our world are rarely the caricatures we see in films. Often, they are the neighbors who smiled across the fence or the leaders who promised salvation while delivering ruin.

Writing these accounts is an exercise in seeking justice through memory. For the victims of the "Summerfield Six," the "Nanjing University Murder," and the many others mentioned in these pages, their stories deserve to be told with the weight they carry. By acknowledging the darkness, we honor the lives that were caught within it.

As you place this book back on the shelf, you carry these twenty-four stories with you. The world may look slightly different now—a little more mysterious, perhaps a little more fragile. But in understanding the darkness, we are better equipped to value the light.

Thank you for walking this path with me. Sleep well, keep your doors locked, and remember: the truth is always out there, waiting in the files.

PART II

TRUE CRIME FILES

24 CHILLING TRUE CRIME STORIES YOU'VE NEVER HEARD OF

INTRODUCTION

Welcome to the shadows.

Most people believe they understand the limits of human depravity. They recognize the names of "household" monsters and the cases that dominate mainstream media. But the true nature of evil doesn't always make the front page; it often lingers in the quiet corners of the world, hidden in cold files that have gathered dust or in stories that were too strange, too local, or too terrifying to be widely told.

True Crime Files: 24 Chilling True Crime Stories You've Never Heard Of peels back the curtain on cases that defy easy explanation. This is an expedition into the darkest corridors of the human psyche, spanning the globe from the desolate "Valley of Death" in Norway to the cryptic, taunting letters of Circleville. These accounts prove that truth is not only stranger than fiction — it is far more ruthless.

Within these pages, you will encounter a diverse gallery of darkness. I explore the manipulative power of belief in chapters like "The Yerba Buena Cult" and the chilling conviction of "Jesus was an Alien." The book dives into high-stakes deception, from the audacity of the "Carnegie Heiress" to the historical fraud of the "Hitler Diaries." For those fascinated by the hunt, I track predators like the "National Forest Killer" and the elusive, faceless entities behind Japan's "Monster with 21 Faces." These are but a few of the twenty-four harrowing accounts waiting for you in these pages.

But the horror doesn't stop with the infamous. Beyond these names lies a deeper, more personal brand of terror — a reminder that the "sleep-walker" in the room down the hall, or the silent van parked in a driveway nearby, might be hiding a secret that would freeze your blood.

Turn the page, lock your doors, and prepare yourself. The world is a much darker place than you imagined.

25

THE SLEEPWALKER

In the world of aspiring online creators, Robert Eugene Crimo III was, for a brief time, a quiet success story. He was a sad, neglected, and lonely kid from an affluent Chicago suburb who found an outlet, and even a small following, through a rap career he built from scratch on YouTube and Spotify. But as his personal life began to unravel under the weight of family dysfunction, financial ruin, and profound depression, the music that was once his salvation began to mirror a much darker internal reality. The mellow, sad-sounding tracks gave way to cryptic videos filled with violent imagery and nihilistic pronouncements. This descent culminated on July 4, 2022, when the rapper known as "Awake" climbed to a rooftop overlooking his hometown's Independence Day parade and rained down a hail of bullets on the unsuspecting crowd below, leaving a trail of casualties, unanswered questions, and bizarre conspiracy theories in his wake.

Robert, who went by Awake later in his rap career, was born on September 20, 2000, and was raised for his entire life in the Lake County area of Illinois, primarily in the city of Highland Park. On the surface, it was an idyllic place to grow up. A wealthy suburb of Chicago, it was known as the picturesque filming location for movies like *Ferris Bueller's Day Off* and as the onetime home of basketball legend Michael Jordan. Awake's family was middle-class; his father, Robert Crimo Jr., was a local businessman, and his mother, Denise, listed her occupation as a homeo-pathic healer. But unlike many of their neighbors in the affluent commu-nity, the Crimo family was deeply dysfunctional, and the signs of neglect began when Awake was just a toddler.

When he was two years old, his mother drove him to a local Toys "R" Us on a hot day and left him alone in the car with the windows rolled up for nearly half an hour. A concerned passerby saw the child and contacted the police. Denise was arrested and charged with child endangerment, to which she pleaded guilty. This incident was a grim foreshadowing of the chaotic and neglectful environment that would define Awake's childhood. While his father was not actively abusive, he was largely absent, consumed by his work. In 2008, after running a few other stores, Robert Jr. opened a popular deli and pantry in town, a "mom and pop" operation that became a local hangout spot. On its opening day, photos captured a seem-ingly happy family, and young Awake was often seen running around the store while his father worked.

But this picture of familial harmony was a facade. The dysfunction that plagued the Crimo marriage was not kept behind closed doors; it was on full public display. Robert and Denise would frequently engage in heated, screaming arguments right in the middle of the deli, in front of friends, customers, and their own children. One of Robert's friends later recalled the intense discomfort these public fights caused, remarking, "If that's the public arguments, I can only imagine the private ones." Soon, the verbal altercations escalated into physical violence. Between 2009 and 2013, police were called to the family home nearly twenty times, with nine of those calls related to domestic violence, usually involving Denise throwing objects at or hitting Robert. The most serious incident occurred in 2010, when Robert called the police to report that his wife had attacked him with a screwdriver. But once at the station, he recanted his story, refusing to press charges — a common pattern in their volatile relationship.

The parents' neglect was also apparent at school. A former coach recalled that Awake and his younger brother were often left behind by their "flighty" mother, who would simply forget to pick them up after their after-school programs had ended, leaving them stranded for hours while their father was busy at the deli. It was in the midst of this turmoil that

Awake, at the age of eleven, sought refuge in music. He decided he wanted to become a rapper, creating online accounts on various platforms and adopting the stage name "Awake the Rapper."

During his middle school years, Awake was described by classmates as a weird, soft-spoken kid who showed little interest in school or his peers. He started to open up a bit after discovering skateboarding, a hobby that allowed him to make a few friends. He also created a YouTube channel, where his earliest videos were mostly do-it-yourself (DIY) tutorials on how to maintain a skateboard. But by the time he entered high school, this brief period of social connection had faded. He reverted to being a loner, a distant figure who was always by himself. He continued to release music throughout his high school years, but his disinterest in academics was profound. Just before his junior year, he dropped out, a decision his father explained to a neighbor was due to his son's "emotional issues."

Now free from the structure of school, Awake dedicated himself completely to his rapper persona. He began to cover his hands, arms, and even his face in tattoos, including the word "AWAKE" inked in block letters just above his right eyebrow. He drove a car emblazoned with anime stickers and the words "Pussy Mobile" written across the back, and he was known to ride an electric bike around the neighborhood while blasting heavy metal music. In 2016, at sixteen, he had his first minor run-in with the law for possession of tobacco. That same year, he had his first taste of viral success with a song called "By the Pond," which he released with another artist named Atlas. The music video for the song eventually garnered around three million views across all platforms before Awake, for reasons unknown, deleted it entirely, an act that only added to his growing online mystique. He released his first full album, *Messages*, in 2017, followed by two more in 2018. He developed a small but consistent following, with his tracks reliably pulling in several thousand views each. His early music was often described as mellow, slow, and sad-sounding rap.

But as Awake's music career was beginning to take off, his family's life was imploding. In 2019, Robert Crimo Jr., facing dwindling business at his deli and mounting debts, launched a bizarre and ill-fated campaign for mayor of Highland Park. He ran against Nancy Roering, who, in a strange twist of fate, had been Awake's Cub Scout leader years earlier. Robert Jr.'s campaign was a non-starter; he was never seen campaigning and received no donations other than one he gave to himself. He was defeated in a landslide. Shortly after, the deli was forced to close, and the family was plunged into financial ruin, with one lender suing Robert for over $750,000. For Awake, who was living in a small apartment on the back of his father's property, the future was looking increasingly bleak.

It was during this period of intense family stress that Awake's own mental health took a nosedive. He had become deeply depressed, and in April 2019, he attempted suicide. Just a few months later, in September, a family member called the police after Awake, brandishing a collection of knives, threatened to "kill everyone." When police arrived, his parents downplayed the incident, and while he wasn't charged with a crime, officers did confiscate sixteen knives, a dagger, and a sword from the home. Crucially, the police also filed a "clear and present danger" report, a legal designation intended to prevent individuals who pose a threat to themselves or others from obtaining a firearm license.

Awake's online persona and real-world behavior began to take a strange turn. He started showing up at Donald Trump rallies, sometimes dressed in a "Where's Waldo?" costume, a goofy act that led many to believe he was simply trolling. At the same time, his music videos grew darker and more cryptic. One video, for a song called "Toy Soldier," featured crude animations of a school shooter, police, and injured victims. Another, for a re-release of his song "On My Mind," depicted Awake in a classroom, first sitting at a teacher's desk, and then suddenly clad in makeshift tactical gear, including a bicycle helmet, as the room is shown littered with what appear to be bullet casings. The video was filled with obscure references to the video game *Call of Duty: Zombies*, a game he was known to be a fan of. Without his own commentary, it was impossible to know if these were artistic expressions, bizarre tributes, or the fantasies of a deeply disturbed young man.

His personal life continued its downward spiral. His parents had separated, and the mortgage company had begun foreclosure proceedings on the family home. He was shot down by a female coworker at Panera Bread whom he had become infatuated with, a rejection that some have speculated was a major contributing factor to his deteriorating mindset. It was in this state of hopelessness and despair that Awake made a fateful decision. He applied for a Firearm Owner's Identification (FOID) card. Because he was not yet twenty-one, he needed a sponsor, and his father, Robert Crimo Jr., agreed to be that sponsor. In a catastrophic failure of the system, the Illinois State Police, for reasons that remain unclear, chose not to act on the "clear and present danger" report they had on file. Within a few months, Awake, having passed a background check, had his license. He immediately began purchasing weapons. Between June and September of 2020, he legally bought five guns, including a Smith & Wesson M&P-15 semi-automatic rifle.

As he was amassing an arsenal, his online activities grew more sinister. Under the username "Awake47," he became a frequent lurker on a gore website called Documenting Reality, a private forum where users share graphic videos and images of real-life violence and death. He began to regularly comment on footage related to mass shootings. By this point, his descent seemed complete.

In February 2021, he self-published a twenty-eight-page book called *Arcturus*, which he described as a manifesto. It was composed entirely of an undeciphered sequence of numbers and remains an unsolved mystery. He was done with music. In his final, chilling video, uploaded just before the attack, he narrated his thoughts over a montage of his previous work. "I need to just do it," he said in a monotone voice. "It is my destiny. Everything has led up to this. Nothing can stop me, not even myself... Like a sleepwalker, walking blindly into the night."

On the morning of July 4, 2022, as the town of Highland Park prepared for its first Independence Day parade in two years, Awake put his plan into action. He prepared his Smith & Wesson rifle and stashed another gun in his mother's car. To conceal his highly recognizable face tattoos and to blend in with the panicked crowd after the attack, he disguised himself in women's clothing. He made his way to the Ross Cosmetics building on Central Avenue, climbed an unsecured staircase to the roof, and set up what he felt was the perfect sniper's nest. At 10:14 a.m., just as the parade began to pass below, he took aim and opened fire. In the span of just a few minutes, he fired eighty-three rounds into the crowd, reloading his rifle twice. The scene below erupted into mass chaos. People screamed, cried, and ran in all directions, scrambling for cover. In total, forty-five people were struck by his gunfire.

His escape plan worked flawlessly. As law enforcement swarmed the scene, Awake, still in his disguise, simply blended in with the terrified parade-goers and walked away, dropping his rifle in the street as he fled. He went home, borrowed his mother's car, and went on the run. The scene he left behind was one of utter devastation. Forty-eight people were injured, one of whom was left permanently paralyzed. Seven people were killed: Katherine Goldstein, Irina McCarthy, Kevin McCarthy, Stephen Strauss, Jacki Sundheim, Nicolas Toledo-Zaragoza, and Eduardo Uvaldo. The parents of a two-year-old boy, Irina and Kevin McCarthy, had both been killed, leaving their son an orphan.

Awake drove north toward Madison, Wisconsin, where he considered carrying out a similar attack on another parade but ultimately decided against it. The manhunt, meanwhile, was in full force. Police quickly found the abandoned rifle and, using security camera footage, identified Awake and the car he was driving. Eight hours after the attack, following a tip from a citizen who recognized the vehicle, police surrounded him and he was arrested without incident. In his confession, he admitted to aiming at people from the waist up, shooting to kill. He referred to the panicked crowd as "sleepwalkers and zombies," a chilling echo of his final video.

The legal fallout was swift. Awake was indicted on 117 felonies, including twenty-one counts of first-degree murder — three for each of the seven victims he killed. His father, Robert Crimo Jr., was also arrested and charged with seven counts of reckless conduct for sponsoring his son's gun license, to which he eventually pleaded guilty and served a brief jail sentence. After a series of bizarre legal maneuvers, including an initial "not guilty" plea and a flirtation with conspiracy theories claiming he was a "patsy" in a false flag operation, Awake finally pleaded guilty to all remaining counts just hours before his trial was set to begin. He was sentenced to seven consecutive life sentences without the possibility of parole.

To this day, we still don't know exactly why he did it. He left no manifesto that could be understood, and in his confession, he offered no clear motive. It was likely a confluence of factors: a lifetime of neglect, profound mental health struggles, personal and financial failures, and a desperate, nihilistic desire to lash out at the world and achieve a dark form of infamy. He is now housed in an undisclosed federal prison, his location kept secret for security reasons. The rapper who called himself Awake has finally been silenced, but the echoes of his final, violent act will haunt the community of Highland Park forever.

26

A CHILDHOOD SENTENCED

It was the last day of school in Lake Worth, Florida, May 26, 2000. An electric buzz of impending freedom filled the hallways of Lake Worth Middle School. Lockers slammed shut for the final time, the sound echoing like a punctuation mark at the end of a long year. Students, their minds already on summer vacation, chattered with an excitement that was almost tangible. In just a few hours, the final bell would ring, releasing them into three months of sun-drenched, unstructured bliss. But inside a classroom, a single moment of a teenage impulse, born from a volatile mix of anger, immaturity, and access to a deadly weapon, was about to rewrite the lives of everyone present. A day that should have been defined by celebration would instead become a nightmare, and a quiet middle school in a Florida suburb would become the epicenter of a fierce national debate about crime, punishment, and the very nature of justice in America.

At the center of this tragedy was thirteen-year-old Nathaniel Brazill. To his teachers, he was no ordinary student. They described him as bright, funny, and at times, even charming. He was an honor student with a perfect attendance record, the kind of kid principals might rely on to help settle minor schoolyard disputes. But beneath that young, likable facade was a simmering anger, a deep well of turmoil fed by a chaotic and abusive home life that no one at the school fully understood. On that fateful last day of school, he had been suspended earlier for a minor infraction — throwing water balloons in the school cafeteria with friends. Upset and fuming, he was sent home before he had the chance to say goodbye to a girl he had a crush on, his first serious girlfriend who had given him his first kiss just six days earlier. In Nathaniel's adolescent mind, this perceived rejection was an unbearable injustice. He rode his bicycle home, but not to begin his summer vacation. He went to retrieve a .25-caliber handgun that belonged to his grandfather, tucked it away, and returned to the school.

He made his way to the classroom of his seventh-grade English teacher, thirty-five-year-old Barry Grunow. Grunow was, by Nathaniel's own account, his favorite teacher, a man he liked and respected. Nathaniel stood at the classroom door and asked to be allowed inside to speak with two female students, including the girl he wanted to see before the summer break began. Grunow, likely seeing a suspended student trying to circumvent the rules, refused his request. The confrontation was brief, a simple exchange between a teacher enforcing discipline and a student pushing back. But Nathaniel was armed. He pulled the small, silver handgun from his pocket. Accounts of what happened next would become the central dispute of his trial. The defense would argue that Mr. Grunow, not taking the threat seriously enough, was met with a cocked gun, an act of intimidation that went horribly wrong. Nathaniel aimed the weapon at his teacher, and in front of a room full of stunned classmates, he fired a single shot. The bullet struck Barry Grunow in the face, killing him instantly. As his favorite teacher lay dying on the classroom floor, Nathaniel ran. The nation was shocked. How could a boy so young, an honor student with no prior history of disciplinary problems, commit such a violent and senseless act? Was this a cold-blooded murder, or a tragic accident born from a child's catastrophic lack of judgment?

The wheels of the justice system turned swiftly. Nathaniel was arrested on the same day as the shooting. The legal framework in Florida at the time, however, was undergoing a dramatic shift. A "tough on crime" mentality had led to changes in laws across the country, blurring the lines between the juvenile and the adult justice systems. There was a time, not so long ago, when a thirteen-year-old who committed even a heinous crime would have been processed through a juvenile system focused on rehabilitation. But by the year 2000, a new philosophy had taken hold: if a child commits an adult crime, they must pay as an adult. In fifteen states, including Florida, the decision of whether to charge a child as an adult was left entirely to the discretion of prosecutors, many of whom were elected officials eager to project a tough image.

Nathaniel Brazill found himself caught in this new legal landscape. The prosecution, brushing aside considerations of his age, mental maturity, and troubled personal situation, decided to try him as an adult for first-degree murder. The case ignited a fierce debate across the country. Should children, whose brains are not yet fully developed and who are legally prohibited from driving, voting, or serving in the military, be locked away in adult prisons for the rest of their lives? Or does a society have a responsibility to seek rehabilitation for its youngest and most troubled offenders? For Nathaniel Brazill, the answer was about to be decided in a courtroom.

The trial became a battle of two starkly contrasting narratives. The prosecution, led by Mark Shiner, painted Nathaniel as a cold-blooded, remorseless killer who was incapable of being rehabilitated. Shiner argued that the killing was premeditated, pointing to statements Nathaniel allegedly made before the shooting that indicated he had planned the act. He repeatedly drew the jury's attention to Nathaniel's stoic and blank demeanor in the courtroom, using it as proof of his lack of remorse. "This defendant's demeanor sends chills up my spine," Shiner told the judge during the sentencing hearing. "Let us not forget a man's life has been taken away," he said after the sentencing, describing the shooting as a "heinous crime committed by a young man with a difficult personality who should be behind bars."

The defense, led by attorney Robert Udell, did not deny that Nathaniel fired the fatal shot. Their entire case hinged on the argument that it was a tragic, unintentional accident. Udell contended that Nathaniel, in a moment of immature fury, only intended to scare his teacher and thought the gun's safety was on when he pointed it at him. They argued that a scared thirteen-year-old boy had been unwittingly thrust into an adult world, and his blank demeanor was not a sign of a sociopath, but rather a coping mechanism for a child accustomed to bottling up his emotions in the face of overwhelming trauma. "He's a child and that's who committed this crime," Udell pleaded with the judge, asking for a sentence of twelve years.

During the emotional sentencing hearing, defense lawyers and psychologists finally revealed the full extent of the turmoil that had been building in Nathaniel's life, painting a picture of a boy drowning in problems that no adult had seemed to notice. His family life was plagued by instability and violence. His mother, Polly Powell, had been in a series of abusive relationships since he was a young boy. Police had been called to their home for domestic incidents on at least seven occasions in the six years leading up to the shooting. Nathaniel had been forced at times to physically intervene in fights between his mother and one of his stepfathers. Another stepfather had refused to let him live in the family home, forcing him to spend nights at his grandmother's house. His biological father was not a constant presence in his life. According to defense experts, Nathaniel learned from a very young age to keep his emotions locked away, to present a stoic exterior no matter what chaos swirled around him.

Just months before the shooting, this fragile stability completely shattered. The month Nathaniel turned thirteen, his mother was diagnosed with breast cancer. His grades, once stellar, began to drop, and in a letter to Mr. Grunow, the very teacher he would later kill, he made references to suicide. He was reportedly fascinated with weapons and dreamed of a career in law enforcement or the military, spending his spare time playing fighter pilot simulation games and visiting military websites. His mother, Polly Powell, took the stand and, between sobs, pleaded for mercy for her son. "I don't know what happened to my baby," she said, adding that if her personal problems and poor choices in men had contributed to his actions, "I take full responsibility."

The highly emotional trial featured the testimony of twenty-three of Nathaniel's classmates, many of whom broke down on the stand as they recalled the horrifying moment when a well-liked, mild-mannered boy shot their beloved teacher. After sixteen hours of deliberation, the jury of nine women and three men returned with a verdict. They rejected the prosecution's argument for first-degree murder, deciding that the shooting was not premeditated. Instead, they found Nathaniel Brazill guilty of second-degree murder with a firearm. While this spared him the mandatory sentence of life without parole, under Florida's sentencing laws, the judge was still required to impose a sentence of twenty-five years to life.

On July 27, 2001, Nathaniel Brazill, now fourteen years old, stood shackled in an orange prison uniform, silent and expressionless, as Judge Richard Wennett pronounced his fate. He was sentenced to twenty-eight years in an adult prison, without the possibility of parole. The sentence would be followed by two years of house arrest and five years of probation. The judge also ordered him to earn his high school equivalency diploma and enroll in an anger management course while in custody. He would be held in a juvenile correction center until he turned eighteen, at which point he would be transferred to an adult prison to serve out the remainder of his sentence.

The reaction to the sentence was deeply divided. The Grunow family, with the exception of the victim's widow, Pam, had asked for the maximum penalty of life in prison and felt the twenty-eight-year term was disappointingly lenient. Barry Grunow's brother, Kurt, told Court TV he was "very disappointed" and felt the jury must have been watching a different trial. Nathaniel's mother, on the other hand, was grateful for what she saw as the judge's leniency. "I was hoping for less," she said, "but I know my son will be home someday."

Nathaniel's life was now defined by prison walls. The months of confinement in an adult county jail while awaiting trial had begun to harden him, forcing him to turn inward in a way that came across as sullen and uncaring. Deputies testified that in his holding cell, he was often unruly, even joking about shooting jurors, a behavior a child psychologist attributed to the false bravado of a scared and overwhelmed child. But there were other moments, away from the prying eyes of others. After the verdict was read, his lawyer recalled that Nathaniel went back to a private room and cried. Later that night, back in the juvenile cell block he shared with other youths accused of violent crimes, he lay on his bunk and cried alone while the others watched an episode of *Law & Order* about a school shooting just like his.

He would spend the rest of his childhood and much of his adult life behind bars, a product of a justice system that had decided he was beyond redemption at the age of thirteen. He will be in his early forties before he is released, a man who has known little else but incarceration since he was a boy. His case prompted an overhaul of the way Florida handles its young violent offenders and became a touchstone in the national debate over juvenile justice. The story of Nathaniel Brazill is a chilling reminder of the devastating consequences of a single, impulsive act of violence. It is the story of a beloved teacher whose life was cut short, of students who lost their innocence in a flash of gunfire, and of a boy who traded the remainder of his youth for a prison cell, his future sealed by a fatal mistake made on the last day of school.

27

A BOTTLE OF LIE

The first known traces of the man who would become the world's greatest wine forger appeared, almost out of thin air, in the early 2000s, under the warm California sun. In Woodland Hills, an outlying district of Los Angeles, a shy, unassuming young man in his early twenties pushed open the door of a renowned local wine shop. He wasn't there to buy wine; he was there to sell a bottle. He was looking for an education, a way into a world of incredible wealth and status. The man, who would eventually be known to the world as Rudy Kurniawan, was a ghost, a chameleon with multiple identities and no verifiable past. But in just a few short years, armed with an almost supernatural palate and an audacious disregard for the truth, he would infiltrate the highest echelons of the fine wine community, perpetrating an international scam of such breathtaking scale that it would take the world's leading experts nearly a decade to bring him down.

The man he met that day in the wine shop was Kyle Smith, a seasoned professional who, for the first time on camera, would later recount the path of the young Asian man who walked into his life. Rudy's request was simple enough. He explained that he had bought a significant amount of 1998 California Cabernet from another merchant, only to discover that it was not a good vintage, and he was hoping to sell the bottles. Smith, seeing a naive but eager young man, agreed. He couldn't have imagined that he was dealing with someone who would one day be sentenced in a New York courtroom for a fraud amounting to tens of millions of dollars.

Beneath his timid exterior, the young Rudy seemed driven by a singular desire: to deepen his knowledge of *Grands Crus*, the great wines of France. His visits to the shop became more frequent, and he peppered the staff with questions. Smith and his colleague, Paul Wasserman, one of California's most renowned wine experts, took the curious young man under their wings. They became his mentors, opening up their encyclopedic knowledge of French wines — their tastes, their grape varieties, their history. It was good timing. In the early 2000s, the American market was dominated by the powerful red wines of Bordeaux, and only a handful of discerning collectors were beginning to bet on the more nuanced and complex wines of Burgundy. Smith and Wasserman encouraged Rudy to venture into this emerging field. They sensed in him a deep-seated need to find something he could excel at, something that would make him important.

Rudy's progress was nothing short of spectacular. In just six months, his palate developed at an astonishing rate. He was a gifted student, a "super taster" with overdeveloped senses and a memory for aroma and flavor that was far beyond average. He would taste, smell, and savor, taking meticulous mental notes to memorize the subtle complexities of every vintage and *Grand Cru* he was introduced to. He had an exceptional memory, learning to identify more than 100 distinct appellations of Burgundy by heart. It was a godsend of a talent, a gift he would later exploit with devastating effect. But Rudy's curiosity extended beyond the contents of the bottle. He questioned his mentors relentlessly about the market for these great French vintages, searching for the unrecognized gems that could be turned into a fortune.

As the American market began its slow pivot from Bordeaux to Burgundy, Rudy understood that this new trend could be incredibly lucrative. To capitalize on it, he needed to immerse himself in the world of those who appreciated these rare beverages. He asked his friend Kyle Smith to introduce him to his exclusive tasting club. The group, known as the "Burg Hounds," comprised twelve of the top wine tasters in Los Angeles, connoisseurs who would meet in the city's finest restaurants to share and critique rare bottles. It was here that the timid young prodigy took his first steps into the closed and rarefied world of the city's finest palates.

From his very first tasting, Rudy was a sensation. In the club's traditional game of blind tasting, the self-taught newcomer, with no formal oenological training, came dangerously close to perfection, consistently identifying wines with an accuracy that stunned the seasoned experts around him. He became an obsessive perfectionist, visiting the wine shop in Woodland Hills daily, tasting everything he could, and beginning to build an impressive wine cellar of his own. These bottles were stored in his modest home in Arcadia, a quiet residential neighborhood north of Los Angeles, where he lived with his mother. It was a place he seemed determined to keep private; Kyle Smith was the only one of his new acquaintances who was ever invited there.

Smith would later recall the strange visit. After having dinner in Rudy's predominantly Chinese neighborhood, Rudy invited him back to the house for a drink. As they approached the front door, Rudy stopped him. "Dude," he said, "when you come into the house, don't freak out when you see what wines I have in there, because my mom thinks they're all $20 or less." Smith was surprised, but he went inside and shared a couple of bottles with his friend. He saw no reason to suspect anything was amiss. But he did realize one thing: the bottles in that house did not cost $20. The average price was closer to $400 or $500 a bottle. In his very first year of collecting, the quiet, unemployed twenty-five-year-old had amassed a collection worth a small fortune, likely around half a million dollars.

The question that hung over Rudy was as potent and unspoken as the aroma of a fine vintage: where was all the money coming from? He was intensely private about his personal life, and he intentionally kept the source of his wealth shrouded in mystery. He told Kyle Smith that his family was involved in liquor distribution in Hong Kong and Indonesia. To others, he presented himself as a "trust fund baby," claiming his wealthy family had essentially exiled him to California, providing him with a million dollars a month to spend as long as he stayed there. His backstory was a shifting narrative of contradictions; at times he was an Indonesian annuitant who had come to the U.S. to study, other times a political exile, other times an aspiring professional golfer. His history was shaky and confused, but in the intoxicating world of high-end wine, where wealth and eccentricity often went hand-in-hand, no one seemed to worry about it. As his lawyer, Jerome Mooney, would later maintain, the story, at least in its broad strokes, was true. The family had money, and they had sent millions to Rudy.

With a seemingly bottomless well of cash at his disposal, Rudy quickly became a dominant and indispensable figure at wine auctions, the arena where the world's wealthiest connoisseurs competed for the rarest bottles. He stood out, employing a killer technique to intimidate his opponents. He would raise his bidding paddle and simply refuse to put it down, automatically outbidding anyone who challenged him until the wine was his. Witnesses from those early sales remember a compelling, relentless young man who, despite being a newcomer, was impossible to ignore. "Who's this guy?" people would whisper, as he spent lavishly, building a collection that was soon being touted as the greatest in California. He even gave his cellar a name: "Magic." In just two years, he had made his name in the wine world, and this was only the beginning.

The turning point that would transform him from a high-rolling collector to a master forger came with his acquaintance with a certain John Kapon, a young, ambitious New York auctioneer barely older than him. The relationship was symbiotic. Kapon, the head of a renowned auction house called Acker Merrall & Condit, began writing effusive emails about the magnificent and rare wines that Rudy would bring to their tastings. Rudy, in turn, understood that through Kapon, he could turn his passion into a massive business. He wanted to become the biggest and most important dealer in history, but to do that, he had to leave Los Angeles. The world's largest auction houses, the ones breaking all the records, were in Manhattan.

In the winter of 2003, at the age of twenty-seven, Rudy flew to New York. The city's wine market was booming. Between 2002 and 2007, the market for rare wine tripled, from 90 million to 300 million dollars. On the tables of the most luxurious restaurants, *Grands Crus* were a must-have status symbol for a new generation of young, wealthy collectors. Tasting clubs formed one after another, each more exclusive and extravagant than the last. Rudy, with John Kapon as his guide, set his sights on this golden youth of Manhattan. He managed to integrate himself into what was probably the wealthiest and most ostentatious tasting group in the city: the "Twelve Angry Men."

This group of twelve wealthy men in their thirties competed weekly to see who could spend the most on rare wine, adopting superhero nicknames like "Big Boy" and "The Punisher." Rudy chose a pseudonym for himself as well, becoming "Dr. Conti" in reference to his favorite wine, the Domaine de la Romanée-Conti, the most expensive and sought-after in the world. Their parties were Dionysian spectacles of excess. Jeroboams — large-format bottles — of Romanée-Conti would be poured around, and members would be told to dump out their glasses of one priceless wine because an even more prestigious one was on its way. They bragged indecently about their exploits online, posting photos of the bottles like trophies. Rudy quickly adapted their gestures, imitated their mannerisms, and copied their flashy dress codes, driving Lamborghinis and wearing white leather jackets. The once-shy young man from Arcadia slipped effortlessly into the skin of a wealthy, arrogant high-roller, and in just one year, he had not only integrated himself into the group but had also become its leader. His technique for retaining power was simple: he brought increasingly rare and astounding bottles to their dinners, wines that none of the other members had ever seen before.

It was during this time that Rudy developed a peculiar obsession that should have set off alarm bells. After each extravagant tasting, he would insist on having all the empty bottles returned to him. He would instruct the sommeliers to wash them clean, being careful not to damage the labels, and then FedEx them to his home in Arcadia. If a bottle was broken in transit, he would fly into a rage. These empty bottles, these "corpses," were the key to his entire operation. While he was playing the part of a wealthy playboy in New York, he was secretly operating a sophisticated counterfeiting workshop out of his mother's kitchen in Los Angeles.

His method, as later uncovered by fraud expert Michael Egan, was both simple and brilliant. He would take the authentic empty bottles and, using a funnel, refill them with a carefully crafted blend of other, cheaper wines.

It was here that his incredible palate and olfactory memory became his most valuable tools. Like a three-star chef with his own secret recipes, he knew exactly which combination of Californian wines, when mixed in the right proportions, could perfectly replicate the taste, color, and aroma of the world's greatest vintages. After filling the bottles, he would turn his attention to the labels. Using photocopying and editing software, the perfectionist would meticulously recreate the labels of the oldest and rarest wines, then artificially age them by baking them in the oven or treating them with liquids to achieve the perfect degree of antiquity. The final, crucial step was the cork. Using a special two-pronged corkscrew, he could remove and reinsert corks without piercing them. A bit of wax around the seal, and the illusion was perfect. In late 2005, after months of perfecting his craft and testing his creations on his unsuspecting acolytes, he was finally ready to launch his global scam.

In 2006, with the help of John Kapon, Rudy organized two anthological sales at Acker Merrall & Condit, which he called "The Cellar" and "The Cellar II." The events were a sensation, drawing the entire elite of the wine world — the most influential critics and the biggest collectors — all eager to get a piece of Kurniawan's legendary "Magic Cellar." He put more than 12,000 bottles up for sale, each one rarer than the next. But some of the offerings were too exceptional to be true. He was selling multiple bottles of wines like the 1945 Romanée-Conti, a vintage of which only 600 bottles were ever produced, the vast majority of which had been consumed decades earlier. The estate's own manager said he had never seen a bottle of it in his life, yet Rudy had several. Despite these glaring incongruities, the plan worked perfectly. The sales grossed a staggering $35 million, a historic record, with the vast majority of the wines sold being fake.

The first real doubts began to surface a few months later, as collectors began to open their expensive purchases. One of Douglas Banzle's friends, a major buyer at the auctions, held a tasting of eleven of his newly acquired wines. Six of them were clearly fake. The whispers had begun, but Rudy continued his unscrupulous business. The mistake that would finally lead to his downfall came in April 2008, at another auction offering several lots from Rudy's cellar. Douglas Banzle, the Burgundy expert, was perusing the catalog when he saw something that stopped him cold: several lots of very old Clos Saint-Denis from the esteemed Domaine Ponsot, with vintages from the 1940s, '50s, and '60s. His first thought was one of excitement; he had never seen those before. His second thought was one of suspicion: he had never seen them before because Domaine Ponsot had not started producing that particular wine until 1982.

Banzle immediately emailed Domaine's owner, Laurent Ponsot, in Burgundy. Ponsot, who had never heard of Rudy Kurniawan, was stunned. He called the auction house and spoke to John Kapon, who dismissively told him that the bottles had all been authenticated by experts. When Ponsot revealed who he was and insisted the wines were fake, Kapon reluctantly agreed to withdraw them from the sale but Ponsot was not convinced. He jumped on the next plane to New York and arrived just in time for the auction, where he discovered that Rudy was offering nearly 100 bottles from his domain, almost all of them fakes, with an estimated value of over a million dollars. Kapon was forced to publicly announce the withdrawal of the lots at Ponsot's request.

The next day, Ponsot arranged a lunch meeting with Rudy, Kapon, and Banzle. When Ponsot asked where the fake bottles had come from, Rudy and Kapon mumbled that they couldn't recall, that they bought so much wine it was impossible to keep track. At that moment, Ponsot knew that Rudy was hiding something. The man who had been described to him as cheerful and urbane was withdrawn, reserved, and haughty. From that day forward, Laurent Ponsot began his own private, two-year investigation, a "Don Quixote"-like quest that took him all over the world, chasing down leads and uncovering evidence of Rudy's massive counterfeiting operation.

Meanwhile, the Federal Bureau of Investigation (FBI), led by prosecutor Jason Hernandez, had also begun to take an interest in Rudy Kurniawan. Their investigation eventually overlapped with Ponsot's, and they joined forces, pooling their research. The evidence they accumulated was damning. The FBI finally had enough to bring him down. On the morning of March 8, 2012, they raided Rudy's home in Arcadia. What they found inside was worthy of a crime film. The house was a counterfeiting factory. The kitchen had been transformed into a laboratory with its windows covered to conceal the activity. Wine-making utensils and empty bottles soaking in the sink were everywhere. In drawers, they found 19,000 fake labels for the world's twenty-seven best wines, thousands of stamps with the logos of the biggest domaines, and hundreds of authentic-looking corks. Rudy Kurniawan, surprised and silent, was arrested on the spot.

His trial began in New York in December 2013. After twenty months behind bars, the man who appeared in court looked nothing like the flamboyant high-roller he had once been. He had lost a significant amount of weight and was calm and silent. But as the trial progressed, it became clear he was in a state of complete denial. Dozens of witnesses took the stand, the forged bottles were displayed one by one, but the accused showed no signs of remorse. He would smile and nod at Laurent Ponsot from across the courtroom, seemingly detached from the reality of his situation. He pleaded not guilty. His lawyers, faced with the mountain of evidence found in his home, were left with little to argue. In a moment of courtroom absurdity that drew laughter from the gallery, his lawyer, Jerome Mooney, claimed that the 19,000 fake labels had simply been used to create a decorative wine-themed wallpaper for his new home. On August 8, 2014, the verdict finally fell. Rudy Kurniawan was found guilty and sentenced to ten years in prison. As the sentence was announced, Laurent Ponsot, who was sitting right behind him, saw his shoulders fall, a final, subtle admission that the game was over. He had played to the very end, and he had lost. A complete mystery still remains. Did he have accomplices? And, most disturbingly, how many of the thousands of bottles created by the forger still lie dormant in the cellars of the world's biggest collectors, ticking time bombs of deceit waiting to be uncorked?

28

CIRCLEVILLE LETTERS

Just thirty miles (about forty-eight kilometers) south of Columbus, Ohio, lies the town of Circleville, a place that proudly proclaimed itself "The Best Little Town Around." In the 1970s, it was a small community of roughly 11,000 people, the kind of place where neighbors knew each other and life moved at a steady, predictable rhythm. But beginning in 1977, this seemingly peaceful town, along with the wider region of Southern Ohio, became the target of a relentless campaign of harassment orchestrated by an anonymous figure known only as the Circleville Letter Writer. Over the next two decades, more than a thousand threatening and accusatory letters, written in distinctive block print, would terrorize residents, poison relationships, and ultimately become entangled with suspicion, tragedy, and a mystery that officially remains closed, yet continues to provoke debate.

The campaign began subtly enough on March 2, 1977, with a letter addressed not to a resident of Circleville itself, but to Gordon Massie, the superintendent of the nearby Westfall High School. The letter, penned in block letters that would become the writer's signature, accused Massie of impropriety with female school bus drivers under his supervision. "Dear sir," it began, "according to my girlfriend, you have asked her to go out many times and have asked the other female bus drivers, too. Due to your position and their jobs with you, you should not do this. This must stop at once for the good of this school and families." The writer threatened to escalate the matter to the school board if the alleged behavior continued, invoking a sense of moral righteousness. "To prey on another man's girl is untouchable, especially when they're out trying to make a living," the letter continued, before taking a sharper, more vulgar turn, "There's also talk of you dating a married woman and taking advantage of them... I suggest you find yourself a pimple-faced whore and start up with her and leave my girls alone."

The initial letter set the tone for what was to come: accusations of infidelity and workplace harassment, veiled threats, and a jarring mix of moral condemnation and crude language. The writer clearly believed they were acting as a moral arbiter, exposing perceived wrongs within the community. A few days later, the threats were carried out; a second letter arrived at the school board, demanding an investigation into Massie's conduct. Simultaneously, a third letter containing the same accusations was sent to Massie's fellow superintendent, spreading the allegations further.

Soon, however, the anonymous writer shifted their focus, zeroing in on one particular individual: Mary Gillispie, one of the school bus drivers working under Massie. Mary was a married mother of two, and the letters accused her directly of having an affair with Gordon Massie, who was also married with a family. The tone immediately became more personal and menacing. "Mrs. Gillispie," one of the first letters addressed to her read, "stay away from Massie. Don't lie when questioned about meeting him. I know where you live. I've been observing your house and know you have children. This is no joke. Please take it serious. Everyone concerned has been notified and everything will be over soon."

The writer seemed obsessed with exposing this alleged affair, positioning themselves as a defender of marital fidelity while simultaneously employing tactics of fear and intimidation. Another letter dripped with contempt, stating bluntly, "Lady, this is your last chance to report him. I know you are a pig and will prove it and shame you out of Ohio. A pig sneaks around and meets other women's husbands behind their backs. It causes families and homes and marriages to suffer." Despite Mary's consistent denials of any affair, the letters continued, flooding her life with anonymous accusations and growing threats.

The harassment soon expanded to target Mary's husband, Ronald Gillispie. Letters arrived informing him of his wife's alleged infidelity with Massie. More disturbingly, the writer began actively inciting violence, recommending that Ron catch Mary and Gordon in the act and kill them, stating that Massie "doesn't deserve to live." When Ron didn't act on these gruesome suggestions, the letters turned threatening toward him as well, demonstrating a chilling knowledge of his personal life, detailing the car he drove and the school his children attended. Ron, deeply disturbed, took the letters to the Pickaway County Sheriff, Dwight Radcliffe. However, according to Ron's brother-in-law, Paul Freshour, the sheriff dismissed Ron's concerns, stating he had more important matters to deal with. It seemed that the authorities offered no immediate recourse against the anonymous tormentor.

The campaign escalated beyond mailed threats. Obscene, crudely made signs began appearing around Circleville, plastered in public spaces for all to see. These signs repeated the accusations against Mary Gillispie and Gordon Massie, but some took a horrifyingly personal turn, describing vile sexual acts supposedly occurring between Massie and the Gillispies' young eight-year-old daughter. According to Paul Freshour, Ron Gillispie became consumed by the need to protect his family's reputation and shield his children from these disgusting public displays. Freshour claimed that Ron began a daily ritual, driving around town for an hour or two before work each morning to find and tear down the signs that had inevitably popped up overnight. The anonymous writer was not just sending letters; they were actively engaging in a public shaming campaign, forcing the Gillispie family into a state of constant vigilance and fear.

The Gillispies, according to Paul Freshour, believed they knew who was behind the relentless harassment. On the night of August 19, 1977, about five months after the first letter was sent, the situation reached a tragic climax. Mary was away, traveling to Florida with her sister-in-law (Ron's sister), Karen Sue Freshour, and some friends. Around 10:00 p.m., Ron received a phone call at home. The contents of that call remain unknown, but whatever Ron heard seemed to confirm his suspicions about the identity of the person tormenting his family. He allegedly told his young daughter that he was going to confront the culprit. He then took his gun, got into his truck, and drove off into the night.

Just ten minutes from his home, on a rural road called Five Points Pike, Ron Gillispie crashed his car into a tree. He hit the tree at 10:25 p.m. Not wearing a seatbelt, he was partially ejected from the vehicle and is believed to have died on impact. He was officially pronounced dead upon arrival at the hospital at 11:15 p.m. Ron was only thirty-five years old. The weather conditions that night were clear, though the road would have been dark. The official coroner's report ruled his death an accident, noting that he had been traveling at excessive speed and missed a curve in the road. A pathology report also revealed his blood alcohol content was 0.16, double the legal limit at the time.

However, Ron's brother-in-law, Paul Freshour, contested the official findings. He insisted that Ron, who he claimed rarely drank heavily, was wildly out of character to be driving drunk. Freshour alleged that Ron hadn't simply crashed but had actually been involved in a high-speed chase, claiming there were bullet holes in the side of the truck. Despite Freshour's urging the sheriff's office to investigate further, no evidence was ever found to support his claims of foul play. The official ruling remained an accident caused by speeding and alcohol impairment.

Ron Gillispie's death did nothing to deter the Circleville Letter Writer; if anything, it seemed to embolden them. New letters emerged, now accusing Mary Gillispie and Gordon Massie of murdering Ron. The writer even claimed that Sheriff Dwight Radcliffe himself was involved in covering up the supposed murder to protect Gordon Massie. Adding another layer of complexity and suspicion to the narrative, Mary Gillispie, who had vehemently denied the affair with Gordon Massie before her husband's death, began a public relationship with Massie afterward. Gordon Massie and his wife eventually divorced, with his wife citing "extreme cruelty" as one of the reasons. While this sequence of events didn't prove the writer's initial accusations, it certainly fueled local gossip and lent a disturbing credence to the idea that there might have been some truth underlying the anonymous harassment.

The threats against Mary continued unabated for years. Then, on the afternoon of February 7, 1983, nearly six years after Ron's death, the writer attempted to escalate their campaign from psychological torment to physical violence. Mary was driving her school bus route, about to turn onto the very same street where her husband had fatally crashed. She spotted yet another sign, this one bearing an obscene message about her daughter, who was now thirteen-years-old. Fed up, Mary stopped the bus, got out, and went to remove the sign, which was crudely attached to a fence. As she pulled at it, she noticed it was connected by twine to a small, nondescript box resting nearby. Apparently not recognizing the potential danger, she detached the sign and took the box home with her. Inside, she found a loaded .25-caliber pistol.

When Mary brought the box containing the gun to Sheriff Radcliffe, the authorities immediately recognized it for what it was: a potentially lethal booby trap that had miraculously failed to detonate. According to the sheriff, the mechanism was designed so that the gun would fire if someone simply tried to rip the sign off the fence. Because Mary had instead removed the entire box along with the sign, the trigger mechanism wasn't activated. The gun itself offered a crucial lead. Its serial number had been crudely filed off, but technicians at the Bureau of Criminal Investigations lab were able to recover it. The number was traced back to a man in Columbus, Ohio. When questioned, the man stated that he had sold the pistol to his coworker and direct supervisor at the local Anheuser-Busch facility: Paul Freshour, Mary Gillispie's brother-in-law, the same man who had been vocal about his suspicions surrounding Ron Gillispie's death.

Suddenly, Paul Freshour, who had been a seemingly peripheral figure offering commentary, became the prime suspect. When confronted by police, Freshour admitted to buying the gun in December 1982, just a few months before Mary discovered it. He claimed he had purchased it for protection because his own wife and children were being harassed. However, he asserted that the gun had been stolen from his garage some-time before the booby trap incident. Despite this claim, he had never reported the gun missing to the police. Adding to the suspicion, he told investigators he knew who had stolen it but refused to name the person. Freshour otherwise cooperated fully with the investigation, allowing searches of his home and car, providing handwriting samples, waiving his right to an attorney, and even agreeing to take a polygraph test. He subsequently failed the polygraph.

The case against Paul Freshour intensified dramatically when his estranged wife, Karen Sue, came forward and told police that Paul was, in fact, the anonymous Circleville letter writer. Paul and Karen Sue were married for twenty years before divorcing in October 1982, during which Paul allegedly abused her and accused her of cheating — echoing the same themes found in the letters. Karen Sue claimed she had discovered evidence of his letter-writing years earlier. She recounted finding pieces of a torn-up letter mentioning the name "Gillispie" in a toilet and finding several other similar letters hidden around the house. She also claimed to have found four letters in the trunk of Paul's car shortly after Ron's death, which Paul allegedly told her Ron had wanted him to mail. A coworker of Karen Sue corroborated parts of her story, confirming to police that Karen Sue had previously mentioned finding letters in her home written in the same block style as the notorious Circleville letters. Paul Freshour vehemently denied his ex-wife's accusations, maintaining his innocence regarding both the letters and the booby trap, and suggested that Karen Sue was attempting to set him up.

While Paul Freshour was the main focus, other potential suspects were briefly considered. Paul himself had apparently suspected his and Karen Sue's adult son, Mark Freshour, of stealing the gun from the garage, though friends claimed Paul would never have implicated his own son to the police. Another theory pointed to William Massie, Gordon Massie's son. He would have been in his late teens or early twenties when the letters started, potentially angered by his parents' impending divorce, for which his mother cited "extreme cruelty." Some later letters were even reportedly signed "Bill Massie," but skepticism remained about his ability to orchestrate the campaign while still living under his father's roof.

Despite the lack of direct physical evidence connecting him to the booby trap and his corroborated alibi for much of the time the trap would have been set, Paul Freshour was arrested and tried for attempted murder in October 1983. He pleaded not guilty. Although he was not formally charged in connection with the letters, the judge allowed thirty-nine of the anonymous missives to be presented as evidence during the trial. The prosecution argued that the handwriting on the chalk box containing the booby trap (an industrial chalk box potentially sourced from Paul's workplace at Anheuser-Busch) was similar to the writing in the letters. Two document examiners testified that the handwriting in the letters *could* have been Freshour's, though it wasn't a definitive match. After deliberating for only two and a half hours, the jury found Paul Freshour guilty of attempted murder. He was sentenced to the maximum term of seven to twenty-five years in prison. Although never proven in court, most people in the community now assumed he was indeed the Circleville Letter Writer.

The conviction, however, did not bring an end to the harassment. In a baffling turn of events, the letters continued, even intensified, while Paul Freshour was incarcerated nearly 100 miles (about 160 kilometers) away in Lima, Ohio. Hundreds more letters were sent during his decade behind bars. The prison warden stated unequivocally that it would have been impossible for Freshour to have written and mailed them from inside. He was kept in isolation, denied access to pens and paper, and all his incoming and outgoing mail was meticulously inspected. Furthermore, the letters continued to be postmarked from Columbus, Ohio, far from the prison. Authorities clung to the theory that Freshour must have had an accomplice on the outside mailing letters on his behalf. The ongoing letters were cited as the reason for his parole denial after seven years. Shortly after the denial, Freshour himself received a taunting letter in prison: "Freshour, now when are you going to believe you aren't getting out of there? I told you two years ago when we set 'em up. They stay set up... No one wants you out... The joke is on you. Ha ha."

The letters finally, abruptly stopped in 1994, the same year Paul Freshour was released from prison after serving ten years. Upon his release, he reportedly contacted the FBI, asking them to investigate the case and clear his name, but received no response. Paul Freshour died in 2012 at the age of seventy, maintaining his innocence to the very end. His son, Mark, who never visited him in prison, died by apparent suicide in 2002.

Despite the glaring questions surrounding the letters sent during Paul's imprisonment, the Pickaway County Sheriff's Office officially considers the case of the Circleville letters closed. Recent investigations by the podcast "Whatever Remains" and the television show *48 Hours* have also concluded that Paul Freshour was the sole perpetrator, somehow managing the letters from prison or having an accomplice. Yet, the identity of a potential accomplice, if one existed, has never been discovered, nor has a definitive explanation been offered for how Freshour could have orchestrated the continued campaign from within the confines of prison. After his release, the Circleville letters stopped, but questions remained — was one man really behind the years of harassment, or does the mystery still hide unanswered truths?

29

THE BONES ON THE MESA

On the evening of February 2, 2009, during a routine walk, a married couple's dog unearthed something unusual sticking out of the sandy soil. Unsure what it was but suspecting the worst, the wife snapped a photo and sent it to her sister, a nurse. The immediate response confirmed their fears: the bone was almost certainly human. They called the authorities, having no idea that this single, protruding bone was merely the first fragment of a nightmare that had lain buried beneath the desert surface for years, a discovery that would expose a horrific series of crimes and reveal a chilling indifference to the lives of some of the city's most vulnerable women.

What the couple had stumbled upon was initially believed to be a single femur or hip bone. Authorities began a careful excavation, expecting to perhaps uncover the rest of a single skeleton. But by February 10th, the scope of the discovery had exploded. They hadn't found one body; they had unearthed the partial remains of three separate individuals. It was sickeningly clear: this was not an isolated burial; it was a mass grave. The realization sent shockwaves through the Albuquerque Police Department and the wider community. Specialists were called in from across the region to assist in the painstaking task of sifting through the disturbed earth.

The location presented immense challenges. The plot had already been significantly disrupted by the heavy machinery used by previous developers who had begun construction before abandoning the project. Investigators knew the bodies could have been buried long before construction started, meaning the developers might have unknowingly unearthed, scattered, and reburied skeletal fragments across the vast site. This was a terrifying thought; keeping the crime scene intact and making sure all the remains were found and correctly matched seemed nearly impossible. Furthermore, the discovery of multiple bodies immediately raised the specter of a serial killer, making the careful collection of any potential trace evidence paramount.

A large-scale operation commenced. Heavy equipment was brought in, but instead of digging aggressively, it was used to slowly move large piles of dirt, which were then meticulously sifted by hand. Cadaver dogs, satellite maps, and ground-penetrating radar were employed to help pinpoint potential burial locations without further disturbing the site. The process was tedious and grim. Some skeletons were found relatively intact, buried as deep as eight feet (about 2.5 meters) below the surface, while others were mere inches down, their bones scattered haphazardly, stark evidence of the construction activity that had churned the earth above them. All the remains found were skeletal; decomposition was complete, leaving only bones. Most were discovered without any clothing or personal items that could aid in identification. Determining the cause of death and simply figuring out who these individuals were would be monumental challenges. As remains were located, their positions were carefully mapped before being handed over to medical examiners.

The first identification came quickly. On February 11th, just a day after the discovery of the third body, dental records confirmed one set of remains belonged to twenty-six-year-old Victoria Chavez. She had been reported missing in March 2005, though her family hadn't actually seen her for nearly a year prior to that report. Like many of the women who would eventually be identified, Victoria had struggled with drug addiction and was involved in sex work. At the time of her disappearance, she was on probation. Her skeletal remains were found relatively close to the surface, buried only about eighteen inches (about forty-five centimeters) deep, suggesting they had likely been disturbed by the construction work. No clothing or identifying items were found with her body.

The grim discoveries continued. By February 18th, the total number of individuals found had risen to six. Victoria Chavez's complete skeletal remains were finally pieced together that day, making her the fourth full set recovered; the other two were still missing significant portions. The destructive impact of the earlier digging was becoming painfully evident. Just six days later, on February 24th, the number climbed again, reaching a staggering ten sets of remains. The Albuquerque Police Department, realizing the scale and complexity of the case, formally requested assistance from the FBI and brought in archaeologists from the University of New Mexico to aid in the recovery and analysis. Profilers were consulted, trying to build a picture of the person, almost certainly a serial killer, who was responsible for this horror.

Among the ten sets of remains was one that held a particularly heart-breaking secret. Inside the pelvic bones of one skeleton lay the tiny, fragile bones of a fetus. The woman had been pregnant when she was killed, esti-mated to be about four months along. Dental records eventually provided a name: twenty-two-year-old Gina Michelle Valdez, known to her loved ones simply as Michelle. Her father remembered her as a kind, giving person who would give you the shirt off her back, and as an amazing mother to the young daughter she already had. She had dreams of becoming a singer or a lawyer, aspirations tragically cut short when she fell into a life of drug addiction she couldn't escape. Her family described a painful pattern: she would disappear for days, then weeks, then months at a time. She would occasionally call her father, usually asking for money, and each time he would plead with her to come home, giving her the money in the desperate hope it might encourage her return. Then, the calls stopped altogether. He reported her missing in February 2005. Shortly after, rumors began to circulate — rumors that Michelle's mother later reported hearing from numerous sources — that Michelle had been stabbed multiple times and her body dumped somewhere on the West Mesa, precisely where she was ultimately found. Disturbingly similar rumors would surface regarding other victims, leads provided by desperate families that were tragically, and perhaps negligently, never adequately pursued by law enforcement at the time.

By February 28th, the final count was reached: eleven adult bodies and one fetus had been unearthed from the makeshift desert graveyard. The third victim to be identified, again through dental records, was thirty-two-year-old Cinnamon Elks. The oldest of the victims found, Cinnamon also struggled with addiction and sex work, primarily in an area of Albuquerque known colloquially as the "War Zone," where most of the victims were known to frequent. She had a lengthy criminal record filled with drug and solicitation charges and led such a transient lifestyle that pinpointing the exact time of her disappearance was difficult. The last confirmed sighting was her arrest in July 2004. When her birthday arrived in August and she failed to make her customary call to her family, they knew something was wrong and tried to report her missing. Initially, police were dismissive, telling her mother that Cinnamon was a grown adult who didn't need to check in. It took until December, months later, for a formal missing person report to be filed. Just like Michelle Valdez's family, Cinnamon's mother also heard chilling rumors. Friends from Cinnamon's circle reported that just before she disappeared, she had spoken fearfully of a "dirty cop" who was picking up sex workers, killing them, and burying them on the West Mesa. This was now the second distinct report mentioning abduction, murder, and disposal in West Mesa, yet these warnings seem to have gone unheeded.

The fourth identification was twenty-four-year-old Julie Nieto, a young mother remembered by her family as caring and well-behaved before drug addiction took hold when she was nineteen. Despite her struggles, she desperately wanted to get clean for her son, making multiple attempts at rehabilitation. Even when she was unable to care for him, she maintained contact, visiting him and bringing presents whenever she could. She was reported missing in August 2004, shortly after Cinnamon Elks was last seen. As with the others, her disappearance was not treated with urgency. A significant connection emerged as these first four women were identified: they all knew each other. This wasn't entirely surprising, given they moved in the same dangerous circles of addiction and sex work in the War Zone. Investigators hoped this link might provide a clue, a reason why these specific women were targeted, but it offered little immediate direction.

In early April 2009, two more victims were named. Twenty-two-year-old Monica Candelaria was remembered as someone always laughing, who adored her family and children. She was last seen on May 11, 2003, and reported missing just two weeks later, making her one of the earliest disappearances connected to the site. Once again, rumors surfaced shortly after she vanished. Friends, including a neighbor named Isaac, told her family they heard Monica had been killed and buried on the West Mesa — the third instance of this specific rumor being reported years before the bodies were found. In Monica's case, there is evidence that investigators did initially follow up on these leads, but the trail went cold, and her case was eventually relegated to the cold case unit. The sixth victim identified was twenty-six-year-old Veronica Romero. She was reported missing by her family on Valentine's Day, 2004.

The large number of remains and their fragmented condition made it necessary to bring in additional experts. Boxes of bones were sent to the Center for Human Identification in Denton, Texas, for advanced DNA analysis, while forensic anthropologists worked tirelessly on-site and in labs to piece together the human puzzle. The task force, now numbering around forty individuals, expanded their search, contacting law enforcement agencies in neighboring states like Arizona and Texas, and even as far as Milwaukee, looking for similar patterns, other serial killers who targeted sex workers, hoping to find a connection.

Soon after, the seventh victim was identified: twenty-four-year-old Doreen Marquez. Her story stood out. Unlike many of the others, Doreen grew up in West Mesa itself, attended West Mesa High School (less than a mile from her eventual burial site), was a cheerleader, and got good grades. She had two children, lived in a nice house, and was known for her style and sassy personality. Her life took a sharp downturn when her boyfriend was incarcerated. Having never previously been involved with drugs or sex work, she suddenly spiraled, leaving her children with family and disappearing for increasingly long periods. The exact date she went missing is disputed; her family last saw her in October 2003, while friends claimed to have seen her in early 2004. She was formally reported missing in December 2004. Although she had no criminal record related to sex work, it was widely assumed she had become involved due to her association with the other victims and the War Zone.

Crucially, all seven victims identified up to this point were Hispanic, local to Albuquerque, and every single one of them had been on the list compiled years earlier by Detective Ida Lopez, the cold case detective whose warnings about a potential serial killer targeting vulnerable women had been largely ignored. Her list, tragically accurate, now became a vital tool for investigators trying to speed up the identification process.

However, one set of remains didn't fit the pattern. They belonged to a Black female, estimated to be in her mid-teens, who didn't match any missing person reports from the Albuquerque area. Clues found with her body included an acrylic fingernail with a very specific, unique design. Police circulated sketches and details — that she had suffered a broken nose and an unrelated stab wound at some point in her life — hoping someone would recognize her. By November 2009, the remains were formally identified as fifteen-year-old Syllannia Edwards, the eighth victim. Syllannia had been in the foster care system since age five, after both her parents were imprisoned. She had run away from her foster home in Lawton, Oklahoma, at some point, though exactly when she was reported missing is unclear. The prevailing theory is that she fell in with a group traveling the I-40 corridor, engaging in sex work to survive. A tip placed her at a hotel in Denver in 2004, after which it's believed she made her way south to New Mexico, where she met her end.

Shortly after Syllannia's identification came the ninth and tenth victims. Twenty-four-year-old Virginia Cloven was remembered as having a hilarious and unique personality, doing well in school while always making people laugh. Her life took a tragic turn when her brother was murdered. Devastated, Virginia, then seventeen, ran away from home, followed shortly after by her other brother. After a brief stay with her grandfather, she moved in with a boyfriend, only to face further tragedy when he was hit by a car and fell into a coma. Homeless and traumatized, she ended up in the War Zone. She maintained sporadic contact with her father, who tried desperately to help her. In June 2004, she called him, sounding enthusiastic, claiming she had met someone she planned to marry and that her life was turning around. Almost immediately after that hopeful call, she vanished completely. She was reported missing four months later.

The final two victims were identified together: Twenty-three-year-old Evelyn Salazar and her fifteen-year-old cousin, Jamie Barela. Evelyn, like most of the others, was involved in drugs and sex work. On a day in late March or early April 2004, after spending time with her family, Evelyn offered to take Jamie to a park located just outside the War Zone. Neither of them ever returned, being reported missing together on April 3rd. Jamie Barela was the tragic anomaly among the victims; she had no involvement in drugs or sex work. She was simply in the wrong place at the wrong time, likely killed because she was with Evelyn when the killer struck. Her death led to speculation that the killer might have known his victims, perhaps targeting Evelyn and killing Jamie only because she witnessed it, or that he viewed any young woman in the War Zone as a sex worker and therefore expendable.

With all eleven victims identified, the grim task of finding their killer intensified, hampered by a near total lack of forensic evidence. No clear cause of death could be determined for any of the victims, though the absence of stab or gunshot wounds led investigators to believe strangulation or suffocation was the likely method. The burial site yielded no foreign DNA, no fibers, no definitive clues linking anyone to the disposal of the bodies. By July 2009, authorities announced they had narrowed their focus to a handful of suspects.

One early person of interest was Ron Erwin, a photographer from Joplin, Missouri, who frequented the New Mexico State Fair near the burial site. A search of his home uncovered thousands of disturbing photographs depicting women posed as if they were dead. While shocking, all the women in the photos were later found alive and well. Erwin cooperated fully, even taking a polygraph, and alibis confirmed he wasn't in Albuquerque during some of the disappearances, leading investigators to largely rule him out.

Another suspect was Fred Reynolds, a local pimp known to associate with several of the victims. He had actively sought information about the missing women from their families, raising initial suspicion. However, Reynolds died of natural causes just a month before the remains were discovered. Family members told police his inquiries stemmed from genuine concern, not morbid curiosity.

Two suspects, however, emerged as far more compelling possibilities. Lorenzo Montoya lived in a trailer just about two miles (three kilometers) from the mass grave. He had a significant history of violence against women and soliciting sex workers. In 1998, police intervened when they caught him attempting to kill a sex worker he had lured to a dead-end road; the case was later dismissed. Crucially, Montoya was killed in December 2006 — around the exact time the disappearances linked to the West Mesa site stopped. He was shot by a pimp, Frederick Williams, while attempting to dispose of the body of nineteen-year-old Shericka Hill, whom he had raped and strangled in his trailer. The method matched the suspected cause of death for the West Mesa victims. Even more damning, satellite images taken between 2003 and 2006 showed tire tracks leading directly from the remote burial site back to Montoya's trailer. A disturbing videotape was also found in his trailer, seemingly recorded at the end of an encounter with a sex worker; while nothing explicit is seen or heard, the distinct sounds of duct tape and a trash bag being handled are audible — items Montoya used when disposing of Shericka Hill's belongings. Despite this mountain of circumstantial evidence, no DNA linked Montoya directly to the West Mesa crime scene, and his death left investigators unable to question him.

The final prime suspect was Joseph Blea. His ex-wife tipped off police shortly after the bodies were found, stating that he frequently visited sex workers but also expressed intense hatred toward them, and that he often dumped trash in the specific West Mesa area where the remains were discovered. Blea had an extensive criminal record, with nearly 140 police contacts between 1990 and 2009, including arrests for breaking into homes to steal women's underwear and jewelry, indecent exposure, and attempted kidnapping of a sex worker. Police surveillance confirmed his ex-wife's claims; he would drive through the War Zone multiple times a day, not soliciting, but slowly cruising and intently watching the women working there. A search of his home uncovered collections of women's underwear and jewelry, potentially connecting him to items reported missing from some of the victims. The strongest physical evidence connecting Blea to the site was a small plastic tree tag, bought from a nursery he often visited between 2003 and 2006 — the same period as the murders. This tag was found buried eight feet (about 2.5 meters) deep, directly with one set of skeletal remains. While highly suspicious, authorities couldn't definitively prove how the tag got there; it could potentially have been moved during construction or discarded as trash, as his ex-wife suggested. Blea was eventually arrested and convicted for a series of unrelated home invasion sexual assaults on middle school-aged children from the 80s and 90s, as well as the murder of another sex worker from the War Zone, linked by DNA. According to a cellmate, while incarcerated, Blea spoke constantly and disparagingly about the West Mesa victims, calling them "trashy" but knowing all their names and admitting to having paid some for sex and hitting at least one of them.

Despite the strong circumstantial cases against Montoya and Blea, the West Mesa Bone Collector case officially remains unsolved. No charges have ever been filed due to the lack of definitive forensic evidence connecting any single individual to all eleven murders. The tragedy spurred community action, including protests demanding better police attention to crimes against marginalized women and the formation of Safe Streets New Mexico by a survivor of another infamous killer, aimed at protecting sex workers. For the families of the victims, the pain lingers, compounded by the knowledge that the system failed to protect them and has yet to bring their killer, or killers, to justice. Authorities still believe other victims may be buried elsewhere, women who disappeared during the same timeframe, their names adding to the haunting list of the forgotten.

30

GLORIAVALE CHRISTIAN COMMUNITY

On March 26, 1997, a former member of a reclusive religious group named Rio D'Angelo received a package in the mail. Inside were letters and videotapes indicating that the members of the group, known as Heaven's Gate, had committed mass suicide. Following the instructions included in the package, D'Angelo drove to the sprawling mansion the cult rented in the affluent San Diego suburb of Rancho Santa Fe. What he found there, and filmed as instructed, was a scene of eerie, meticulously staged death that would soon shock the nation and the world. Thirty-nine bodies lay peacefully in bunk beds and on mattresses throughout the house, all dressed in identical black uniforms and black-and-white Nike sneakers, their faces and torsos covered with purple shrouds. It was the quiet, orderly culmination of a bizarre journey that began over two decades earlier, a journey led by a charismatic former music professor and a nurse who believed they were extraterrestrial beings sent to lead humanity to salvation aboard a UFO. The Heaven's Gate cult operated for years in near-total seclusion, stripping its members of their identities not through violence or overt coercion, but through a gradual, insidious process of psychological manipulation, preparing them for a final "graduation" from their human existence.

The story of Heaven's Gate is linked to the life of its co-founder, Marshall Herff Applewhite Jr., born on May 17, 1931, in Spur, Texas. He went by his middle name, Herff, in his youth. His upbringing was steeped in religion; his father, Marshall Herff Applewhite Sr., was a Presbyterian minister who moved the family frequently around South Texas, establishing new churches every few years. While outwardly Herff Sr. and his wife, Louise, were seen as kind and devoted parents, some family members recalled the senior Applewhite as a strict authoritarian, particularly hard on young Herff, whom he pressured relentlessly to follow him into the ministry. Herff Jr. desperately wanted to make his father proud and aspired to become a minister himself from a young age, once walking into his father's church and telling the parishioners that he couldn't wait to preach the word of God one day.

By all accounts, Herff was a charismatic and intelligent child, always smiling and full of life, often described by his sister Louise as the comedian of the family, always able to get everyone laughing. As a teenager at Corpus Christi High School, he blossomed into a tall, good-looking young man with piercing blue eyes, known by his classmates as an outgoing overachiever who was always smiling. After graduating, he enrolled at Austin College, still intending to pursue the ministry. He excelled in college, becoming the leader of the acapella choir and participating in the Judiciary Council before graduating with a degree in philosophy in 1952. That same year, he married his high school girlfriend, Anne Francis Pierce, and enrolled at the Union Theological Seminary of Virginia, seemingly on track to fulfill his father's expectations.

But after only one semester, Herff made a decision that would alter the course of his life. He left the seminary to pursue his true passion: music. He possessed a remarkable singing voice, particularly suited for opera, and he set out on a new path. He and Anne moved to North Carolina, where he took a job as the Director of Music at the First Presbyterian Church. Life seemed good until 1954, when he was drafted into the army. He served for two years, stationed briefly in Austria and then in New Mexico, rising to the rank of sergeant before being honorably discharged in 1956. Upon his return, he immediately enrolled at the University of Colorado to pursue a master's degree in music with an emphasis on musical theater. There, he became heavily involved in the local theater scene, even acting alongside an eighteen-year-old Joan Van Ark in a community production of *Annie Get Your Gun*.

After graduating, Herff landed a position as a music professor at the University of Alabama in 1959. He quickly became a beloved and respected faculty member, known for his upbeat personality, laid-back teaching style, and ability to captivate students. He and Anne settled into the community, raising their two young children, Mark and Lane. They appeared to have the perfect, idyllic life. But beneath the surface, Herff was hiding a profound internal struggle. In 1965, his carefully constructed world fell apart when Anne suddenly left him, taking the children with her. The reason soon surfaced: Herff had been having an affair with a male graduate student. He had been living a double life, torn between the expectations of his religious upbringing and his own sexuality. Anne filed for divorce, which was finalized in 1968.

The revelation and the subsequent collapse of his marriage marked the beginning of a deep psychological decline for Herff. He left his position at the University of Alabama and moved back to Texas, becoming the chair of the music department at the University of St. Thomas in Houston. He threw himself into his work, becoming deeply involved with the Houston Grand Opera and starring in fifteen productions alongside famous artists like Plácido Domingo, a Spanish opera singer, earning rave reviews. He was at the height of his musical career but the internal conflict continued to fester. Eventually, he gathered the courage to tell his parents he was gay. Their reaction was exactly what he had feared, his strict father reportedly being appalled and asking, "What kind of sins have I committed for the Lord to scorn me this way?" Herff felt utterly rejected, not only by his parents but by the Presbyterian Church that had been the bedrock of his entire life.

He fell into a deep depression, even contemplating suicide by jumping off a bridge. His colleagues noticed a dramatic shift in his personality; the articulate, mild-mannered man they knew became paranoid, agitated, and seemed to have a "perpetual crazed look in his eyes." It was around this time that he began hearing voices and having visions. During a trip to Galveston beach, he claimed to have received a divine vision revealing the origins and destiny of the human race. Simultaneously, he developed a fervent interest in UFOs and extraterrestrials, a common fascination in the 1960s and '70s, but one that took on a more ominous significance in the context of his deteriorating mental state. By 1970, after suffering several mental breakdowns, Herff was let go from his job at the University of St. Thomas, ostensibly due to "health problems of an emotional nature." The death of his father in 1971 sent him spiraling further.

Everything came to a head in 1972 when Herff was admitted to a hospital in Houston. The exact reason for his admission remains unclear; his sister claimed it was for a near-fatal heart blockage that caused brain damage, cementing his psychosis, while others suggest he voluntarily checked himself into the psychiatric ward seeking a "cure" for his homosexuality. Regardless of the reason, his hospital stay proved to be the most pivotal moment of his life, for it was there that he met Bonnie Lou Nettles, the forty-four-year-old nurse who would become his spiritual partner and co-founder of Heaven's Gate.

Bonnie Lou Trousdale was born in Houston in 1927 and raised in a strict Baptist home. She graduated from nursing school in 1948 and married Joseph Nettles the following year, eventually having four children. As she grew older, Bonnie turned away from her Baptist roots and became deeply immersed in New Age practices. She participated in séances, believed she was clairvoyant, interpreted astrological charts with the help of a ghostly 200-year-old monk named "Brother Francis," and shared Herff's fascination with UFOs. In 1966, she joined the Houston Lodge of the Theosophical Society, an organization that encourages belief based on individual experience rather than tradition, delving deeper into esoteric beliefs. Her growing obsession with these alternative spiritualities caused a rift in her marriage. In the late 1960s, a fellow seer gave Bonnie a prophecy: in 1972, she would meet a tall, slender man with fair skin and blonde hair and when she laid eyes on Herff Applewhite in the hospital that year, she knew instantly that he was the man from the prophecy.

Bonnie approached Herff, who was in an extremely vulnerable mental state, and offered him a reading. She told him that he was a prophet sent by God, destined to guide humanity away from sin and toward the kingdom of heaven. For Herff, who felt rejected and purposeless, Bonnie's words were a lifeline. He latched onto this new identity, and the two became inseparable, their relationship described as entirely platonic. Herff moved in with the Nettles family, a bizarre situation that soon led to Bonnie and Joseph's divorce, setting them free to pursue their divine quest. They pooled their money, opened a short-lived metaphysical bookstore, and started a business teaching theosophy, a mystical belief system that tries to understand the nature of divinity and spiritual enlightenment. However, by 1973, they were broke, living out of campsites, stealing food, and dining and dashing, justifying their actions by believing they were above human laws. During this time, they consumed a wide range of literature, from religious texts to fantasy novels, and became avid watchers of *Star Trek*. Bonnie adopted Herff's short hairstyle, creating the androgynous look that would later become the cult's signature.

Their defining "epiphany" occurred in July 1973 while camping on the Oregon coast. Reading the *Book of Revelation*, they became convinced that they were the "two witnesses" described in Chapter eleven, destined to be martyred, resurrected after three and a half days, and then ascend to heaven in a cloud — which they interpreted as a UFO. This marked the birth of their core doctrine: only their most loyal followers, those who could shed their "humanness," would be allowed to transcend with them to the "Next Level" aboard the spaceship. This ascension, which they called "the demonstration," would signify the coming apocalypse. However, in August 1974, Herff was arrested for failing to return a stolen rental car and Bonnie for possessing stolen credit cards. Herff spent six months in jail.

Upon his release, the pair, now calling themselves "Bo and Peep" or simply "The Two," launched their first major recruitment effort. They traveled across the United States, posting flyers inviting people to meetings where Herff, the primary speaker, would preach their message: abandon your earthly lives, families, possessions, and desires, especially sexuality, to purify yourselves for the journey to the Next Level. They emphasized that their martyrdom and resurrection were imminent, and the spaceship could arrive any day, creating a sense of urgency. Their message resonated with a surprising number of people. In September 1975, after a single meeting in Waldport, Oregon, twenty locals vanished, leaving everything behind to join the group. People from various backgrounds, many well-educated and from comfortable families, walked away from their lives, captivated by the promise of ascension. Couples like Suzanne and Wayne Cook left their ten-year-old daughter Kelly, telling her they were going away on a spaceship and she would never see them again.

Sociologist Robert Balch, intrigued by the reports of the missing Oregonians, infiltrated the group with a colleague in 1975. They followed cryptic instructions involving a zip code book in a post office and a meeting atop Mount Diablo before being integrated into separate nomadic encampments. They spent three months living undercover within the cult. Balch noted that, at this early stage, Bo and Peep didn't employ typical coercive cult tactics; membership was voluntary, and people were free to leave at any time. Life was communal and unstructured, moving between campsites, with daily meetings where the members were given tuning forks and instructed to tune their minds to the frequency of Note A (440 Hz), though no one, including Bo and Peep, seemed to know quite what to do with them. However, when Balch published his findings, the media attention exploded and Bo and Peep's real names were revealed. The press began associating them with sinister groups like the Manson Family, even accusing them of bizarre acts like cattle mutilations. Attendance at their meetings plummeted, members started leaving, and Bo and Peep declared, "The Harvest is closed," retreating with their remaining followers into nearly two decades of seclusion.

During these years underground, the group evolved significantly. The Members stabilized at around forty core followers, mostly well-educated individuals from middle-to-upper-class backgrounds, ranging in age from sixteen to individuals in their 70s, and among them was Thomas Nichols, brother of actress Nichelle Nichols, who portrayed Uhura in *Star Trek*. They continued their nomadic existence, eventually settling into rented mansions funded by the trust fund of member David Van Sinderen, living in strict secrecy within suburban neighborhoods. It was during this period that Bo and Peep adopted their final, most enduring names: Ti (Bonnie) and Do (Herff), inspired by Bonnie's favorite movie, *The Sound of Music*.

Life inside the "craft," as they called their homes, became highly regimented and focused on stripping away individuality. Bonnie and Herff were the "teachers" in a "classroom" designed to help members shed their human "vehicles" and prepare their alien consciousnesses for graduation to the Next Level. Any pre-existing relationships were severed, and members were assigned "check partners" for constant mutual monitoring, sometimes even accompanying each other to the bathroom. Everything was a test, and perfection was the goal.

They developed their own terminology to avoid triggering memories of their past lives: bedrooms were "rust chambers," the laundry room was a "fiber lab," bras were "slingshots," and heaven was the "Next Level." Sexual organs were referred to as "plumbing," and any sensual thought or romantic feeling was completely forbidden. Celibacy was strictly enforced, underscored by the humiliating "nocturnal emission" logbook where men had to record involuntary nighttime occurrences. Meals were strictly controlled, even pancakes had to be the exact same size. Makeup was forbidden, and everyone adopted the same short haircut and uniform-like clothing — button-up shirts, slacks, and athletic shoes — to achieve a genderless, collective identity, mirroring the Borg from *Star Trek*, a collective Herff became fascinated with. Members were given new names ending in "-ody," meaning "little member of the kingdom of heaven," further erasing their pasts. Physical abuse was absent, and members remained technically free to leave, often given bus money if they chose to depart, but the psychological control was profound and pervasive.

This secluded existence was shattered in 1985 when Bonnie was diagnosed with eye cancer. Despite surgery to remove her eye, the cancer spread rapidly to her liver, and she died on June 19, 1985, just three weeks after informing the group. Her death created a major doctrinal crisis: if they were aliens merely inhabiting human vehicles, why hadn't Bonnie simply shed her failing body and ascended? Herff quickly reformulated the narrative and explained that Ti's vehicle had simply "broken down" and that her advanced Next Level consciousness had effectively "burned up" her human form from the inside. The transformation, he now claimed, was purely spiritual; their physical bodies would be left behind on Earth. Because of cognitive dissonance (the discomfort of holding conflicting beliefs), the remaining members accepted the change, letting their need to believe outweigh the clear contradiction.

With Bonnie gone, Herff became the sole leader, assuming an even more controlling and messianic role. He declared himself Jesus Christ and

Bonnie God the Father, and conducted a bizarre ceremony where he "married" every member of the group, placing a gold band on each of their fingers. However, his own struggles with his repressed sexuality continued to torment him. This culminated after Herff experienced a nocturnal emission himself, expressing intense frustration over his inability to control his urges. An enthusiastic member, Stephen McArthur (Sarody), suggested castration as a definitive solution. Herff seized upon the idea, offering it as a voluntary option to the male members. After a dangerously botched first attempt performed within the group by former nurse Julie LaMontagne (Livody), which resulted in Sarody being rushed to the hospital and his removed testicles being thrown into the ocean, they found a doctor willing to perform the procedures. Ultimately, Herff and six other men opted for castration which, due to the extremity of the action, caused some long-term members, including Wayne Cook, to leave the group, though his wife Suzanne remained.

In the early 1990s, fueled by the widespread anxiety surrounding the upcoming turn of the millennium (the "Y2K scare"), Herff decided it was time for one final recruitment effort. They launched a satellite TV series called *Beyond Human*, took out a $30,000 full-page ad in the *USA Today*, sent out VHS tapes, and even returned to holding in-person meetings. This time, however, the public was overwhelmingly skeptical and often openly hostile, mocking their beliefs and criticizing them for abandoning their families. The recruitment drive was largely a failure, attracting only a couple of new members and reinforcing Herff's belief that humanity had rejected its final chance for salvation. Influenced by the tragic events of the Waco siege in 1993 (a fifty-one-day standoff between Branch Davidians, a religious sect founded in 1955 by Benjamin Roden, and federal agents where seventy-six people died), the discussion within the group turned definitively toward planning their "exit." An initial idea to provoke a deadly confrontation with authorities was rejected by the members as too uncertain. Suicide became the agreed-upon plan, leading five members to leave the group.

The arrival of the Hale-Bopp comet in 1996 provided the final catalyst. When unfounded rumors circulated online about a massive, unidentified object four times the size of Earth trailing the comet, the members of Heaven's Gate seized upon it as the sign they had been waiting for — the spaceship carrying Bonnie had arrived to take them home to the Next Level. Though they couldn't see the non-existent object through their own high-powered telescopes, their belief was unshaken. They set their "graduation" date for March 1997, coinciding with the comet's closest approach to Earth and the Easter holiday. In their final weeks, they took celebratory trips to Sea World, Las Vegas, and Mexico. They recorded cheerful exit interviews expressing their joy at leaving their "vehicles" behind; they updated their website with a final "Red Alert" message, proclaiming Hale-Bopp as the long-awaited marker for their departure. After enjoying a last meal together at a local Marie Callender's restaurant, they methodically carried out their plan over several days starting March 22nd. They ingested a lethal cocktail of phenobarbital, a medicine used to control seizures, mixed with applesauce or pudding, washed down with vodka, and then placed plastic bags over their heads to ensure asphyxiation. They died in three staggered groups, with members of the later groups carefully cleaning and shrouding the bodies of those who had gone before. Herff himself is thought to have been in the second group. It was a calm, orderly, and deeply tragic conclusion to a twenty-two-year journey into delusion, leaving a shocked public to grapple with the incomprehensible reality of thirty-nine individuals willingly following their leader into oblivion.

The aftermath saw further tragedy, as several former members, including Wayne Cook and Chuck Humphrey, committed suicide in an attempt to "catch up" with the group they believed was now aboard the spaceship. A 1998 reunion of former members devolved into anger when letters revealed that Bonnie Nettles had secretly maintained contact with her own daughter throughout the cult's existence, a stark betrayal of the sacrifices demanded of her followers.

The story of Heaven's Gate stands as one of the most haunting examples of how faith, isolation, and psychological manipulation can intertwine to devastating effect. What began as a quest for spiritual enlightenment became a descent into delusion, driven by the insecurities and unhealed wounds of a man seeking purpose and acceptance. Through Bonnie and Herff's teachings, ordinary people were slowly reshaped into instruments of a shared fantasy, surrendering individuality, identity, and ultimately life itself in the belief that death would bring transcendence.

31

THE CARNEGIE HEIRESS

In the dazzling, often deceptive world of America's Gilded Age (a period from about the late 1870s to the late 1890s), fortunes were made, empires were built, and high society guarded its gates with fierce exclusivity. It was an era defined by staggering wealth and rigid social structures, yet it was also a time ripe for manipulation by those audacious enough to exploit the era's assumptions and vanities. Into this glittering landscape stepped a woman of humble origins and boundless nerve, a master chameleon who, through sheer force of will and a breathtaking series of lies, convinced the financial titans of her time that she was the secret, illegitimate daughter of Andrew Carnegie, then the richest man on the planet. Armed with forged documents and an uncanny ability to project an aura of immense wealth and social standing, she conned bankers and businessmen out of millions, leaving a trail of financial ruin and shattered reputations in her wake. Her name, or at least the one under which she perpetrated her most famous frauds, was Cassie L. Chadwick. Her real story, however, was a far cry from the privileged life she fabricated, a decades-long saga of deception that began long before she invoked the Carnegie name and ended behind prison walls.

Before she adopted the Chadwick persona and began weaving her elaborate Carnegie fantasy, she was Elizabeth Bigley, born in Eastwood,

Ontario, Canada, on October 10, 1857. From a young age, she reportedly displayed a "mania for fine clothing," an early indicator, perhaps, of her aspirations for a life beyond her means. Her criminal career began in early adulthood. At the age of just twenty-two, she was arrested for forgery in Woodstock, Ontario. Facing prison time, she deployed a tactic that would serve her well throughout her life: she feigned mental instability. Pleading not guilty by reason of insanity, she convinced the court of her diminished capacity and walked free.

Undeterred, Elizabeth, now operating under various aliases, set her sights on bigger targets. Three years later, in 1882, she surfaced in Cleveland, Ohio, presenting herself as a wealthy heiress. Her performance was convincing enough to capture the attention and affection of a local physician, Dr. Wallace S. Springstein. They were quickly married, but the union lasted a mere eleven days. Dr. Springstein, upon discovering his new wife's fabricated background and criminal history, promptly threw her out of his house. Her brief foray into legitimate society had ended abruptly.

Cast out but ever resourceful, the woman now known as Cassie embarked on a series of smaller, transient scams. In Erie, Pennsylvania, she adopted the name "Madame LoRuse" and cultivated friendships, hinting at vast sums of money that were temporarily inaccessible. Playing on their sympathy, she claimed to be suffering from a severe hemorrhage requiring an urgent, costly operation. To make her fictitious illness appear real, she employed a grotesque but effective trick: she would surreptitiously make her gums bleed, presenting the blood as evidence of her internal ailment. Her concerned friends, convinced of her dire situation, lent her the money she requested. She took their cash and vanished, leaving them with nothing but empty pockets and the story of her supposed affliction.

A couple of years later, now using the name "Lidley Baggley," she settled into a boarding house in another town, owned by Mrs. Hoover. By this time, Cassie was pregnant. Ever the manipulator, she wrote back to her mother and sister in Canada, claiming she had married a wealthy, elderly man named C. L. Hoover, who was conveniently deceased, and that he was the father of her child. She named her son Emil Hoover, giving him the surname of his entirely fictitious father. Motherhood, however, did not align with her ambitions. At some point, young Emil was sent to live with Cassie's mother and sister in Canada, freeing her to continue her relentless pursuit of wealth and status through deception.

Seeking a new angle, Cassie reinvented herself yet again, this time as a clairvoyant and fortune teller, operating first as "Lydia Scott" and then as the more exotic "Madame Lydia De Vere." This profession, built on illusion and suggestion, perfectly suited her talents. However, her old habits soon resurfaced. While practicing her mystical arts, she committed forgery against one of her clients, a crime that finally landed her a significant prison sentence. She was sentenced to nine and a half years in the Ohio State Penitentiary. Yet, her knack for escaping consequences persisted. After serving only four years, she was granted parole by the Governor of Ohio, William McKinley. In a strange twist of fate, just five years after granting her early release, McKinley would become the 25th President of the United States, only to be assassinated four years into his term. Cassie, meanwhile, walked out of prison, ready for her next act.

Upon her release, she once again sought the security and legitimacy of marriage to a respectable man. Working under another alias at a massage parlor, she encountered Dr. Leroy S. Chadwick, a prominent and highly respected physician in Cleveland. Whatever transpired during that initial massage appointment sparked a whirlwind romance and shortly after their meeting, in 1897, they were married. Dr. Chadwick came from a well-known and esteemed family, members of Cleveland's "400," the city's equivalent of New York's elite social register. Crucially, Dr. Chadwick knew absolutely nothing about Cassie's real family, her background, or her extensive criminal past. His relatives and friends were immediately suspicious of this mysterious woman who had appeared seemingly out of nowhere. They worried that Dr. Chadwick, known for his reserved and trusting nature, was being taken advantage of.

In the same year she married Dr. Chadwick, Cassie launched her most audacious and elaborate scheme yet. She began a fraudulent borrowing spree, securing hundreds of thousands of dollars in loans from multiple Cleveland banks. While her husband's medical practice was successful, the Chadwick name alone wouldn't qualify her for the massive sums she sought. So, she invoked a different name, one synonymous with unimaginable wealth and power: Carnegie. She boldly claimed to be the illegitimate daughter of Andrew Carnegie, the steel magnate who stood as the wealthiest man in the world at that time.

Astonishingly, the right people — people with money, bankers susceptible to the allure of prestige and connection — believed her. Her story played perfectly into the social dynamics and technological limitations of the era. Illegitimacy, particularly among the wealthy, was a scandalous but not uncommon secret, something whispered about but rarely confirmed. Cassie's willingness to confide this sensitive detail lent her story an air of authenticity, and thanks to the rudimentary identification systems, as there were no driver's licenses or sophisticated databases to verify her claims, she got away with it. After all, who would dare to question Andrew Carnegie directly about such a delicate personal matter?

Cassie played her part flawlessly. She dressed in the finest clothes, displayed impeccable manners, and moved through society with the practiced ease of inherited wealth. She presented herself as Carnegie's cherished but secret daughter, well-provided for by a father who felt a sense of obligation, even if he couldn't publicly acknowledge her. To back up her claims, she produced forged documents: promissory notes and securities certificates purportedly signed by Carnegie himself, promising repayment and listing collateral supposedly worth millions. She even fabricated evidence of a trust fund established for her, valued at over $10 million (about $350 million today). Faced with these seemingly legitimate documents bearing the signature of the world's richest man, and charmed by Cassie's convincing portrayal of a discreetly cared-for heiress, the bankers readily opened their vaults.

Her audacity grew with each successful loan. She secured large sums from prominent Cleveland institutions like the Euclid Avenue Savings and Trust, which gave her $382,000 (about $13 million today) and the American Exchange National Bank, which gave her $8,800 (about $313,000 today), as well as smaller banks like the Wade Park Banking Company, which gave her $40,000 (about $1.4 million today) and the Savings Deposit Bank of Elyria, which gave her $10,000 (about $350,000 today). But her most significant victim was Charles Beckwith, the president of the tiny Citizens National Bank in Oberlin, Ohio. By the time Cassie encountered him, her confidence was absolute. She wasn't asking for tens of thousands; she requested a staggering $340,000 (about $12 million today), including $100,000 (about $3.5 million today) as a personal loan. Beckwith, reportedly smitten with her, and reassured by the forged Carnegie notes, gave her everything she asked for. This single act of reckless lending, based entirely on Cassie's lies, would ultimately bankrupt his small bank. Altogether, Cassie Chadwick managed to steal an estimated $2 million (about $70 million today) by jumping between cities in Ohio, Massachusetts, and New York, all while claiming to be Andrew Carnegie's secret love child.

Her extravagant charade finally began to unravel in 1904. A Massachusetts man named Herbert B. Newton, a broker she had duped, filed a lawsuit against her, claiming she had stolen $190,800 (about $7 million today) from him using the same forged Carnegie notes as security. Newton's public accusation acted like a dam breaking; suddenly, other bankers and businessmen who had been quietly trying to recover their losses, perhaps too embarrassed to admit they had been swindled, came forward with their own lawsuits. The cumulative claims quickly reached over a quarter of a million dollars, and that only accounted for those willing to publicly admit their folly.

With her web of deceit collapsing, Cassie fled, but the law caught up with her on December 2, 1904. Police tracked her down to a room at the Hotel Breslin in Manhattan, apparently preparing to flee the state or even the country. When they arrested her, they discovered $100,000 (about $3.5 million today) in cash strapped around her waist. Her time playing the role of an elite socialite was over.

Cassie's trial was a sensation, laying bare the full scope of her decades-long criminal career. Details of her previous aliases, frauds, the faked hemorrhage, the fabricated wealthy husband, the fortune-telling scams, her earlier prison sentence, and even a faked death notice she sent to friends in 1883 were all brought to light. The sheer audacity and longevity of her deception shocked the public. Her estranged husband, Dr. Chadwick, who had moved to Europe with his daughter, was initially charged alongside her, under the assumption that he must have been complicit. However, he sailed back to the United States for the trial and was quickly exonerated, proving he had been as clueless as everyone else about his wife's elaborate deceptions.

Despite the overwhelming evidence against her, Cassie maintained an air of detachment throughout the proceedings. Due to hearing loss she had developed, she didn't even hear the clerk read the guilty verdict on seven counts of conspiracy. When her attorney finally leaned in and told her, "We have lost, Mrs. Chadwick," the color drained from her face. She sank into her chair, and as she was led away to her jail cell, she cried out, "Let me go! Oh my God, let me go! I'm not guilty! I'm not guilty, I tell you! Let me go!" before fainting.

Her sentencing hearing drew considerable attention, notably attended by Andrew Carnegie himself, the man whose name she had so brazenly exploited. She was sentenced to fourteen years in prison and fined $70,000 (about $2.5 million today) — a paltry sum compared to the millions she had stolen. The true cost of her crimes was borne not just by the banks, but by their everyday account holders. This was before the establishment of the Federal Deposit Insurance Corporation (FDIC) in 1933; when a bank failed due to fraud like Cassie's, depositors lost everything.

One group of victims was Oberlin College, which had deposited its funds in Charles Beckwith's now-closed Citizens National Bank. At the sentencing hearing, when it was revealed that Cassie's fraud had cost the college $50,000 (about $1.7 million today), Andrew Carnegie stepped in — whether out of responsibility or his usual philanthropy — to cover the loss. He replaced the lost funds and donated an additional $100,000 (about $3.5 million today) for the construction of a new library on campus, a building that still stands today. Carnegie reportedly felt horrible for the victims and assisted others as well.

The most tragic figure in the aftermath was Charles Beckwith. Financially ruined, his bank shuttered, and having served jail time himself for his reckless mismanagement of depositors' funds, he remained inexplicably loyal to Cassie. He visited her in prison, telling her, "I am not convinced that you are a fraud, and I look for the time when everything will be straightened out." He pleaded with her to make a statement that could clear his name, but she refused, reportedly laughing in his face. Just weeks after that prison visit, Beckwith died in shame — blind, paralyzed, and delirious, using his last breaths to speak of Cassie. When news of his death reached Cassie in her cell, she initially feigned indifference to the press but later confided to a cellmate that the news left her "pained beyond expression."

Cassie Chadwick began serving her sentence on January 12, 1906, and on October 10, 1907, on her fiftieth birthday, she died. The prison doctor attributed her death to a "bad heart," a diagnosis few who knew her story would have disputed. The woman who had charmed, manipulated, and swindled her way through life, leaving a trail of broken banks and broken men, had finally run out of time and illusions.

32

THE BOY WHO BURNED DOWN THE LAW

It was a sweltering summer night in Lawrence County, Alabama, the kind where the heat clings heavy and damp, refusing to yield even after the sun dips below the horizon. In the small, rural community, the air hung thick with the sounds of cicadas and the distant bark of dogs. But the oppressive stillness of that July night in 2003 was about to be shattered by an act of shocking brutality, forever altering the lives of everyone involved and igniting a legal firestorm that would eventually reach the highest court in the United States. At the center of this maelstrom was a skinny, unassuming fourteen-year-old boy named Evan James Miller, a child whose broken past and momentary, monstrous actions would inadvertently place him at the forefront of a landmark battle over juvenile justice in America.

Evan Miller's young life had been a chaotic shuffle through poverty, neglect, and violence. Bouncing between foster care placements and a home environment saturated with abuse and instability, he carried the visible and invisible scars of a deeply troubled childhood. His mother struggled, and his father's presence was marked more by harm than help. Evan had attempted suicide multiple times, cycled through psychological programs, and developed a dependency on drugs — all before he was old enough to legally drive a car. He was a child adrift, shaped by chaos and trauma, lacking the guidance and stability necessary to navigate the treacherous path to adulthood.

On the night of July 15, 2003, Evan was spending time with a slightly older friend, sixteen-year-old Colby Smith. They ended up at the nearby mobile home of a neighbor, fifty-two-year-old Cole C. Cannon. Cannon had only recently moved into the Country Living trailer park, occupying the trailer just in front of where Evan lived with his mother. According to later testimony, Cannon appeared to have been drinking heavily that evening; Colby Smith recalled that he smelled of alcohol and was staggering. He had come over to the Millers' trailer earlier, complaining he'd burned his dinner and asking for something to eat. While Evan's mother, Susan, prepared some spaghetti for Cannon, Evan and Colby slipped over to Cannon's trailer. Their initial intent, according to Smith, was to look for drugs, but they found none. Instead, they stumbled upon Cole Cannon's baseball card collection — a remnant from years prior when he owned a card shop — and pocketed some of the cards, hiding them away before returning to Evan's trailer.

When Cannon finished eating and went back to his own trailer, Evan and Colby followed him a short time later. Their plan, Smith testified, was now to get Cannon drunk and steal his money. They shared marijuana with him, smoked a joint, and played drinking games until Cannon, heavily intoxicated, eventually passed out on his couch. While Cannon was unconscious, Evan found his wallet, took it into the bathroom, and removed the cash inside, a little over $300, which he then split with Colby. The theft should have been the end of it, a petty crime committed by two troubled teenagers against an incapacitated man. But the situation took a sudden, violent turn.

As Evan attempted to slide the now-empty wallet back into Cannon's pocket, the older man abruptly woke up and lunged, grabbing Evan by the throat. Colby Smith, witnessing the altercation, reacted instantly. He grabbed a nearby baseball bat and struck Cannon hard on the head. The blow stunned Cannon, releasing his grip on Evan. But the violence didn't stop there. Evan, now free, climbed onto Cannon and began pummeling him furiously with his fists. Cannon pleaded with them to stop, but his cries went unheeded. Evan picked up the baseball bat that Colby had dropped and continued the assault, striking Cannon repeatedly with brutal force. The beating was merciless, fueled perhaps by Evan's own history as a victim of abuse, now tragically transformed into a perpetrator. At some point during the assault, Evan reportedly placed a sheet or shirt over Cannon's battered head and uttered chilling words: "Cole, I am God. I come to take your life."

After Evan delivered a final blow with the bat, he and Colby fled back to the Miller trailer, leaving Cannon broken and bleeding on the floor. But within minutes, they returned, perhaps realizing the gravity of what they had done or simply trying to cover their tracks. They made a cursory attempt to clean up the blood that was splattered on the walls and furniture. Then, their thoughts turned to destroying the evidence entirely. They decided to set the trailer on fire. Colby used a lighter to ignite a couch in the back bedroom, while Evan started another fire on a different couch. As they were leaving the rapidly burning trailer, Colby saw Cannon still lying helplessly on the floor. In a fleeting moment of what he later described as pity, Colby placed a towel under Cannon's head in a futile attempt to stanch the bleeding and turned on the kitchen faucet, stopping up the sink in a desperate, illogical hope that the water might extinguish the flames. As they finally exited the burning trailer, they heard Cole Cannon's faint, haunting question drift through the smoke: "Why are y'all doing this to me?" About ten minutes later, Colby returned to the trailer alone, perhaps driven by guilt or morbid curiosity. He could hear Cannon coughing inside, but smoke was pouring out, and he saw Evan approaching, so he turned and fled back to the Miller residence for good. Cole Cannon was left to die in the inferno.

Firefighters from the Speake Volunteer Fire Department responded to the blaze in the early morning hours of July 16th. While extinguishing the fire, they noticed blood spatter on a wall and blood saturating a coffee table, immediately indicating that this was more than a simple house fire. Their search led them to the discovery of Cole Cannon's body in the hallway. The fire marshal, Richard Montgomery, conducted the initial investigation and quickly determined the fire was suspicious, noting multiple points of origin, and turned the case over to Investigator Tim Sandlin of the Lawrence County Sheriff's Department.

Investigator Sandlin began piecing together the events. After speaking with Cannon's family, he learned that certain items were missing from the trailer, including his wallet and some baseball trading cards. The wallet was later found stuffed under the couch, but Cannon's driver's license was gone. Sandlin also recovered the baseball bat from beneath the couch. These findings led him directly to the neighboring trailer occupied by Evan Miller and his mother, Susan. Susan Miller voluntarily gave Investigator Sandlin a box of trading cards, and both she and Evan agreed to accompany him to the sheriff's office to provide statements.

At the station, Evan was read his rights from a juvenile Miranda form, which both he and his mother signed. Initially, Evan stuck to a simple story: he had been home watching a movie, admitted Cannon had visited their trailer earlier, but denied ever going over to Cannon's trailer himself. He claimed he only learned about the fire when the fire department arrived the next morning. However, as Investigator Sandlin pressed him, asking him to recount the events backward from the morning, Evan became agitated. "Forget all that," he snapped, "that wasn't true." He then requested that everyone except Investigator Sandlin leave the room. With his mother and juvenile officers gone, Evan provided a second statement. He admitted going to Cannon's trailer, finding the trading cards, and returning later with Colby to drink beer. He described Cannon becoming heavily intoxicated and falling, then claimed Cannon grabbed him by the throat when he tried to help. He stated that Colby pushed Cannon off him, Cannon grabbed the bat, hit Evan with it, Colby then took the bat and hit Cannon, before Evan kicked the bat under the couch. He admitted to punching Cannon several times and finding the wallet on the floor, taking the cash and the driver's license. He ended his account by claiming he and Colby ran out the back door when they heard his mother knocking, warning that the police were coming, and heard Cannon ask why they did it as they fled. Significantly, this second statement made no mention of the brutal beating with the bat after the initial altercation, nor did it include any admission of setting the fires.

Evan's partial admission, however, was enough to prompt a full fire investigation at Cannon's trailer on July 24th. Deputy Fire Marshal Bo Lynden Blackton confirmed the extensive blood spatter and identified four separate points of origin for the fire, clearly indicating arson. Meanwhile, the initial external examination of Cannon's body by forensic pathologist Dr. Adam Craig had yielded a perplexing result. Seeing no obvious signs of foul play beyond what could be attributed to the fire, Dr. Craig initially ruled the death an accident caused by smoke and soot inhalation and did not perform a full autopsy. However, based on the developing evidence from the investigation, Investigator Sandlin requested that Cannon's body be exhumed for a more thorough examination. On August 1st, 2003, Dr. Craig performed the full autopsy. He discovered significant injuries hidden beneath the fire damage: a two-inch (about five centimeters) contusion on the forehead caused by blunt force, and six rib fractures on both sides of the body. Hemorrhaging confirmed these injuries occurred before Cannon died. Dr. Craig revised his findings, reaffirming smoke inhalation as the primary cause of death but adding multiple blunt force injuries and ethanol intoxication as significant contributing factors that likely prevented Cannon from escaping the burning trailer.

While the forensic evidence mounted, Evan Miller made further incriminating statements, seemingly unprompted. During transport to mental health evaluations on July 31st and August 4th, he spoke with Deputy Tim McWhorter. Though not interrogated, Evan initiated conversations about the case. He asked the deputy if he would get in trouble for changing his story to tell the truth, admitted he was "not innocent" and had been involved in the assault, and stated he deserved to serve time. He claimed he had been "really messed up" on Klonopin and whiskey that night. He repeated the story of Cannon grabbing him by the neck but added that he then "slammed Mr. Cannon really hard" because he was "really pissed off," and admitted they had "roughed him up pretty good," acknowledging the autopsy would show bruises. He claimed memory lapses but conceded, the more he thought about it, the more it made him think he started the fire.

DNA analysis provided further corroboration. Nancy Jones, head of the DNA section at the state forensic lab, testified that blood found on a cushion and the wall matched Cole Cannon's DNA profile. Bloodstains consistent with Evan Miller's DNA were found on two T-shirts recovered from the scene; one of these shirts also possibly contained Cannon's blood, and the spatter patterns were consistent with impact from an object, not a gunshot. While usable DNA could not be obtained from the bat itself or the towel placed under Cannon's head, the collective evidence painted a damning picture.

Evan Miller, now seventeen years old, after lengthy juvenile proceedings and certification as an adult, finally went on trial for capital murder in October 2006. His defense claimed he was not guilty due to mental illness, with his mother and a psychologist testifying about his troubled past — suicide attempts, time in foster care, drug use, and diagnoses such as conduct disorder, personality disorder, depression, and oppositional defiant disorder. His accomplice, Colby Smith, had accepted a plea deal the previous week, pleading guilty to felony murder in exchange for a life sentence with the possibility of parole, contingent on his testimony against Evan. The prosecution presented the forensic evidence, Smith's testimony, and Evan's own incriminating statements.

On October 20th, 2006, the Lawrence County jury returned their verdict. After initially returning confused, having found Evan guilty of everything including lesser charges, they were reinstructed and sent back. They ultimately found Evan Miller guilty of capital murder committed during the course of first-degree arson. Under Alabama law at the time, this conviction carried a mandatory sentence: life in prison without the possibility of parole. Circuit Judge Philip Reich imposed the sentence immediately. Before being led away, Evan offered a muffled apology to Cannon's family. Candy Cheatham, Cannon's oldest daughter, responded with a raw and powerful victim impact statement, showing Evan pictures of her father as a child that she had salvaged from the ashes. "You say you're sorry," she said, her voice thick with grief and anger. "You have no idea what kind of pain we went through... He was a person and he mattered to us. I do hope when you're in prison, you will find Jesus. But I can't forgive you right now. And I don't think my family can either." Evan's own family wept, his sister Aubrey later telling reporters that while her brother deserved punishment, he shouldn't have been tried as an adult and that their parents shared the blame for the neglect and abuse that shaped him.

The mandatory life-without-parole sentence imposed on a seventeen-year-old for a crime committed at fourteen placed Evan Miller's case at the center of a burgeoning legal challenge to juvenile sentencing practices. Advocacy groups, notably the Equal Justice Initiative (EJI), took up his cause, arguing that sentencing children to die in prison violated the Eighth Amendment's prohibition against cruel and unusual punishment. The case eventually made its way to the United States Supreme Court. Candy Cheatham expressed frustration with how the EJI presented the facts of the case in their briefs, feeling they downplayed Evan's culpability and unfairly maligned her father's character.

In June 2012, the Supreme Court delivered its landmark ruling in *Miller v. Alabama*. The Court held that mandatory life-without-parole sentences for individuals under the age of eighteen at the time of their crimes are unconstitutional. The ruling did not ban life-without-parole sentences for juveniles outright, but it required that sentencing judges consider the unique circumstances of the child offender — their age, maturity level, background, and the nature of the crime — before imposing such a severe sentence. The decision fundamentally reshaped juvenile justice, affirming the principle that "children are different" and possess a greater capacity for change and rehabilitation than adults. For Evan Miller, the ruling meant his mandatory sentence was vacated, and he was entitled to a new sentencing hearing where his youth and background could be properly considered. Eventually, he received his new sentencing hearing in Alabama and, in March 2017, Evan Miller was re-sentenced to life with the possibility of parole after serving thirty years. His story, which began with a brutal act in a small Alabama town, had inadvertently led to a profound shift in American law, forcing the justice system to confront the complex question of whether a child, no matter how heinous their crime, can ever truly be beyond redemption.

33

THE MAN WITHOUT A NAME

On the morning of June 16, 2009, a father and his son went for an early morning swim at Rosses Point, a scenic beach in County Sligo, Ireland. The Irish coast, even in June, can be brisk and bracing, a place of rugged beauty where the Atlantic meets the shore with a steady, rhythmic pulse. As they made their way along the sand, they saw a figure washed up at the water's edge. It was the body of a middle-aged man, and it was immediately clear that he was dead. By 8:10 a.m., he was officially pronounced dead at the scene, and his body was transported to the morgue at Sligo University Hospital for an autopsy. There was no identification found on or near him, no wallet, no phone, nothing to give a name to the face of the man who had met his end on that quiet beach. He was a ghost, a John Doe whose final moments were a complete mystery. Later, he would be buried in an unmarked grave in Sligo, his funeral attended only by police officers who had been tasked with the impossible job of figuring out who he was.

Thanks to CCTV, investigators were able to piece together the man's last few days with remarkable clarity. But the copious amounts of video evidence they uncovered did not solve the mystery; instead, they deepened it, revealing a man who moved through the world with a singular, chilling purpose: to systematically erase himself from existence. Who was this man, how did he manage to leave no trace of his life behind, and what was the significance of the mysterious purple plastic bag he was seen carrying all over town? The case that unfolded was a modern-day echo of the famous Tamám Shud mystery, a perplexing tale of a man who seemed to materialize out of thin air only to vanish into the great unknown, leaving behind a trail of carefully curated questions.

The first confirmed sighting of the mystery man was on Friday, June 12, 2009, when he arrived in the city of Derry by bus. From there, he immediately caught another bus to Sligo, a popular coastal town in the northwest of Ireland. Upon his arrival, he hailed a taxi and asked the driver to take him to a cheap hotel. The first option was fully booked, so the driver took him to his next suggestion, the Sligo City Hotel. Hotel security cameras captured his entrance. He was a man of medium build, dressed neatly in dark trousers, a shirt, and a leather jacket, carrying a black shoulder bag and another larger black bag in his hand. He approached the front desk, paid cash in advance for a three-night stay, and gave his name as Peter Bergmann. In the hotel register, he wrote down an address: Ainstettersnstrasse 15, Vienna, 4472, Austria. Both the taxi driver and the hotel staff noted that he spoke with a thick German or Austrian accent. In what would later become a critical point of frustration for investigators, the hotel, apparently against its own policy, did not ask him for any form of identification. Peter Bergmann, a man with no verifiable past, had officially checked in.

The next day, Saturday, June 13th, the man began a strange and methodical ritual. He was captured on CCTV coming and going from the hotel a total of thirteen times. Each time he left, he was carrying a full purple plastic bag. The contents were impossible to see on the grainy footage, but the bag was clearly weighted with objects. And each time he returned to the hotel, the purple bag was gone. He was also seen visiting the local post office that Saturday, where he purchased eight stamps for overseas postage and a corresponding number of airmail stickers. Sligo has an extensive network of surveillance cameras covering its town center, and Bergmann was visible on many of them as he walked the streets. But in all that footage, he was never once caught in the act of disposing of the contents of the purple bag. What he was getting rid of and where he was leaving it remains a complete mystery.

The following day, Sunday, June 14th, Bergmann's activities took a different turn. He hailed another taxi and asked the driver to recommend a quiet, secluded beach where he might go for a swim. The driver took him to Rosses Point, about five miles (about eight kilometers) out of town. Bergmann got out of the cab, took a brief look around the beach, and then, without explanation, got right back in and asked to be driven back to Sligo. It was a reconnaissance mission. The driver later confirmed that during their conversation, Bergmann mentioned he was from Austria, reinforcing the identity he had constructed at the hotel. His use of taxis seemed at odds with his choice of a cheap hotel, a small detail that suggested he was not without funds but was perhaps being careful and deliberate in his choices.

Monday, June 15th, was Peter Bergmann's last full day of life. He requested a late checkout from the hotel and then went out one last time, again carrying the full purple plastic bag for its final emptying. When he checked out of the hotel later that day, the CCTV footage showed him with his black shoulder bag and the purple plastic bag, but the larger black bag he had arrived with was now gone. In its place was a much smaller bag, something that looked more like a wash bag. He walked to the bus station, and by the time he appeared on the cameras there, this smaller black bag had also disappeared. Inside the station, he ordered a cappuccino and a toasted cheese and ham sandwich, a classic meal for someone waiting to travel. He then took a piece of paper from his pocket, wrote some notes on it, folded it up, and then meticulously tore it into tiny pieces, scattering the confetti remains into a nearby public bin. Finally, he boarded the bus for Rosses Point, the beach he had scouted out the day before. When the driver asked if he wanted a single or a return ticket, he asked for a single.

The bus arrived at Rosses Point in the mid-afternoon, and Bergmann disembarked, carrying what little he had left. Several people confirmed seeing him on the beach over the course of that afternoon and evening. He stood out. Most witnesses remembered him being quite smartly dressed for a day at the beach, wearing his dark trousers, shirt, and leather jacket. One witness later said that he looked "almost out of place and out of time." He was seen walking parallel to the water's edge with his trousers rolled up, pacing up and down the sand with his hands clasped behind his back, as if he were "in another world." He responded to brief greetings from fellow beachgoers but otherwise kept to himself. The last confirmed sighting of him alive was after 10:30 p.m., with some sources placing it as late as 11:50 p.m. It was only the fact that he was there so late that made anyone remember seeing him at all. The next morning, his lifeless body was found washed up on the sand. He was wearing Speedo-style swimming trunks, but strangely, he had his underwear and a T-shirt over them. His other clothes, including his leather jacket, were found in a neatly folded pile further up the beach. There was no form of ID on his body, only a few coins and some minor personal items. And just like his other belongings, every single tag had been cut from his clothing.

The initial assumption was that he had drowned, a logical conclusion for a man found washed up on a beach in swimming gear. But the autopsy revealed a far more complex picture. The medical examiner confirmed there were no signs of foul play, but also, crucially, no evidence of salt-water drowning. Further examination revealed that Bergmann was a very sick man. He had advanced prostate cancer, with tumors that had metastasized into his bones and other organs. He had also suffered from at least two previous heart attacks. Yet, the toxicology report came back with no trace of any painkillers in his system, something the examiner found highly unusual for someone who must have been in a considerable amount of pain. Given the advanced stage of his cancer, it was likely he had only weeks, if not days, to live. The official cause of death was listed as acute cardiac arrest. He had intended to go into the sea, but it seemed his own failing heart had claimed him before the water could.

The name Peter Bergmann and the Austrian address were quickly found to be fictitious. Searches of European, North American, and South American passport databases yielded no matches. Stills from the CCTV footage and an artist's rendering based on his autopsy photos were circulated throughout Ireland and Europe, but no family member, no friend, no former colleague ever came forward to identify the man. None of his bags or any of the items he had so carefully disposed of around Sligo were ever found. It was as if Peter Bergmann was a ghost who had walked the earth for a few days and then simply dissolved.

Everything about his behavior pointed to a man who had come to Sligo with the sole intention of ending his life and leaving no trace of his existence behind. But why go to such extraordinary lengths to ensure his anonymity? One theory revolved around insurance. In some countries, life insurance policies are voided in the event of a suicide. By making it seem as though he had simply disappeared, he could eventually be declared legally dead, allowing a potential payout for his family. This theory, however, has a significant flaw: he seemed to have no dependents or anyone he wished to notify of his death, so who would the insurance policy benefit?

A more plausible, and far more depressing, theory centers on the contents of the purple plastic bag. The sheer number of trips he made — at least thirteen — suggested he was disposing of more than just a few changes of clothes. One of the most poignant theories is that he was getting rid of items related to his illness that he found embarrassing, such as adult diapers, a common necessity for those with advanced prostate cancer. He may not have wanted the hotel staff to see them in his room's bin, and so he took it upon himself to dispose of them discreetly in public trash cans around the town. The police did search public areas, but without knowing what they were looking for, such items would have been easily overlooked. His apparent knowledge of the CCTV camera locations, which some have suggested points to spy training, is more likely the common sense of a man who was simply observant. The cameras in Sligo are highly visible, and it would not take a trained operative to notice where they were and, more importantly, where they were not.

The letters he mailed from the post office add another layer to the mystery. Were they final farewells to loved ones, explaining his decision and asking them to respect his wish for anonymity? If so, it would explain why no one ever came forward. It's a sad thought, a man so alone at the end that his final resting place is an unmarked, shared grave, his funeral attended only by strangers. It's also possible that his family and friends simply never saw the media appeals, which were largely confined to Ireland and parts of Europe.

Every potential clue seemed to lead to another dead end. While the labels on his clothes were cut off, the brands were still identifiable: his shoes were

German-made, and his jacket and trousers were from C&A, a Dutch store popular across Europe. The items in his pockets — plasters from the German brand Hansaplast, German-distributed aspirin, and a generic bar of hotel soap not available in Ireland — all pointed to a European, likely German-speaking, origin. But these items are so widely available that they provided no concrete leads. His fingerprints and DNA were taken, but they matched no one in any criminal database. In a move that has frustrated online sleuths for years, the Gardaí have officially stated that they will not submit his DNA to commercial ancestry sites, citing privacy concerns.

In the end, the most probable conclusion is also the simplest and the most tragic. Peter Bergmann was likely a quiet, lonely man, ravaged by a terminal illness and in immense, unmedicated pain, who decided to take control of his own end. He traveled to a place he had perhaps visited before, or maybe just picked from a map, and spent his final days meticulously erasing his past to spare anyone the burden of his death. The letters he posted were his true goodbyes, sent to the few people who mattered, asking them to respect his final wish. The heart attack may have been unplanned, a sudden end to a journey that was meant to conclude in the cold embrace of the Atlantic, but the end result was the same. In an age of total surveillance, digital footprints, and international communication, the man known as Peter Bergmann achieved something remarkable: he gave himself a new name, and then he disappeared, leaving behind only the ghost of a story and the enduring question of whether we should even be trying to find him at all.

34

THE NATIONAL FOREST KILLER

In the quiet woods of Cherokee County, Georgia, a sheriff's deputy noticed a white van parked conspicuously on private hunting lands. Assuming it was likely a simple case of trespassing, he approached the vehicle, where an older man with a scruffy beard was arranging maps. The man explained he was just preparing to camp briefly before moving on, chatting amiably about the strictness of the landowners and even joking lightly about hunters mistaking his colorful gear for game. Beneath this friendly, almost folksy demeanor, however, lurked a calculating predator, a man whose recent past was marked by murder and whose mind concealed far darker intentions. When the deputy requested identification, the man retrieved a fanny pack and assured him there were no weapons, casually pointing out an expandable police baton in the van as he did so. Finding no outstanding warrants or immediate cause for concern, the deputy allowed Gary Michael Hilton to leave, unaware that he had just released a dangerous killer back into the wild.

The first sign that something was terribly wrong emerged further south, in Leon County, Florida. On Sunday, December 2, 2007, forty-six-year-old Cheryl Dunlap, a dedicated nurse at Florida State University and a devout Christian active in her church, failed to show up for her Sunday school class. Concern grew the following day when she missed work, an uncharacteristic absence that prompted a friend to report her missing. Her adult son went to her home, hoping for a simple explanation, but found only her beloved dog, alone and unsettled. Police soon determined that no one had heard from Cheryl since the morning of Saturday, December 1st, when she told a friend she was heading to the library. Records confirmed she had logged onto a computer at the Wakulla County Public Library at 9:45 a.m. and cashed a check for $100 at a bank around 11:15 a.m. After that, she vanished.

Friends initially considered the possibility that Cheryl, who had recently expressed a desire for more adventure in her life, might have simply decided to leave town abruptly. But that scenario seemed increasingly unlikely given her strong ties to her community, her job, her sons, and her deep faith. Any hope for an innocent explanation evaporated that afternoon when Cheryl's car was discovered abandoned off a road near Leon Sinks Geological State Park, a popular area for hiking. There was no sign of Cheryl. Her purse and keys were still inside the vehicle, her belongings scattered across the seat, and ominously, one of the rear tires was flat. A closer examination revealed the tire hadn't just gone flat; it appeared to have been deliberately punctured. Signs of foul play were mounting, sending waves of fear and turmoil through her circle of friends and family. Her son recalled his last, brief phone conversation with her weeks earlier, a missed connection that now felt like a haunting regret.

Cheryl Dunlap's picture was quickly disseminated through local media. A couple came forward, reporting they had seen her at Leon Sinks on the afternoon of December 1st, sitting peacefully on a bench, reading a book. This placed her at the park but offered no clue as to what happened next. The investigation took a sinister turn when police checked her bank records. Cheryl's ATM card had been used five times between December 2nd and December 4th, withdrawing a total of over $700. Her family knew Cheryl would never have willingly given up her PIN. Investigators rushed to the bank, hoping surveillance footage might reveal who was accessing her account, finding their worst fears confirmed. The grainy ATM video showed not Cheryl, but a tall, thin figure, their face obscured by a disturbing, crudely made mask, methodically withdrawing cash from her account. The identity of the person behind the mask was a complete mystery, leaving Cheryl's loved ones grappling with dread and help-lessness.

A month later, the nightmare seemed to repeat itself, this time over 300 miles (about 480 kilometers) north in the mountains of Georgia. On January 1st, 2008, twenty-four-year-old Meredith Emerson, an avid hiker, left a note for her roommate saying she was taking her black Labrador retriever, Ella, for a hike on Blood Mountain, one of her favorite spots along the Appalachian Trail. When she failed to return by the next morning, her roommate reported her missing. Meredith's boyfriend found her car parked at one of the trailheads, covered in snow. A frantic search began, involving friends, police, the Georgia Bureau of Investigation (GBI), and eventually, scores of volunteers.

As news of her disappearance spread, investigators spoke to several people who had been hiking on Blood Mountain on New Year's Day. They recalled seeing Meredith and Ella, but they also noticed something else: an older man lurking nearby. One witness described coming across a disturbed section of the trail shortly after seeing Meredith and the man, suggesting a struggle had taken place. Left behind on the ground were several items: Meredith's water bottles, Ella's leash, and, most ominously, an expandable police baton. Witnesses provided a consistent description of the man: white, around sixty years old, roughly 5'10" (about 177 centimeters) and 160 pounds (about seventy kilograms), with graying hair. They also mentioned another crucial detail: he had a large, reddish-colored dog with him.

Police shared these details, and tips began pouring in. Could this man be responsible for Meredith's disappearance? Could he even be the same sinister figure in the mask who had drained Cheryl Dunlap's bank account just a month earlier? The parallels were chilling: two women, alone in national forest areas, both now missing under suspicious circumstances.

Back in Leon County, Florida, the investigation into Cheryl's disappearance was also receiving tips that took on a disturbingly familiar shape. Multiple witnesses independently reported encountering a specific man in the Leon Sinks area in late November 2007, just days before Cheryl vanished. Their descriptions matched the man seen on Blood Mountain: older, skinny, scruffy, sometimes described as homeless-looking, often accompanied by a large reddish dog, variously identified as an Irish Setter or a dark Golden Retriever. Several witnesses noted feeling unnerved by him; one mentioned a long knife strapped to his side, another simply said, "He gave me the creeps." One hiker, disturbed by the encounter, had even joked grimly to her companion, "Man, that guy's killed like ten people." An older man, a white van (mentioned by some Florida witnesses), a red dog — the details were strikingly consistent across both states.

The critical break came when a Georgia businessman named John Taber heard the description of the man sought in connection with Meredith Emerson's disappearance. He immediately called the GBI tip line. Taber explained that the man they were looking for had worked for him intermittently for years, selling house siding, right up until he had recently demanded money and threatened to kill Taber. He confirmed the man drove a white Chevrolet Astro van and had a reddish Golden Retriever named Dandy. His name, Taber told the stunned investigators, was Gary Michael Hilton.

Armed with a name and driver's license photo, the GBI issued an updated "Be On the Lookout" alert. Gary Michael Hilton was officially named a person of interest in Meredith Emerson's disappearance. The race to find him intensified, fueled by the desperate hope that Meredith might still be alive.

Tragically, in Florida, that hope had already been extinguished. On December 15, 2007, two weeks after Cheryl Dunlap was last seen, a hunter walking his dogs deep in the Apalachicola National Forest stumbled upon a gruesome scene. Buzzards circling overhead led him to what appeared, at first glance, like animal remains partially covered by tree limbs and palmetto fronds. But as he got closer, he realized the horrifying truth: it was a human body, nude and significantly decomposed. The body had been horrifically mutilated. The hands and head were missing, and the nipples had been cut off. Due to the advanced decomposition and decapitation, the medical examiner could only determine the cause of death as "undetermined homicidal violence." Later, by comparing a DNA profile generated from a thigh muscle sample to known records, it was determined that the body belonged to Cheryl Dunlap.

The search for Hilton in Georgia reached a critical point on January 4th, three days after Meredith vanished. Ella, Meredith's black lab, was spotted wandering into a Kroger supermarket in Cumming, Georgia, nearly fifty miles (about eighty kilometers) south of Blood Mountain. Her microchip confirmed her identity. While Meredith's family was relieved Ella was safe, her discovery so far from the mountain, without Meredith, was deeply concerning. Later that same day, police received another crucial tip: a woman reported that Gary Hilton had called her demanding money. The call was traced to a payphone at a QuikTrip gas station, located directly across the street from the Kroger where Ella had been found. Investigators rushed to the scene, but Hilton was gone. However, in the dumpster behind the gas station, they made a grim discovery: bloody clothing, Meredith's purse, and her wallet containing her driver's license and student ID cards. The hunt for Gary Hilton had become a desperate race against time.

That night, the 911 calls police had been waiting for finally came in. Multiple callers reported seeing a man matching Hilton's description, along with his distinctive white van and red dog, at a Chevron gas station in nearby Chamblee. Witnesses described him acting suspiciously, pulling items out of his van and throwing them into the dumpster. "He's going to be gone if somebody doesn't get here," one caller urged. Police converged on the location. As officers arrived, Hilton went flat on the ground and was taken into custody without a struggle. His van and his dog, Dandy, were secured. But the relief of his capture was immediately tempered by a stark, unsettling reality: Meredith Emerson was nowhere to be found.

Hilton was transported to GBI headquarters, where he initially proved utterly uncooperative, lying prone on the floor, refusing to answer questions, and complaining of pain from multiple sclerosis. Investigators noted fresh scratches on his face and neck, along with a badly swollen right hand — possible defensive wounds. With Meredith's fate hanging in the balance, they needed Hilton to talk. Agent Clay Bridges appealed to his conscience, "You need to go ahead and just tell us where she's at." But Hilton remained silent.

While Hilton stonewalled, evidence continued to mount. Investigators processing his van found blood that matched Meredith's DNA. Meanwhile, in Florida, police searching campsites near where Hilton had been seen around the time of Cheryl Dunlap's disappearance made a horrifying discovery: a burn pit containing charred human finger bones and skull fragments. DNA identification was impossible due to the condition of the remains, but authorities were almost certain they belonged to Cheryl. At one of these campsites, investigators also found zip ties, matching the description of those potentially used on Meredith, and crucially, a cigarette butt containing Hilton's DNA. Further solidifying the link between the two cases, forensic analysis confirmed that the bayonet-style knife recovered from the struggle scene on Blood Mountain was an exact match to the puncture marks found in Cheryl Dunlap's slashed tire.

Faced with overwhelming evidence for kidnapping and the high probability of multiple murder charges across states — potentially involving the death penalty — Hilton's resolve finally broke. His lawyer negotiated a deal: in exchange for leading investigators to Meredith Emerson's body and providing a full confession, the state of Georgia would take the death penalty off the table. Hilton agreed.

Over hours of recorded interviews, Gary Hilton presented a complex and often contradictory self-image in his interviews, revealing a worldview steeped in cynicism, perceived superiority, and detachment from societal norms. He portrayed himself as a philosopher, soldier, scientist, and artist, framing even extreme acts, like pulling out his own teeth, as both practical intimidation and an "artistic-philosophical statement." He viewed ordinary people as shallow, labeling them "posers" or "schmuck townspeople," and believed his intelligence came from reflection rather than formal education. A preoccupation with death, which he traced to age four, underpinned his view that most human neuroses stemmed from existential anxiety.

Hilton expressed profound alienation, identifying as a loner and a sociopath, describing himself as a "round peg in a square hole" unable to find satisfaction in human relationships. His bond with animals, first manifested in the dog he acquired at twenty-one, was far stronger than any with humans, a distinction highlighted in his care for Meredith Emerson's dog Ella even while he abducted and ultimately murdered her. His views on women were harsh and misogynistic; he described them as manipulative, greedy, and heartless, using their sexuality to control men while retaining a nurturing instinct only for children and animals.

Eventually, Gary Michael Hilton laid bare the chilling details of Meredith Emerson's abduction and murder. He described encountering Meredith on the trail, drawn initially by their dogs meeting. He admitted forming the intent to abduct her almost immediately, driven, he claimed, solely by the desire to obtain her ATM card and PIN. He recounted the violent struggle when he confronted her, producing first the knife, then the baton, both of which she bravely fought him for. He admitted to beating her severely to gain control, described securing her first with zip ties, then with a nylon cord leash around her neck, and leading her off the trail. He detailed retrieving her purse from her car, securing her with chains in his van, and his surprising decision to go back for her dog, Ella, because Meredith was voicing concerns.

He described the subsequent days, driving around North Georgia, making repeated, failed attempts to use her ATM cards as Meredith deliberately gave him incorrect PINs — a desperate strategy that likely prolonged her life. He spoke of camping with her in Dawson Forest, bizarrely insisting she was "at ease" and "having a good time," even going hiking with him, despite being his captive. Finally, he recounted the horrifying end. Believing he was about to release her, he led her into a secluded part of the woods, secured her to a tree with a chain, returned to his van for coffee and the iron handle from a car jack, then walked back and brutally bludgeoned her to death. He confessed to decapitating her afterward, claiming it was purely for "forensic" reasons to prevent fiber transfer from her hair, and to pouring bleach over her body to destroy DNA evidence. He admitted he knew from the moment he abducted her that he would have to kill her, and described the act of killing and decapitation as "dreadful," "surrealistic," and like an "out-of-body experience," something so horrific he had to go on "autopilot" to complete it.

Following his confession, Hilton led investigators through the dark woods of Dawson Forest directly to Meredith's mutilated body and, separately, to where he had disposed of her head. On January 31, 2008, less than a month after his arrest, Gary Michael Hilton pleaded guilty to the murder of Meredith Emerson and was sentenced to life in prison without the possibility of parole.

But Hilton's reign of terror extended beyond Meredith and Cheryl. During his interviews, he alluded to his "rampage" starting earlier. A federal investigation soon connected him to the disappearance of John and Irene Bryant, a retired couple from North Carolina who went missing while hiking in Pisgah National Forest in October 2007. Hilton later confessed to these murders as well. He admitted to accosting the couple, demanding their credit cards, beating John with his baton when he refused, and killing Irene on the spot. He then kidnapped John, forced him to withdraw $300 from an ATM (captured on surveillance footage wearing the same yellow jacket), drove him to Nantahala National Forest, and shot him in the head. In 2011, Hilton was indicted in federal court for the Bryant murders, ultimately pleading guilty in 2012 and receiving four additional consecutive life sentences.

He was also considered a suspect in the 2005 disappearance of Rossana Miliani, another hiker who vanished from North Carolina after being seen with an older man matching Hilton's description. However, when detectives interviewed him about her case, Hilton vehemently denied involvement, and a polygraph test indicated no deception, though the reliability of such tests is questionable.

Finally, Hilton faced trial in Florida for the murder of Cheryl Dunlap. Despite his earlier agreement in Georgia, he pleaded not guilty. The prosecution presented the damning evidence: Cheryl's DNA in his van, his DNA on the cigarette butt at the campsite where her likely remains were found, the ATM footage, and the puncture marks on her tire matching his knife. They also played excerpts from his own bizarre home videos, recorded just days after Cheryl vanished, where he seemed to ramble about killing someone. In April 2011, the jury found him guilty of first-degree murder, kidnapping, and grand theft. Gary Michael Hilton, the man who fancied himself a lone wolf philosopher-artist living outside society's rules, was sentenced to death. His "rampage," as he called it, born of a chilling blend of sociopathy, misogyny, and perceived existential insight, left a trail of terror across the national forests of the southeastern

United States, a brutal counterpoint to the natural beauty he claimed to cherish.

35

THE VAN IN THE DRIVEWAY

On September 11th, 2021, police officers in Northport, Florida, pulled up to a quiet, suburban home, the residence of the Laundrie family due to an urgent call. They were investigating the disappearance of twenty-two-year-old Gabby Petito, and this house was their only solid lead. They did not have a warrant, but they did not need one to see what was parked in the driveway: a white 2012 Ford Transit van. It was instantly recognizable as the vehicle Gabby had meticulously converted into a DIY camper, the mobile home that was supposed to carry her and her fiancé, Brian Laundrie, on a dream road trip across the country.

When investigators spoke with Brian's parents, Christopher and Roberta Laundrie, the conversation was brief and cold. They insisted they had no idea where their future daughter-in-law was. They did, however, know where their son was: inside the house. The admission was a shock to the officers because the van and Brian were here, but Gabby was not. The simple question hung in the air: Why? When the officers asked to speak with Brian, the Laundries offered no explanations. Instead, they handed over the contact information for their family's lawyer. With no warrant, the police were stonewalled, forced to leave with more questions than they had arrived with. Why did this family already have legal representation? What were they hiding?

The police, however, were not the first to be met with this suspicious, uncooperative silence. The day before, Gabby's mother, Nicole Schmidt, was descending into a state of panic. She had not heard from her daughter in two weeks. She sent a text message to Brian's mother, Roberta, pleading for information: Was Gabby okay? The message was marked as "read," but no reply came. Nicole waited, trying to give Roberta the benefit of the doubt, but when she followed up, the message status turned a stark, definitive green. She had been blocked. Roberta Laundrie had seen the pleas from Gabby's mother and had actively, deliberately, cut off all communication. Gabby's father, Joe Petito, also tried to contact Brian's parents and his sister, Cassie, but was met with the same impenetrable silence. Joe's final, desperate message warned them that if they refused to respond, he would be forced to call the police. The threat was met with nothing.

This behavior was a terrifying betrayal to Gabby's parents, who had, despite their reservations, entrusted their daughter to this family. Gabby had introduced Brian to them in 2019. He seemed quiet, a subdued counterpart to Gabby's vibrant, outgoing personality. When she announced her intention to move in with him and his parents in Northport, they hesitated, gently warning her that the relationship was moving too quickly. But Gabby was determined. In December 2019, she packed up her life in New York and moved over a thousand miles south, taking a leap of faith to begin a new chapter with Brian.

Frustrated and terrified, Nicole Schmidt turned to the only tool she had left: the internet. She created a "Where's Gabby" poster using a joyful, recent picture from the road trip and shared it on Facebook. Gabby had already cultivated a decent following on Instagram by documenting her travels, and the missing person post began to circulate quickly. The next day, September 11th, her parents officially filed a missing person's report in New York. After the Northport police were rebuffed at the Laundrie home, they learned the most critical piece of information: Brian hadn't just returned. He had been back in Florida, with Gabby's van but without Gabby, since September 1st. He had been home for ten days and said nothing, while Gabby's parents were sick with worry. Gabby's parents immediately demanded that the police seize their daughter's van as evidence. This time, the Laundries had no choice but to comply.

On September 12th, the FBI formally opened an investigation, coordinating a wide search in the areas where Gabby was last known to be: Grand Teton National Park and the Bridger-Teton National Forest in Wyoming. The following day, Gabby's parents held a press conference, their faces etched with strain as they revealed the distressing timeline of their last communications. Her father, Joe, confirmed she was in Utah on August 21st. The couple then traveled to Grand Teton, where Gabby FaceTimed her parents on August 25th. That was the last time they ever heard her voice. Her mother, Nicole, received a text from Gabby's phone on August 27th. Then, after three agonizing days of silence, a final, strange text arrived on August 30th. It read, "Can you help Stan? I just keep getting his voicemails and missed calls."

To an outsider, the message may have seemed innocuous, but for Nicole, it was a blaring alarm bell. Stan was Gabby's grandfather, but she had never once in her life referred to him by his first name; he was, and always had been, "Grandpa." Nicole shared her chilling fear with the media, stating plainly, "I don't know if that was her texting me or not."

The press conference ignited a digital wildfire. A new subreddit, "Gabby Petito," was created and quickly had 90,000 members in a single week. This online community became a virtual command center, a massive, crowdsourced detective agency dedicated to compiling information, discussing the case, and inevitably, speculating. The primary focus of that speculation was the absolute, deafening silence from Brian Laundrie and his family. Their refusal to provide any answers soon led to real-world consequences, as protestors gathered outside their Northport home, their voices rising in anger, shouting for Brian to come out and tell them where Gabby was.

Online, users tirelessly debated the family's cold behavior. Some suggested their attorney had simply advised them to invoke their Fifth Amendment right to remain silent. But others countered this argument forcefully, pointing out that while Brian had the right to silence, his complete lack of any apparent desire to help find his missing fiancée was, in itself, a damning admission. He was the only person on Earth who could provide answers, and he was choosing to hide behind his parents and his lawyer. On September 15th, law enforcement made it official, formally naming Brian Laundrie a person of interest in Gabby's disappearance.

In response, Brian's lawyer, Steven Bertolino, released a statement that only poured gasoline on the fire. He explained that "intimate partners are often the first people law enforcement focuses their attention on" and that "any statement made will be used against you," regardless of his client's involvement. He concluded that on the advice of counsel, Mr. Laundrie would not be speaking. People saw the statement as cold, insensitive, and strategically evasive. It never once flatly denied that his client knew where Gabby was.

With direct communication rendered impossible, Gabby's family took their plea to the national stage. On September 16th, their lawyer stood before a bank of news cameras and read aloud a letter addressed directly to Christopher and Roberta Laundrie. "We believe you know the location where Brian left Gabby," the letter began. "We beg you to tell us. As a parent, how could you let us go through this pain and not help us?" The family's words were heavy with grief, reminding the Laundries that Gabby had lived with them for over a year and was set to become their daughter-in-law. "All we want is Gabby to come home," it concluded. "Please help us make that happen."

That same day, the case grew infinitely more complicated. The Moab City Police Department in Utah released bodycam footage from August 12th, just two weeks before Gabby's last known communication. Officers Danielle Robbins and Eric Pratt had pulled over Gabby's white van after a 911 call reported a domestic dispute — specifically, a man hitting a woman outside a food co-op. The footage was difficult to watch. It showed the officers separating the couple; Brian appeared preternaturally calm, while Gabby was a wreck, visibly shaking, crying, and distraught. She admitted to striking Brian and described being in a state of high stress, referencing her obsessive-compulsive disorder (OCD). Instead of probing deeper or treating the incident as a potential domestic abuse case, the officers ruled it a "mental health crisis." Their solution was to separate the couple for the night, sending Brian to a hotel and leaving a vulnerable, weeping Gabby alone in the van.

The footage went viral, and the officers faced a tidal wave of criticism. Viewers felt that if the police had truly deemed it a mental health crisis, Gabby should have been offered a hospital visit, not abandoned in the van. While some users speculated that Gabby may have been the aggressor, pointing to scratches on Brian's face, most found her behavior inconsistent with that of an abuser. They noted how she immediately took all the blame and belittled herself, while Brian seemed to be putting on a charming, calculated act for the officers. Then, the online sleuths noticed a glaring omission: there were two officers at the stop, but only one officer's footage had been released. They began to demand, loudly, that the Moab Police release Officer Pratt's footage, speculating that it contained something the department was trying to hide.

Just as the public was dissecting this disturbing video, Brian's family dropped their bombshell. On September 17th, they called the police, not with information, but with another disappearance: Brian Laundrie was missing. The news exploded online, with the public immediately voicing suspicion that he had not gone "missing" but had fled. It was then revealed that police had made a critical surveillance error. Investigators had mistakenly believed Brian was still at home because they had seen him drive off in his gray Mustang on September 13th and then saw the same car return on September 15th. They had confidently, and incorrectly, reported to the press that he was accounted for. It turned out the person who drove the car back was not Brian, but his mother, Roberta, her face partially obscured by a baseball cap.

This revelation raised a new, urgent set of questions. If Brian had been missing since the 13th, why did his parents wait until the 17th to report it — two full days after they had retrieved his car and, with it, his only means of transportation home? The Laundries claimed Brian had gone hiking in the nearby Myakkahatchee Creek Environmental Park, which borders the sprawling, 25,000-acre (about 101 square kilometers) Carlton Reserve. They said he often went there for a few days at a time to "unwind," but this time he had not returned. The location itself was forbidding — a wild, swampy, and vast expanse of Florida wilderness, an impenetrable labyrinth of dense brush, water moccasins, and alligators. A local rancher assisting with the search stated bluntly that no one could survive out there for two weeks on foot. This led to widespread speculation that the parents had pointed police to the uninhabitable reserve as a diversion, a way to fake his death and help him escape.

The official timeline was later clarified. The family's attorney, Bertolino, had in fact informed the FBI on the morning of September 14th that Brian had not returned home. It was the FBI, seeing Roberta drive the car back on the 15th, who mistakenly assumed he had returned. The family had reportedly gone to the park on the 14th, found the Mustang, and left it there for Brian. When he still hadn't returned the next day, they found the car ticketed and drove it home to prevent it from being towed.

With both Gabby and Brian now missing, investigators were desperate for leads and pleaded with the public to use the dedicated tip line. The online community mobilized, and the line was flooded with hundreds of tips per day. Amidst a torrent of false sightings and misinformation from people seemingly chasing online clout, a few credible, chilling witness accounts emerged. A woman named Nina Angelo reported seeing a couple she later identified as Gabby and Brian at the Merry Piglets Tex-Mex restaurant in Jackson, Wyoming, on August 27th — the last day Gabby's phone had contact with her mother. She described Gabby as visibly distressed and crying, while her partner was aggressive, pacing in and out of the restaurant and lashing out at the staff.

Another witness, Jessica Schultz, reported seeing the white van multiple times. On August 26th, she was driving behind it on a road in Grand Teton National Park. She saw it again, parked at a trail in Spread Creek, on the evenings of August 27th and 28th, noting it appeared to be empty. She later recognized the van from the Moab bodycam footage because of a distinctive straw hat on the dashboard, and she urged the FBI to search Spread Creek.

Then, a series of sightings placed Brian alone. On August 29th, Miranda Baker and her boyfriend picked up Brian Laundrie near Colter Bay. He told them his fiancée was back at their van working on social media content and offered them $200 for a ride to Jackson. However, when Miranda mentioned their destination was Jackson Hole, Brian "panicked" and insisted they drop him off immediately near Jackson Lake Dam. Shortly after, another driver, Norma Gene Jalivc, picked him up. He again asked for a ride to Jackson but, learning she was going the opposite way, insisted she drop him at the Spread Creek campsite where his fiancée was supposedly waiting. As she approached the entrance to the park, Brian jumped out of the car before it had even fully stopped, seemingly desperate that she not drive all the way in.

These witness accounts were compounded by the release of the original 911 call from Moab, which confirmed the caller's report: "We drove by and the gentleman was slapping the girl." This directly contradicted the narrative the officers had constructed, in which Gabby was the primary aggressor. But the most pivotal clue, the one that would break the case open, came not from a witness but from a camera lens. A traveling couple, Kyle and Jen Bethune, who documented their trips on YouTube, were reviewing their footage from late August. As they scanned their video from the evening of August 27th, they spotted it: Gabby's white Ford Transit van, parked in the Spread Creek dispersed camping area. This footage corroborated Jessica Schultz's sighting and gave investigators a precise, time-stamped location to focus their search.

On the second day of the FBI's intensive search in Spread Creek, they found a body. It was located just off a gravel road, not buried or hidden, but simply left there, abandoned to the elements. It was the moment the entire nation had been dreading. Gabby's stepfather, Jim Schmidt, who had flown to Wyoming to assist in the search, was the first to be contacted. The officers did not need to show him the body; they only had to describe the sweater she was found in. He knew, instantly, that it was her. On September 21st, the FBI made the official, heartbreaking announcement. The Teton County Coroner confirmed the remains belonged to Gabrielle Petito. The initial determination was homicide. The final autopsy would later confirm the cause of death as blunt force injuries to the head and neck, with manual strangulation.

The world's worst fears were confirmed. Gabby had been murdered, and the only person who knew the full story was gone. The following day, a federal arrest warrant was issued for Brian Laundrie. It was not for murder but for the use of unauthorized access devices. He had used Gabby's debit card between August 30th and September 1st, withdrawing about $1,000. As the manhunt for Brian reached a fever pitch, neighbors of the Laundries revealed a shocking detail: after Brian returned home alone, his parents had taken him on a family camping trip to Fort De Soto Park from September 6th to 7th, acting as if nothing was wrong. This discovery led to rampant speculation that the trip was a ruse to destroy evidence, including Gabby's missing cell phone.

On October 1st, the public finally saw why the Moab police had been so reluctant to release the second officer's bodycam footage. The new video showed Officer Pratt asking Gabby if the 911 report of Brian hitting her was true. Through heartbreaking sobs, she replied, "I guess, yeah, but I hit him first." She then added the crucial, whispered detail: "Well, he grabbed my face." The footage also captured the officers laughing about the incident with Brian, commiserating with him, and mocking Gabby's obvious distress. The disparity in treatment was chilling.

Meanwhile, the search for Brian in the Myakkahatchee and Carlton reserves had become a waterlogged, seemingly impossible task. Relentless rainstorms had submerged the entire area under water. Then, on October 20th, the park finally reopened to the public as the floodwaters began to recede. Brian's parents, Chris and Roberta, informed law enforcement they wanted to join the search that day. Shortly after they entered the park, the case came to its grim conclusion. Chris Laundrie ventured off the trail and found a dry bag belonging to his son. At roughly the same time, in a different area, authorities located a second, water-damaged backpack near human skeletal remains. Also at the scene were a rusted revolver, a white metal ring, and a wilted notebook. The remains showed a clear bullet wound to the skull. The following day, dental records confirmed the remains were Brian Laundrie's. His death was officially deemed self-inflicted.

Investigators hoped the notebook, damaged but partially legible, would provide the final answers. Inside, Brian had written his final, self-serving story. He claimed the death was an "unexpected tragedy." He wrote that while rushing to cross Spread Creek, Gabby fell and was gravely injured. He claimed she had a growing bump on her forehead, was freezing cold, and was "begging for an end to her pain." "I ended her life," he wrote. "I thought it was merciful, that it is what she wanted."

This confession, however, was immediately scrutinized and dismantled by the public and investigators, who found it riddled with glaring inconsistencies. The couple was not far from their van, and cell service was available in the area; he could have called 911. Furthermore, the severe injuries he described in the note were not found in Gabby's autopsy report. The timeline also directly contradicted his story. Gabby's last text and laptop activity on the night of August 27th indicated she was alive and well in the van, not dying of injuries in a creek. The very next day, August 28th, Brian was already on the phone with his parents and hiring a lawyer. He was also discovered to have been texting himself between his and Gabby's phones in an attempt to create a false alibi. He sent the deceptive "Stan" text on August 30th and used her card to Zelle himself $700 with the note, "Goodbye, Brian." The evidence was overwhelming: his confession was a lie, crafted to paint a killer as a merciful partner.

While the case was officially closed, several mysteries lingered, fueling continued online debate. Some theories suggested Brian had faked his death, though these were largely disproven by the DNA analysis and the advanced decomposition of the remains, which was consistent with being submerged in a swamp for weeks. A more persistent theory, one publicly shared by Gabby's own mother, was that Brian's parents were somehow involved in his death. Suspicion centered on the fact that his remains were found so quickly on the very day his parents joined the search. This, however, was likely a grim coincidence, as the floodwaters had only just receded that day, finally making the previously inaccessible area searchable.

One discrepancy, however, remains stubbornly unexplained. The autopsy determined the fatal gunshot wound was to Brian's left side. Yet, according to his sister and autopsy confirmations, Brian was right-hand dominant. A retired FBI agent, Jennifer Coffender, commented that this was "bothersome" and statistically inconsistent with a self-inflicted wound. She offered three possibilities: Brian was ambidextrous, he was holding something in his right hand, or the gun was held by someone else.

The suspicion surrounding the Laundries was further cemented by the discovery of an undated letter from Roberta to Brian, found among his belongings from the van. The letter was ominously marked "Burn after reading." In it, she made a dark promise: "If you're in jail, I will bake a cake with a file in it. If you need to dispose of a body, I will show up with a shovel and garbage bags." Roberta insisted the letter was written long before the trip and had no connection to Gabby. While the Petito family lawyer argued the content suggested it was written after the murder, its location in the van's belongings makes it more likely it was written before. Regardless of the timing, the letter demonstrated a chilling, enabling attitude that many felt explained the family's actions.

In the aftermath, the Petito family filed a $3 million wrongful death settlement, which was approved in November 2022. A separate civil suit against the Laundries for emotional distress, claiming they knew Brian had murdered Gabby while they were issuing messages of hope, was settled privately. Every dollar recovered from these lawsuits went directly to the Gabby Petito Foundation.

Gabby Petito's family created a foundation after her death to support searches for missing persons from overlooked communities and assist survivors of domestic violence. Her case's intense media attention had revealed that many other missing persons were previously ignored, highlighting disparities in law enforcement focus. In 2024, the Gabby Petito Act was enacted in Florida, requiring officers to conduct standardized lethality assessments during domestic violence calls — a measure that came too late for Gabby but aims to protect others in her memory.

36

THE WORM THAT TURNED

On the outside, they were the perfect family. Rahan Arshad was a thirty-six-year-old taxi driver, a husband, and a father of three young children who filled their quiet home in Cheadle Hulme, Manchester, with laughter. But behind the closed doors of the house on Turves Road, a different story was unfolding. It was a narrative poisoned by jealousy, paranoia, and a suffocating need for control, one that was about to explode into one of the most shocking family murders in modern British history.

The end began on July 28th, 2006. On that day, Rahan Arshad, consumed by a rage he had been nurturing for years, picked up a rounder's bat. He first went to the bedroom, where he confronted his thirty-two-year-old wife, Uzma Rahan. He bludgeoned her to death, striking her with such ferocity — more than twenty-three times — that investigators would later describe it as one of the most brutal domestic killings they had ever witnessed. His violence, however, was not over. He then went to his children and brought eleven-year-old Adam, eight-year-old Abbas, and six-year-old Henna downstairs to their playroom and, one by one, beat them to death with the same bat.

After slaughtering his entire family, Arshad did not panic. He did not call the police. Instead, he calmly packed his bags, cleaned his car, and drove to London's Heathrow Airport. He had planned his escape with chilling foresight. More than two weeks earlier, he had booked a one-way ticket to Thailand. The day before the murders, he had purchased the rounder's bat. He had even told his family and friends that he was taking Uzma and the children on holiday to Dubai. This lie was his final, cruel masterstroke. On Saturday, July 29th, he boarded his flight and fled the country, leaving the bodies of his wife and three children to decompose inside the sealed family home.

For nearly four weeks, the house on Turves Road stood silent. Neighbors noticed the family was gone but assumed they were on their promised holiday in Dubai. Friends wondered why Uzma, who was normally so communicative, had not called. But as August wore on, a foul stench began to emanate from the property, a smell so overpowering it finally led concerned neighbors to contact the police.

On Sunday, August 20th, 2006, officers arrived and forced their way inside. They were met with a nightmare frozen in time. The bodies of Uzma, Adam, Abbas, and Henna were discovered where they had been slain. They were so badly decomposed after weeks in the summer heat that police would need to use dental records just to formally confirm their identities. The devastating murders of a mother and her three children shocked the entire community.

An immediate manhunt was launched for Rahan Arshad, who was now the sole suspect. Police discovered his BMW 320 car abandoned at Heathrow Airport, confirming he had fled the country. Detectives from Greater Manchester Police, working with Interpol, quickly traced his flight to Bangkok, Thailand. They issued an international appeal, and Arshad's own brother, Razan, made a public plea for him to surrender.

The search intensified, with authorities in Thailand on high alert. The breakthrough came on August 30th, 2006, just over a month after the murders. Rahan Arshad was questioned by Thai authorities at the Thai-Malaysian border as he was attempting to re-enter Thailand. He agreed to return to the United Kingdom voluntarily and was flown from Bangkok to Heathrow, where he was met by detectives as he stepped off the plane. He was immediately arrested on suspicion of four counts of murder and transported to Manchester for questioning.

Upon his arrest, Arshad displayed no hint of remorse. His confession to the officers was calm and detached, leaving no doubt about his guilt. He admitted to the murders in chillingly vulgar terms, expressing brief sorrow only for his children before reverting to cold indifference. Detectives later noted that this fleeting moment was the only sign of emotion he ever showed. Afterward, he refused to answer any further questions.

His trial at Manchester Crown Court began in early 2007. Despite his initial confession, Arshad pleaded not guilty to all four counts of murder. He presented the jury with a desperate, fabricated story: he claimed he had returned home to find that his wife, Uzma, had bludgeoned their three children to death, and that he, in a fit of rage, had then killed her.

The prosecution systematically dismantled his defense, painting a portrait not of a grieving father, but of a cold and calculating killer. The jury heard how Arshad had been consumed by jealousy. During his own testimony, Arshad claimed he was "the worm that turned," attempting to portray himself as a long-suffering victim. He described his wife as a "bad-tempered, materialistic spendaholic" who constantly put him down and thought herself superior. He said he struggled to keep her in the lifestyle she demanded, working long hours as a private hire driver. He told the jury he "adored her," but his words were laced with resentment and a deep-seated need for control.

He grew increasingly angry over her new preference for Western-style clothing, often criticizing her for wearing tight jeans and tops, which he claimed were inappropriate for a Pakistani mother. Their marriage — an arranged union between first cousins who had never met before — had long been troubled. His paranoia focused on the belief that Uzma was being unfaithful. He said his suspicions began when she received phone calls during shopping trips and told the caller she couldn't talk because she was with her husband. Uzma, who worked part-time as a beautician, maintained that these were simply work-related calls. Arshad later claimed to have seen text messages that confirmed his fears, though she continued to deny any affair.

The court learned that his paranoia was, in fact, based in reality. Uzma had indeed begun an affair with a neighbor's husband, a man named Nikki. But the affair was a symptom of a marriage that was already broken, largely by Arshad's own actions. In February 2004, while Uzma was in Pakistan grieving the death of her father, Arshad decided to "teach her a lesson." He sold their family home, flew to Lahore, dumped their three children with her, and then filed fake divorce papers before going traveling. He even allegedly married another woman, a claim he denied in court. He would later admit this was a big, massive mistake.

After his travels, Arshad claimed he wanted a reconciliation. Uzma's brother, Rahhat Ali, acted as a mediator, and Arshad agreed to buy a new house on Turves Road, putting the property in both their names. But the reconciliation was a sham, a final, desperate act of control. He embarked on a lavish spending spree to win her back, but his gestures were empty and laced with deceit. He bought a £30,000 (about $35,000) BMW 320, telling Uzma it was an early birthday present. In reality, he had bought it on hire-purchase, paid only one installment, and insured it solely in his own name. He bought a new computer for the children, gold jewelry for his wife, and redecorated the house with new wardrobes and carpets.

The sudden burst of generosity did nothing to ease Uzma's fears. She wasn't confused — she was frightened. To those closest to her, she revealed her growing dread, her words carrying an eerie sense of inevitability. She told friends that her husband had either truly changed or was on the verge of killing her. To one, she said grimly, "Count the days until he kills me."

The prosecution presented the jury with the evidence of his cold premeditation: the rounder's bat purchased the day before the killings, and the plane ticket to Thailand booked two weeks in advance. The jury did not believe his story for a second. On March 13th, 2007, Rahan Arshad was found guilty on all four counts of murder.

When the verdicts were announced, the courtroom was heavy with emotion. In the public gallery, Uzma's mother and two brothers sat together, their grief and anger barely contained. Her brother, Rahhat Ali, cried out as the guilty verdict was delivered, his voice breaking the tense silence. Judge David Clark addressed Arshad directly, calling the evidence against him "overwhelming." He condemned Arshad's actions as acts of "great brutality," describing how he had beaten his wife to death in their bedroom before coldly leading his sleepy children downstairs to kill them as well. The judge noted there was no indication of mental illness, declaring that life imprisonment would truly mean life. Rahan Arshad was sentenced to spend the rest of his days behind bars, with no possibility of release.

After the hearing, Detective Superintendent Martin Bottomley, who led the investigation, called the case one of the most brutal and devastating murders he had ever encountered. He then read a statement from Uzma's grieving family, their words capturing the depth of their loss. They spoke of Uzma as a best friend, a beloved sister, and a devoted daughter whose absence had left a void no one could fill. Her mother, they said, could not comprehend how Arshad could destroy the very family he was meant to protect. The statement ended with a final, resolute sentiment — relief that justice had ensured he would never walk free again.

The murders sent shockwaves through the community, leaving friends and neighbors struggling to comprehend the horror that had unfolded behind closed doors. To those who knew the family, Arshad had always appeared to be a devoted husband and a doting father who adored his children. His closest friend told reporters he could not believe Arshad was capable of violence, insisting there was "no way he would ever hurt those kids." At the school where Uzma worked as a dinner lady and where the children were pupils, the grief was equally profound. Staff and parents remembered the children as kind and well-mannered, and Uzma as a respected, gentle woman who brightened the lives of those around her.

Behind the facade of a happy, ordinary household lay a man consumed by jealousy, paranoia, and a desire for absolute control — an obsession that culminated in one of the most horrific family murders in modern British history. The brutality of his actions, the calculated planning, and the cold detachment he displayed left a community reeling and a family irreparably shattered. For Uzma, Adam, Abbas, and Henna, there was no escape from the violence within their own home. For Arshad, justice was swift and unyielding, ensuring he would never have the opportunity to harm again. The case would leave an enduring mark, not only on the city of Manchester but on all who struggle to understand how a man so seemingly ordinary could commit such an unspeakable atrocity.

37

THE YERBA BUENA CULT

Yerba Buena, a communal farming settlement at the edge of the Sierra Madre in the early 1960s, was small enough that a newcomer's footsteps carried. Fewer than a hundred people lived there, arranged in a handful of families who had been sent to establish cropland for the state of Guanajuato. The village had no police post, no school, no phones, no electricity, and no formal government presence. People were skilled at agriculture and short on money, literacy, and outside contact. In 1962, brothers Santos and Cayetano Hernández arrived as strangers and immediately became the center of attention because strangers were rare. They had spent years roaming Mexico with petty frauds and amateur magic, and they had decided they wanted something larger and more lucrative. In Yerba Buena, they saw isolation and vulnerability and moved to occupy the space.

The brothers announced that they were prophets of ancient gods and that the community had been chosen. If everyone obeyed, the gods would reveal treasure hidden in the nearby mountains; if anyone refused, the gods would punish heresy. The promise made use of a popular regional myth about gold in the hills. To dress the claim, the brothers performed simple stagecraft, the same sleights of hand they had used to sell smaller cons elsewhere. The villagers, who already believed in the possibility of treasure, turned over their savings and personal valuables and installed the men in the best hut, at the mouth of a cave that would become the center of ritual life. In short order, the brothers were being fed and waited upon. Money was thin in Yerba Buena, and the initial take disappointed them. They pivoted to sex and control.

Santos and Cayetano began selecting girls — typically fourteen to sixteen — and told parents that the gods had commanded sexual initiation as part of divine instruction. The girls were abused and then sold into brothels in nearby towns, generating cash. The brothers also forced adult women and some men to serve as sex slaves. With their authority fixed in daily life, they moved the community's focus into the cave and built a pattern of ceremonies: incense and chants, peyote tea passed from hand to hand, marijuana smoke, the slaughter of a goat by throat-cutting, and then an orgy conducted on the cave floor. The setting was damp and dark, and the logic was simple — ritual obedience would bring treasure.

As weeks passed without the promised reward, villagers began to talk. Doubt spread quietly, and word reached the brothers. They needed to pull the village back under tight control. They left for Monterrey to see an associate from their trafficking business, a local pimp named Eleazar Solís. The idea was to return to Yerba Buena with a woman who could appear as an incarnate goddess, a living sign that the prophets had, in fact, been in contact with the supernatural. Eleazar said he had someone perfect for the role: his eighteen-year-old sister, Magdalena Solís. There is very little about her early life beyond the fact that she had been forced into sex work at twelve and that she sometimes worked as a fortune-teller and medium, selling contact with the dead. The brothers explained the scheme, and Eleazar and Magdalena agreed. A role offering constant deference and a change of circumstances was attractive.

They chose an Aztec figure this time — a correction from the brothers' earlier confusion between Andean and Mesoamerican pantheons — and prepared Magdalena to appear as Coatlicue. They dressed her with a headdress and bones, built the scene, and included Eleazar as "high priest." The brothers, still planning to be ultimate decision-makers, would continue as prophets. On the appointed night the villagers filed into the cave. The familiar sequence began: chanting, incense, peyote. Then a third man announced himself as a high priest of the ancient goddess. Flash powder ignited, smoke filled the cave and when it cleared, Magdalena stood where no one had been a moment before. The villagers fell to their knees, convinced the gods had, at last, responded.

For a short while, the structure remained the same. Magdalena presided over ceremonies that looked like the old ones: drugs, sacrifice, and sex. But the social dynamic changed quickly. Worship and deference concentrated on her. The villagers brought her needs and waited for her in the hut. She took sex slaves for herself. In a matter of days the attention hardened into conviction; she began to believe the role and the chain of command inverted. Instead of advising and directing the pageant from behind the scenes, Santos and Cayetano found themselves on the outside of the true authority. Even Eleazar's claims as brother and handler fell away. Magdalena had the village, and with it the capacity to command.

With that shift came new practices. She replaced peyote tea with blood mixed into a ceremonial cup. At first she cut herself to provide it, blending her blood with the hallucinogen and passing the vessel around. Then the rites changed tone. During ceremonies, she forced participants into acts designed to obliterate taboo: incest, bestiality, sexual assaults on children. The point was not only gratification but proof of control. If she could order what people had never imagined doing and watch them do it, she knew there was nothing beyond her reach. But soon the objections started to come when two villagers questioned the direction of the cult. Not having any of this, Magdalena had them lynched. Their deaths, carried out by their neighbors, reset the terms of disagreement inside a tiny community where every family was tied to every other.

From that moment human sacrifice replaced animal sacrifice. The records are unclear about the numbers, and mostly, identify at least six victims later found dismembered in the caves, with possibilities as high as fifteen or sixteen. Selection was described in two ways by sources: sometimes random, sometimes aimed at those who thought to harbor doubts or plans to leave. However chosen, victims were cut apart, blood was drained, mixed with chicken blood and peyote, and passed to the congregation. Orgies followed. Hearts were torn from chests; in some cases, the victims were still alive when the chest was opened. The cadence of ceremonies settled: assemble, ingest, kill, drink, dismember, copulate, disperse. This phase lasted roughly six weeks.

On the night of May 31, 1963, a fourteen-year-old boy named Sebastián Guerrero was moving through the area around Yerba Buena. He had no connection to the village and knew nothing about the cult. He saw lights flickering in a cave and went to see what was there. As he approached, he heard sounds he later described as part human, part wild animal. Inside, he hid behind a rock and watched a woman at an altar holding what looked like a human heart. People on the floor were engaged in sexual acts. A chalice passed from hand to hand. On the altar lay a dismembered body. When Sebastián understood what he was seeing, he ran, fifteen miles (about twenty-five kilometers) to the nearest police station in Vallegrande and told officers what he had witnessed.

At first the officers doubted the story because it sounded impossible. Sebastián insisted. An officer named Luis Martínez volunteered to check. He and the boy drove toward Yerba Buena and did not return. After a day without contact, colleagues reported Martínez missing and asked the state to open an investigation. Officers canvassed the region's fringe settlements and heard consistent rumors about ancient ceremonies and devil worship in the caves near the village. The pattern in the reports matched Sebastián's account. Police requested military support. A joint force moved on Yerba Buena.

They went straight to the farmhouse where Magdalena and Eleazar were living. Inside, they were found both in bed and heavily intoxicated. Santos ran from the house and a pursuit began. During the exchange of gunfire, police shot and killed him. Searches of the house and grounds found the bodies of Sebastián Guerrero and Officer Luis Martínez. Martínez's chest had been opened and his heart removed. His brother, Cayetano, was already dead, killed by cult member Jesús Rubio, who later said he wanted a piece of the high priest's body as protection. Several cultists who had barricaded themselves inside a cave died in ensuing shootouts.

With the principal figures accounted for, police and soldiers searched the cave complex. They recovered the physical evidence that matched Sebastián's description: ritual arrangements, blood traces, and bodies. Six dismembered victims were found there. The arrests included Magdalena and Eleazar and a number of villagers. Prosecutors sought testimony from members of the cult to build a broad case against the leadership for multiple murders. No one agreed to testify. Whether out of loyalty, fear, or both, the villagers stayed silent. The absence of insider witnesses shaped the charges. Magdalena and Eleazar were tried for the murders of Sebastián Guerrero and Officer Luis Martínez. They were convicted and sentenced to fifty years in prison. Several villagers were convicted of gang murder and lynching and received thirty-year sentences. By the calendar, Magdalena's term would have ended in 2013 but no reliable public update exists on her status; it has been speculated that she died in prison.

What happened in Yerba Buena did not depend on elaborate theology, only on the conviction that an authority stood above question and could be enforced in a dark place at a distance from ordinary scrutiny. The cave was close to the village in miles and far from it in every other way. When soldiers and police walked its floor after the raid and counted bodies, the distance collapsed. Everything that had been done in secrecy was measured. The rest was the work of courts and calendars. The village returned to itself with the knowledge of what had happened inside it. The record that remains is spare: names, places, sequences, sentences — but it is enough.

38

THE MONSTER WITH 21 FACES

The evening of March 18, 1984, began like any other for Katsuhisa Ezaki. As the president of Ezaki Glico, one of Japan's largest and most beloved candy manufacturers, his life was one of success and routine. He was in his home in Osaka, enjoying a quiet evening bath, when that routine was violently interrupted. Two hooded, armed assailants suddenly burst into his home, stormed the bathroom, and kidnapped the naked executive. The audacious crime marked the beginning of a bizarre and theatrical extortion campaign that would baffle Japanese authorities and hold the entire nation in a state of anxious fascination for seventeen months.

The day after the abduction, a ransom note arrived. The demand was staggering: 1 billion yen (about $6.5 million) and 100 kilograms of gold worth about $10 million. The kidnappers specified a drop-off at a particular phone booth, but the elaborate plan collapsed almost immediately. Just two days after his capture, before any money could be paid, Ezaki escaped. In a dramatic account of his break for freedom, he described how he managed to loosen his bindings, break down a door of the isolated warehouse where he was being held, and find two railroad employees who helped him contact the police. He was still wearing the clothes his assailants had given him. While Ezaki was safe, the ordeal was far from over. He had no idea who his captors were, and they, it turned out, were just getting started.

Though their initial kidnapping plot had failed, the perpetrators simply shifted their tactics. They issued a new demand for $480,000, but this time, the threat was aimed not just at the company's president, but at the public itself. If the money was not paid, they would begin poisoning Glico candies with potassium cyanide. To prove their seriousness, the group reportedly snuck into Glico headquarters and set some of the property on fire. The escalation from a targeted kidnapping to a threat of mass public poisoning was a shocking development, one that left authorities scrambling.

Despite the growing list of crimes, authorities were at a loss. In the Japan of the 1980s, an unsolved case of this magnitude was a rarity and a professional embarrassment. The Japanese police force was famously effective; in 1983, they had solved 97.1% of all murder cases and 55.3% of thefts, statistics that dwarfed the clearance rates in the United States. Failing to get to the bottom of the Glico case was seen as a public failure, a "black eye" on the police's stellar reputation. The *Yomiuri* newspaper ran an editorial that captured the growing public sentiment, stating, "We do not recall a case in which criminals have made such fools of the police."

Perhaps no one was more frustrated by the police's incompetence than the criminals themselves. On April 8, 1984, the press received the first of what would become over 100 letters sent over the next year and a half. The letter was a masterpiece of public taunting, addressed "To the stupid police." It openly mocked their efforts, asking if they were idiots and stating that if they were professionals, the case would already be solved. Because the police had such a high handicap, the letter offered to provide some hints. The writers proceeded to debunk the prevailing theories, clarifying that the kidnapping was not an inside job and that the owners of the warehouse Ezaki escaped from were not involved. They even offered new clues, stating that the car they used was gray and naming the grocery store where they bought their food. The letter ended with a final barb, suggesting that if the police could not catch them with this much information, they were just thieves of taxpayer money, and perhaps the criminals should kidnap the head of the prefectural police instead.

The letters continued to pour in, each one a public performance. Critics at the time categorized the group's actions as *gekijo hanzai,* or "crime as theater." The group had a brilliant knack for capturing public attention and leveraged the media to ensure their threats and taunts were widely reported. The letters often provided seemingly specific but ultimately useless details, such as the exact gate they used to enter a factory or the model of typewriter they were using. None of the clues ever led to a breakthrough, and all the physical evidence left at the crime scenes was either stolen or mass-produced, rendering it untraceable. The police looked more and more incompetent. The only clue that seemed to hold any weight was linguistic; the dialect used in the letters pointed to someone from the Osaka region. But this theory, while interesting, did not bring authorities any closer to an arrest.

By June of 1984, the criminals had given themselves a name, one drawn directly from Japanese popular fiction. In their letters, they began referring to themselves as *Kainin Nijūichi Mensō* — The Monster with 21 Faces. It was a direct reference to a 1936 children's story by the famed mystery writer Edogawa Rampo, titled "The Mystery Man with the 21 Faces." The name was fitting. Rampo's story featured a master thief who stirred up the newspapers daily and was so adept at disguise that he could be anyone. One excerpt from the story seemed to describe the group's philosophy perfectly. It told of a gang that, without fail, would send a letter of warning announcing the date, place, and object of their planned crime. They did this, the story suggested, either because they did not want an unfair battle or simply to show that no matter how many precautions are taken, they can still commit the crime with their great skill. The fictional thief had become a real-world boogeyman.

After months of tormenting Glico, the Monster with 21 Faces expanded its operations. In September 1984, another major Japanese confectioner, Morinaga & Company, began receiving extortion letters. The group threatened unspecified action if they did not receive $410,000. According to police, Morinaga refused to pay. The Monster's response would be their most terrifying act yet.

On October 8, Japanese newspapers received a chilling new letter, this one addressed "To moms throughout Japan." It began with a mocking tone, noting that in autumn, when appetites are strong, sweets are delicious. It then declared that when thinking of sweets, one thinks of Morinaga. "We've added some special flavor," the letter continued, "The flavor of potassium cyanide is a little bitter." The Monster announced they had placed twenty boxes of these "bitter sweets" in stores from Hakata to Tokyo, and that they had attached a notice on them that they contained poison.

That same day, a frantic search began. Sure enough, packages of Morinaga cookies and candy were discovered in grocery stores across Japan. Attached to them were typewritten labels that read, "Danger. Cyanide!" In total, eighteen packages were found, one in a supermarket just thirty-five yards (about thirty-two meters) from Katsuhisa Ezaki's home. When tested, not all contained cyanide, but at least one was found to contain a lethal dose. Thanks to the warning labels, no one was harmed. But the letter that warned of the tainted sweets also contained a far more sinister threat: the next time, there would be thirty boxes, and they would not be labeled.

The threat of unlabeled, poisoned candy sent a wave of panic across the country. For the next two weekends, a reported 40,000 police officers staked out grocery stores, a massive and desperate mobilization. The stakeouts yielded nothing. Thankfully, it did not appear the group ever went through with their threat of unlabeled poison.

Investigators did, however, find two new potential clues. The first was surveillance video from October 7, the day before the poison letter arrived. It showed a suspect with permed hair, glasses, and a baseball hat placing something on a shelf where poisoned candy was later found. But this promising lead quickly dissolved. The camera was bad, the lighting was poor, and the security tape had not been changed in over a year, resulting in a grainy, useless image. Photos of this "Video Man," as he came to be known, were released to the public, but he was never identified.

The second clue was a set of audio recordings from phone calls attempting to extort money. When released, the public was disturbed to hear that the voices on the tapes were not those of hardened gangsters but of a woman and a child. At one point, the child's voice could be heard giving clear instructions for a money drop, telling the company representative to leave the money "behind the seat of the bus stop bench." The involvement of a woman and child forced everyone to reconsider just who, or what, the Monster with 21 Faces truly was.

By March 1985, a full year after the kidnapping of Ezaki, the list of harassed companies had grown to thirty-one. Japan's finest detectives were still completely baffled. On several occasions, a company would actually pull together the demanded ransom, but the Monster with 21 Faces never picked it up. They seemed to have an uncanny ability to spot a trap. In one instance, the group instructed Glico representatives to wait for a phone call at a specific truck stop. Plainclothes policemen went in their place, but the call never came. The follow-up letter from the Monster was particularly humiliating. They mocked the police for thinking they could be fooled, dressed up in their "nice businessmen's blue suits." The group wrote that they could tell immediately they were cops, that "those shifty eyes gave you away." At every turn, the Monster was one step ahead.

Then, as abruptly as it began, it was over. On August 12, 1985, a year and a half after they first kidnapped a candy man from his bathtub, the Monster with 21 Faces sent their final letter. They announced they were stopping. The case had become one of the largest and most expensive in Japanese history. According to Japan's National Police Agency, authorities had received over 28,000 tips and had utilized over 130,000 police officers in the investigation. And they had nothing.

The economic damage was immense. A year after the kidnapping, the Japanese Ministry of Agriculture claimed sweets consumption across the country was down 10%. Both Ezaki Glico and Morinaga suffered massive losses. After the public poisoning threat, all Glico products were pulled from the shelves, forcing the company to temporarily shut down production and lay off two-thirds of its part-time employees. Morinaga's sales were estimated to have plummeted by as much as 60%. The Monster had failed to collect a single yen in ransom, but they had cost the corporations millions and terrorized the public.

In the aftermath, with a stack of taunting letters and a humiliated police force, theories about the Monster's identity flourished. The first, and one of the most popular at the beginning of the crime wave, was that the entire affair was an inside job, and that Katsuhisa Ezaki himself was in on the plot. This theory was based almost entirely on public disbelief that Ezaki had been able to escape his kidnappers so easily. However, no actual evidence ever surfaced to support this. Furthermore, the theory buckled under logical scrutiny. Glico's business was devastated by the ordeal. It made little sense for Ezaki to orchestrate a scheme that involved setting his own property on fire, pulling all of his products from the shelves, and laying off a huge portion of his workforce.

A second, more compelling theory pointed to an act of long-simmering revenge. Nearly thirty years earlier, in 1955, the Morinaga company had been at the center of a horrific tragedy. A stabilizing agent used in their dry milk product was accidentally contaminated with arsenic. By 1956, over 12,000 infants had been injured and 138 had died from the poisoning. A 1969 report showed that survivors continued to suffer related ailments. By the time the Monster began its campaign in 1984, the survivors of the dry milk incident would have been in their late twenties or early thirties, perhaps, this theory suggested, ready to seek revenge on the company that had poisoned them. This, however, failed to explain the full scope of the crimes. Why would a group seeking revenge on Morinaga target Ezaki Glico first and most aggressively, and why would they go on to harass dozens of other unrelated food companies?

The final and most tantalizing theory centers on a single man: Manabu Miyazaki. In November 1984, a drop of 100 million yen (about $650 million) was arranged in Kyoto. Police surveilling the drop-off spotted a suspicious man, later described as the "fox-eyed man," and gave chase. In what had become a predictable pattern, the suspect eluded capture. The police did, however, find the stolen car he had been driving, and inside was a police scanner, explaining how the group had stayed one step ahead. In January, authorities released a police sketch of the "fox-eyed man." The likeness was reportedly so strong that it led to his identification as Manabu Miyazaki. Even Miyazaki's own mother, who happened to be from Osaka, allegedly believed the sketch was of her son.

Miyazaki fit the profile. He was the son of a yakuza boss, a known criminal who had organized anti-police actions in college and had already been arrested several times. It seemed the police had finally made a face-saving break in the case, but charges were never brought against him. Miyazaki apparently produced a rock-solid alibi, and no hard evidence ever tied him to the case.

Miyazaki would later write a memoir detailing his life of crime. The book was released, perhaps tellingly, shortly after the statute of limitations for the Monster with 21 Faces case had expired. The cover of the book was the very police sketch that had made him famous. Though he confessed to other crimes, Miyazaki never mentioned any involvement in the 21 Faces spree. But in a final, ironic twist, the book went on to earn the known criminal over 100 million yen (about $650 million) — a sum comparable to the ransoms he was suspected of trying to collect.

In the end, the Monster with 21 Faces got away with it. Even with the statute of limitations long expired, no one has ever come forward to claim responsibility. The identities of the group members, their true motives, and the face of the man in the surveillance video all remain a mystery. Unless the real faces behind the crime someday decide to reveal themselves, the case of the Monster with 21 Faces remains one of Japan's most fascinating and audacious unsolved crimes.

39

THE GIRL WHO CARRIED A SKULL

On the crisp, cold morning of January 13, 1995, a husband and wife were out for their routine jog along the wooded trails near the University of Tennessee's agricultural campus in Knoxville. As they moved through the quiet landscape, their conversation was cut short by a jarring sight. Splattered across the path, stark against the dead winter leaves, was something unmistakably red. It was blood. In a more secluded, wooded section of the trail, they saw that the splatters formed a grim path leading away from the trail and into the gray, thickening trees of the park. They called over a nearby groundskeeper, and together, the three of them followed the trail of blood deeper into the woods. It led them to a scene of unimaginable horror. Lying in a muddy clearing was the battered and bloody corpse of a young woman.

The police were called, and the area was quickly cordoned off. The crime scene was extensive, a chaotic tableau of violence. There were signs of a desperate struggle: broken foliage, multiple footprints churned into the mud, and discarded articles of clothing strewn about. A large pool of blood was found about thirty feet (ten meters) from where the body lay, suggesting the victim had been attacked, had managed to fight off her assailants and run, only to be overcome and dragged back to her final resting place. The woman, nude from the waist up, had been subjected to a brutal and prolonged assault. Her head had been bludgeoned, her face and body were covered in cuts, and her throat had been slashed. But it was the final, deliberate mutilation that spoke to a motive beyond simple violence. Carved deep into the victim's chest was a pentagram. This was not just a murder; it was a ritual.

The epicenter of this dark story was the Knoxville Job Corps, a federally funded educational program located just off Dale Avenue. In the mid-1990s, Job Corps centers across the country served as a last chance for young people, typically from low-income or troubled backgrounds, who had dropped out of high school and were seeking a way to get their lives back on track. The Knoxville center, however, had developed a notorious reputation for crime, drugs, and mismanagement. In fact, the murder that January morning would be the final straw, the horrific event that would lead to the center's permanent closure just a few months later. It was this troubled institution that brought together the three central figures of the crime: a victim looking for a future, and two killers bound by a shared obsession with the occult.

Christa Pike was born in West Virginia in March 1976, into a world that offered her little in the way of stability. Her mother was an alcoholic, and her father was largely absent, leaving Christa to be raised by her grandmother. For a time, under her grandmother's care, she was a bright and promising young girl. But when she was twelve, her grandmother passed away, and Christa was forced to return to her mother's chaotic and destructive orbit. Her life quickly spiraled downward. Her mother introduced her to drugs at a young age, she dropped out of school, and she was arrested numerous times for stealing, eventually landing in juvenile detention. But by the time she was seventeen, she claimed she wanted to change her ways. The Job Corps was going to be her path to a different life. She moved to the dorms in Knoxville with the stated goal of studying to become a nurse. In reality, she had little interest in hitting the books. She was far more interested in the social scene, and in one young man in particular.

At the Job Corps center, Christa met and fell deeply in love with Tadaryl Shipp. Like Christa, Tadaryl had a rough upbringing. He had grown up in Memphis, dropped out of school at a young age, and had been involved with gangs. He, too, had come to Job Corps in an effort to turn his life around, enrolling in the culinary arts program with the dream of becoming a chef. But Tadaryl had a dark side, an intense fascination with Satanism, the occult, and all things demonic. He kept a small shrine to Satan in his dorm room, and it was over this shared interest that he and Christa bonded. They became inseparable, attached at the hip, spending their time performing seances, chanting, and poring over occult texts. She became, in her own words, his "little devil." Their twisted romance was the crucible in which the murder would be forged.

Into this volatile mix walked Colleen Slemmer. Originally from Jacksonville, Florida, Colleen did not have the same troubled background as Christa and Tadaryl. She was at Job Corps to study computer technology, a quiet and unassuming nineteen-year-old focused on building a future for herself. But from the moment Colleen arrived, Christa saw her not as a fellow student but as a rival. She became convinced, with a jealousy that quickly festered into paranoid obsession, that Colleen was trying to steal Tadaryl away from her. Colleen and her friends vehemently denied this, but Christa's perception was her reality, and that reality was becoming increasingly violent.

After the students returned from the Christmas break in early 1995, Christa's rage toward Colleen reached a boiling point. On January 11th, she confided in a friend named Kim, telling her that she was going to kill Colleen because, as she put it, "she just felt mean that day." The next day, January 12th, Christa put her plan into motion. She enlisted Tadaryl and another friend, Shidola Peterson — who was also interested in Satanism — to help her. That evening, around 8:00 p.m., the trio lured Colleen away from the dorms with a promise of smoking marijuana together. They walked for about twenty minutes, making their way to the secluded, wooded trails of the nearby university agricultural campus.

Christa would later claim that she had only planned on fighting Colleen, roughing her up a bit to warn her away from Tadaryl. But she admitted to bringing a box cutter with her. Shidola Peterson was posted as a lookout, and in the dark woods, the attack began. It was not a fight; it was a methodical and sadistic torture session that lasted for nearly an hour. Christa and Tadaryl unleashed a torrent of violence on the terrified young woman. As Colleen pleaded for her life, Christa slashed at her with the box cutter and beat her relentlessly. Each time Colleen managed to break free and run, Tadaryl would chase her down and drag her back. At one point, they grabbed a large, heavy chunk of asphalt and slammed it into her head multiple times, fracturing her skull.

According to Shidola, who would later turn state's witness, the attack was not just a spontaneous burst of jealous rage. She testified that days earlier, she had overheard Christa and Tadaryl talking about wanting to perform a human sacrifice for the devil, and Colleen's name had come up. In the woods that night, Christa seemed to be channeling something dark and otherworldly, later claiming that she had heard voices telling her what to do. As Colleen lay dying, Christa and Tadaryl carved the pentagram into her chest. It took a long time for Colleen to die. When it was finally over, Christa took a final, gruesome souvenir: she used a piece of the asphalt to break off a small piece of Colleen's shattered skull, which she wrapped up and put in her pocket.

Around 10:00 p.m., two hours after they had left the dorms, Christa, Tadaryl, and Shidola returned. Colleen was not with them. Later that night, Christa went to her friend Kim's room. In a state of manic excitement, she confessed to the murder, laughing, singing, and dancing as she recounted the horrific details. To prove her story, she proudly showed Kim the piece of Colleen's skull she had taken. Her lack of remorse was absolute and chilling. The very next morning, around the same time that the joggers were discovering Colleen's body, Christa was in the Job Corps cafeteria, brazenly showing off her grisly souvenir to other students while she ate breakfast. She was overheard telling another student, in reference to her shoes, "That's not mud, that's blood." Her complete inability to conceal her crime, or perhaps her overwhelming need to brag about it, would lead to her swift capture. One of the students she had boasted to called their mother, who immediately called the police.

The investigation, which had barely begun at the crime scene, now had a clear direction. Detectives arrived at the Job Corps center and, after confirming that Colleen Slemmer was missing, they consulted the dormitory's sign-out logs. The records showed that Christa, Tadaryl, and Shidola had all checked out and back in at the exact same time on the night of the murder. Colleen had only checked out. On January 15th, the police brought them in for questioning. During a search of their rooms, they found Tadaryl's satanic shrine. Faced with the evidence and the testimony of the students Christa had confessed to, all of them were arrested and charged with first-degree murder. They did not deny their involvement. Christa, in particular, seemed almost proud of what she had done, even walking investigators through the entire event, calmly pointing out where they had dumped Colleen's clothing and identification.

Christa Pike's trial began in March 1996. The prosecution had a mountain of evidence against her, including her own confession and the damning testimony of Shidola Peterson, who had agreed to testify in exchange for a lighter sentence. The defense team tried to argue that Christa was a product of a broken home, a deeply troubled young woman suffering from a host of mental illnesses, including bipolar disorder and post-traumatic stress disorder but any sympathy the jury might have had was erased by the sheer barbarity of the crime and Christa's chilling lack of remorse. On March 22, 1996, after only a few hours of deliberation, the jury found her guilty of both first-degree murder and conspiracy to commit murder. She was sentenced to death by electrocution, becoming the youngest woman in the United States to be sentenced to death at the time.

Days after receiving her death sentence, she sent a letter to Tadaryl, which was intercepted by prison authorities. The letter was a shocking testament to her unrepentant and sociopathic nature. "Hey love," she wrote, "I just want you to know how much I love you... you see what I get for trying to be nice to a hoe? I went ahead and bashed her brains out so she'd die quickly, instead of letting her bleed to death and suffer more... and they fry me. Ain't that stupid?"

Because he was seventeen at the time of the murder, Tadaryl Shipp escaped the death penalty and was sentenced to life in prison with the possibility of parole after twenty-five years. Shidola Peterson, for her cooperation, received six years of probation. Christa Pike was sent to death row, where she has remained for the past quarter of a century, a source of constant trouble and bizarre legal maneuvering. She has filed and withdrawn numerous appeals, at one point even requesting to have her execution date sped up, only to have her attorneys immediately file arguments against it. Her capacity for violence did not end with her incarceration. In August 2001, she attempted to murder a fellow inmate, strangling her with a shoelace, an act for which she received an additional twenty-five-year sentence. In 2012, she was at the center of a foiled escape plot, which involved a former prison guard and another man she had been corresponding with.

Today, Christa Pike remains the only woman on death row in the state of Tennessee. Now in her late forties, she has spent more of her life behind bars than not. In recent interviews, she has expressed a kind of muted regret, stating that she knows she did something horrible and deserves to be in prison for the rest of her life, but that she does not deserve to die. But for the family of Colleen Slemmer, and for a justice system confronted with the sheer, remorseless evil of her crime, any punishment short of the one she was given seems inadequate. The story of Christa Pike is a chilling saga of jealousy, obsession, and a teenage romance that devolved into a ritual of torture and human sacrifice, a crime so brutal that it not only ended a young woman's life but also shuttered an institution and left an indelible stain on the community of Knoxville.

40

HITLER DIARIES

In 1983, one of the most significant and explosive historical discoveries of the twentieth century was presented to the editors of *Stern*, an internationally respected German news magazine. A trusted, longtime journalist on their staff, Gerd Heidemann, brought them two black leather-bound volumes. Heidemann claimed they were the authentic, handwritten personal diaries of Adolf Hitler. This, he explained, was just the beginning. In total, sixty-two volumes existed, a complete personal record written by Führer himself throughout the war.

The potential value of such a find was immeasurable. These volumes were not just military or political documents; they were the purported private thoughts of one of history's most infamous and reviled figures. The appetite for such a discovery was massive. It was a find that promised to rewrite history, offering insights not only to academics and military historians but to an entire world still grappling with the man's legacy. It was, in short, the scoop of the century.

Born in 1938 in Löbau, Saxony, Kujau grew up during the final years of the war and came of age in its aftermath. His family was poor, and like many in East Germany, they lived amid the ruins of a defeated nation. In the years after the war, Nazi memorabilia flooded black markets, and Kujau developed an early fascination with it. By the time he reached adulthood, he had already shown a talent for imitation — first as an artist, then as a forger. He could copy handwriting, mimic paper aging, and create convincing replicas of wartime artifacts. He also had a talent for deception. His early life was marked by small crimes and aliases; he stole food, forged signatures, and spent time in prison for petty theft. When he fled East Germany for the West in the late 1950s, he carried that skill for duplicity with him.

Settling in Stuttgart, Kujau reinvented himself as a businessman and art dealer. By the 1970s, he had built a modest trade selling Nazi-era memorabilia — medals, uniforms, and personal items said to have belonged to prominent officials. His clients were collectors, often nostalgic or obsessed with the war's dark history. Many were gullible, and Kujau quickly learned how easily they could be fooled. He began producing fake Hitler signatures and letters, claiming they came from secret caches hidden by SS officers. His forgeries were so convincing that even experienced collectors were deceived. To maintain the illusion, he cultivated a network of contacts, aliases, and stories. When skeptics questioned his sources, he claimed he was dealing with a high-ranking East German general who possessed Hitler's personal items. Over time, his small operation grew into a lucrative business built entirely on lies.

Around the same time, another man's obsession was taking shape — one that would soon intersect fatally with Kujau's. Gerd Heidemann was a journalist for the German magazine *Stern*, known for his work on historical subjects. Born in Hamburg in 1931, he was too young to have fought in the war but old enough to have been shaped by its aftermath. He collected Nazi memorabilia and even bought Hermann Göring's old yacht, the *Carin II*, which he restored and filled with artifacts. His fascination with the Nazi elite bordered on fixation. By the late 1970s, his career at *Stern* had stagnated. Heidemann needed a story that would restore his reputation — something monumental, something that would make history. When he began hearing rumors about the lost diaries of Adolf Hitler, it felt like destiny.

In 1980, Heidemann learned from a contact in the collectors' world that certain private dealers claimed to possess secret writings by Hitler. The source was mysterious, allegedly linked to an East German officer who had smuggled the materials out of the Soviet zone. Intrigued, Heidemann arranged a meeting. The man who eventually appeared before him was Konrad Kujau, using one of his aliases, "Dr. Fischer." Kujau showed him what he said was one of the recovered notebooks — a small black volume embossed with the initials "A.H." The pages were filled with neat, slanted handwriting in old-style German script. To Heidemann's astonishment, it appeared authentic. Kujau explained that there were many such volumes, each representing a year of Hitler's life. He claimed they had been recovered from the crashed plane near Dresden decades earlier and smuggled to the West through secret channels. This process, he warned, would involve costly and dangerous trips across the border.

The strategy was brilliant. It created a sense of scarcity, danger, and exclusivity, allowing Kujau to produce the forgeries on demand rather than having to create sixty-two volumes upfront. It also allowed him to escalate his price with each new delivery. Heidemann, a trusted and well-respected journalist, took the bait completely. He brought the initial volumes to his editors at *Stern*, who, taking their star reporter at his word, were immediately convinced.

Stern magazine essentially gave Heidemann a blank check. They opened a bank account containing millions of marks, from which Heidemann was authorized to withdraw vast sums of cash to pay Kujau for each new volume. No receipts were required. It was the perfect setup for Heidemann to exploit, so he began skimming off the top, siphoning millions for himself while giving Kujau his cut. On the other hand, Kujau, realizing he had found the biggest sucker in the world, was no longer dealing with small-time collectors but with a major corporation.

The diaries themselves were, by most accounts, banal. They were little more than appointment books filled with mundane observations. Those who read the translations were not confronted with the rants of a sociopath, but with entries about Eva Braun's bad breath or the need to get tickets for the Olympics. But the banality, paradoxically, lent them an air of authenticity. This, the thinking went, is what a real diary would look like — a day-to-day accounting, not a manifesto. The content did not matter; the fact that they were believed to be Hitler's, written in his own hand, was what mattered.

For Heidemann, it was the story of a lifetime. If true, it would be one of the most important historical discoveries since the end of the war. He presented the idea to *Stern's* editors, emphasizing the need for secrecy. The magazine's management, tempted by the potential for global exclusivity, approved initial funds to obtain the materials. The first notebook was purchased for a substantial sum. Handwriting experts hired by *Stern* — though given limited samples for comparison — declared that it could indeed be authentic. The paper looked old, the ink faded appropriately, and the writing style consistent with Hitler's known correspondence. Encouraged, *Stern* continued to buy. Between 1981 and 1983, the magazine paid millions of marks for what eventually became sixty forged volumes — each meticulously produced by Kujau. To protect his cover, he wrote them using fountain pens and old-style paper, soaking the sheets in tea or chemicals to simulate aging. He even manufactured artificial burn marks to suggest the books had survived the plane crash.

As the deal grew, both men were drawn deeper into deception. Kujau enjoyed the money and attention, while Heidemann convinced himself that the diaries were genuine. To others, he repeated the story about the East German source, hinting at secret political connections. The secrecy within *Stern* became extreme. Only a few editors knew the full details, and even they operated under coded references, calling the project "Heiligtum" — "the holy relic." Payments were routed through hidden accounts. The editors dreamed of publishing an exclusive that would elevate *Stern* to global prominence.

In April 1983, after months of negotiation, *Stern* finally decided to go public. A press conference was arranged in Hamburg on April 25. The event drew reporters from around the world. The magazine's editors announced that they had secured Hitler's personal diaries, authenticated by experts, and that the documents would soon be published in serial form. *Stern* sold international rights to major outlets, including *The Sunday Times* in London and *Newsweek* in the United States. The news exploded across headlines. Newspapers described the find as "the greatest historical discovery of the century." Scholars began speculating about what new insights the diaries might reveal into Hitler's mind — his private thoughts, doubts, and daily routines.

At *The Sunday Times*, a senior journalist named Magnus Linklater was tasked with reading the first installment and preparing it for publication. The team was immediately appalled, but not for the reasons one might expect. They were not horrified by the content but bored by it. They had expected world-shaking revelations — why Hitler called off the invasion of England, or his true plans for the Jews. Instead, they found what Linklater called "day-to-day tittle-tattle," with entries complaining about Göring's ill-fitting suits. The material was, by all journalistic standards, terrible.

Furthermore, *Stern's* conditions of sale made proper authentication impossible. Desperate to prevent a leak, they refused to allow anyone from the outside to access the physical diaries. This meant the *Sunday Times* team was kept from the very people and processes that could have exposed the fraud. They were given only facsimiles of some pages and an English translation.

Still, *The Sunday Times* needed some form of authentication to protect its reputation. Murdoch sent Hugh Trevor-Roper, a revered Cambridge historian and a director on News International's board, to validate the purchase. Trevor-Roper was flown to Switzerland, where the diaries were kept in a bank vault. The scene that greeted him was, by design, overwhelming. Dozens of the black, leather-bound volumes were stacked impressively on a table. The sheer scale of the forgery was one of its most convincing elements; no one could believe that a single person would, or could, forge so much.

But the authentication was fatally flawed. Trevor-Roper was the first to admit that his comfort with the German language was limited, and he was completely unfamiliar with the specific Sütterlin script used in Germany in the 1930s and 1940s — a script Kujau was brilliant at forging. Overwhelmed by the spectacle and the pressure, Trevor-Roper made his assessment. When Linklater later called him, desperate for reassurance, the historian said he was 99% convinced they were authentic. For a story of this magnitude, 99% was not good enough.

While Murdoch was negotiating, *Stern* executives, unaware of his internal doubts, were shopping the rights to *Newsweek* in America, asking for $3.6 million. Murdoch, in a brilliant tactical move, called *Newsweek* and suggested they work together on a single, collective bid of half a million dollars. *Newsweek* agreed, and *Stern*, finding its leverage gone, was forced to accept the lowball offer. Murdoch had secured the scoop of the century for a pittance. He had the reassurances of one of the world's leading historians, and that was enough.

In the weeks leading up to publication, Hugh Trevor-Roper began to have serious doubts. He frantically tried to call the paper's editors, stating he was no longer comfortable and wanted to withdraw his backing. When Murdoch was eventually told that his expert now suspected they were fake, his alleged reply was blunt. He went with publication.

On Sunday, April 24, 1983, *The Sunday Times* ran the story with banner headlines, proclaiming the massive exclusive. The issue was a huge success, gaining an extra 60,000 in sales. The editorial team was congratulating itself on one of its greatest front pages when the phone rang. It was Hugh Trevor-Roper. Magnus Linklater and the other editors listened in horror to their editor's side of the conversation. At that moment, the entire foundation for their story collapsed.

The next day, *Stern* magazine held its own triumphant press conference in Hamburg to reveal the source of the diaries to the world. At the press conference, both Trevor-Roper and Weinberg voiced doubts about the authenticity of the Hitler diaries, insisting that German experts must verify them. Trevor-Roper admitted his skepticism stemmed from the lack of evidence linking the books to the 1945 plane crash and lamented that journalistic haste had replaced proper historical verification. *The Guardian* later praised his reversal as an act of "moral courage." Meanwhile, historian David Irving, dismissed by Koch as having "no reputation to lose," challenged the diaries' legitimacy, questioning how Hitler could have written after his arm injury in 1944. Waving photocopied pages, he demanded to know if the ink had been tested — receiving no answer. Chaos erupted as reporters surged forward, and security dragged Irving out as he shouted, "Ink! Ink!"

Suddenly, historians and experts who had been shut out of the process began to point out the obvious. No one in Hitler's surviving inner circle had ever recalled the Führer keeping a diary. Within days, the German Federal Archive (Bundesarchiv) in Berlin was given access to the physical volumes. It did not take them months or years to find the truth; it took a few days. The diaries, they declared, were a laughable and clumsy fake.

The smoking gun was in the material itself. The paper used was from the 1970s. The glue in the bindings was modern, post-war glue. The ink was from a modern pen. The forgery was not clever at all; it was simply audacious. The only reason it had not been exposed immediately was that, in the rush to publish, no one had bothered to conduct the most basic scientific tests.

The most notorious and bizarre mistake, however, was on the cover of each volume. Kujau, attempting to create an official monogram, had embossed the initials "FH" in a fancy German script. He had mistaken the gothic letter "A" for an "F." The initials on the diaries of Adolf Hitler should have been "AH." This simple, glaring error had been missed by Heidemann, by the editors at *Stern*, and by the world-renowned historian Hugh Trevor-Roper.

The scandal that followed was immense. Within weeks, *Stern's* reputation collapsed. The magazine had spent more than nine million marks on the hoax and staked its credibility on it. Public outrage was matched by ridicule. The editors responsible for approving the project were forced to resign. Across Europe and the United States, newspapers that had purchased rights to the diaries faced humiliation.

The subsequent investigation revealed an extraordinary trail of deceit. Police discovered Kujau's workshop filled with pens, inks, papers, and reference books on Hitler's handwriting. He had studied authentic letters in archives and copied phrases from published documents. His imitation was careful but not perfect; he often inserted anachronistic words or repeated phrases that Hitler never used. Kujau admitted that he had forged every volume himself. Heidemann, however, insisted that he too had been deceived — that he had believed the diaries to be genuine and had merely acted as an intermediary. Prosecutors disagreed. Evidence showed that Heidemann had siphoned off large sums of the money *Stern* provided for purchases, claiming the funds were needed for secret payments to East German couriers. In reality, much of it had gone to his personal accounts, spent on luxuries and debts.

The trial began in August 1984 in Hamburg. It was a spectacle. Reporters filled the courtroom, eager for details about how one of Europe's most respected magazines had been fooled. Kujau, dressed neatly and sometimes smiling for the cameras, seemed to enjoy the attention. He admitted his guilt readily and even demonstrated his forgery techniques for the court. Heidemann maintained that he had acted in good faith, though his credibility was destroyed by the financial evidence. In July 1985, the verdict was delivered. Kujau was sentenced to four and a half years in prison; Heidemann to four years and eight months. The sentences were surprisingly light, with the judge noting that the "stupidity" and negligence of the *Stern* management meant they had to share in the culpability. Both served about half their terms before being released. *Stern's* editors who had approved the project were dismissed from their positions, and the magazine's reputation never fully recovered.

After his release, Kujau briefly became a minor celebrity. He appeared on talk shows, opened a small art gallery, and even sold authorized "Kujau copies" of famous paintings — this time openly labeling them as reproductions. He seemed to revel in the absurdity of his fame, often mocking the very people who had once been deceived. Heidemann, by contrast, withdrew from public life, embittered and financially ruined. The "Hitler Diaries" episode haunted him for the rest of his life.

The legacy of the hoax was uneven. Hugh Trevor-Roper's career was destroyed; the historian never recovered from the public humiliation. Gerd Heidemann was left ruined, professionally and financially. Konrad Kujau died in Stuttgart in 2000, but not before his book, detailing his life of crime, earned him the millions the diaries never had.

And Rupert Murdoch? *The Sunday Times*, like *Stern*, had to print a massive retraction. But in the media world, scandal sells. After the initial "Hitler Diaries" exclusive, the paper sold just as many copies, if not more, with the follow-up headline: "The Hitler Diaries Hoax." Murdoch's paper reportedly retained 20,000 of the new readers they had gained from the debacle. For him, it didn't matter if the story was fake, because he was still making money. The hoax was a disaster for journalism, but for a press baron, it was just another profitable news cycle.

41

THE CARTEL HUNTER

In a small diner, three people sat at a table, existing in separate worlds. On one side sat Miriam Rodriguez, a middle-aged mother, her back straight, staring at the two young men opposite her as if in a tense business meeting. The man directly across from her, Sama, was focused on her, but his attention was constantly split by the walkie-talkie buzzing on the table. Through its static, Miriam could hear voices calling out street names, tracking police and military patrols in the area. It was the only reason she knew his name. The third man, oblivious to the tension, was scarfing down his food like it was his last meal. When he finished, he eyed Miriam's untouched sandwich. "You going to eat that?" he asked. She pushed the plate toward him.

Sama leaned forward. "Your daughter smoke weed or something?" Miriam was taken aback. "Excuse me?" He explained that her daughter, Karen, was surprisingly relaxed for a kidnap victim, super chill. He said he liked that, and it made him want to let her go. Miriam knew she had to play along, but a cold certainty had already settled in her heart. Her daughter had been taken by the Zetas, one of the most dangerous cartels in Mexico. No one got out alive.

Sama told her the decision wasn't his, but for $2,000, he could try to convince the big boss to spare her. Miriam smiled, a hollow gesture. She knew these men, the ones sitting in front of her eating her food, had already killed her daughter. And in that moment, she knew she would not stop until every single one of them paid for it.

The Zetas were not always a cartel. They began as Hired Guns, an elite paramilitary wing of the Gulf Cartel, one of Mexico's oldest and most powerful criminal syndicates. The original Zetas were former members of the Mexican Army's elite Special Forces, many of whom had received extensive training in urban warfare, sniper tactics, and explosives from the United States military, ironically to fight the cartels. The leader of the Gulf Cartel recruited thirty of these agents to be his personal bodyguards, offering them pay the government could never match. This private army was lethally effective, but soon, they realized their strength. If they were the part that made the Gulf Cartel so special, why did they need the Gulf Cartel?

The Zetas split off and declared war on their former employers on March 31, 2010. The battle for control of the northeastern border, a prime smuggling route, began in Miriam's hometown of San Fernando. In the early morning hours, the Zetas staged a fake highway accident to lure police and firefighters to an isolated road. Once the authorities were gathered, a convoy of makeshift tanks — modified trucks, SUVs, and even a school bus, all spray-painted with the letter "Z" and outfitted with gun mounts — appeared on the highway. For six hours, from 4:00 a.m. to 10:00 a.m., they drove block by block, firing into every public building, riddling police stations and courthouses with bullets. The message was clear: the Gulf Cartel was no longer in charge.

The Gulf Cartel fought back, plunging San Fernando into a full-scale war. Civilians became collateral damage in a conflict that saw tens of thousands of innocent people die. The Zetas' initial, surgical violence soon gave way to a new philosophy. As they ran out of elite Special Forces to recruit, they began forcing younger, more volatile, and more sadistic members into their ranks. To keep them loyal, Zeta leadership gave these new cells a free-for-all: they could earn their own money through any means necessary — extortion, theft, human trafficking — as long as they did not interfere with the cartel's primary business of drug and oil smuggling.

This policy unleashed a new kind of terror. The Zetas, who had once left civilians alone, now targeted them. They weren't just violent; they were theatrical in their cruelty, specializing in torture, decapitation, and dissolving bodies in acid, a practice they called "cooking." They posted their executions online. They ruled not just through power but through psychological warfare. They were accused of not following the "gentleman's code" of other cartels, killing pregnant women and dismembering victims alive in front of their families.

In this atmosphere of fear lived Miriam Rodríguez. Born and raised in Tamaulipas, she was known for her stubbornness and her courage. She had survived cancer, built a small business selling cowboy hats, and raised her children with discipline and warmth. Her home in San Fernando sat near the main road leading to the U.S. border, a route that traffickers and migrants shared in uneasy proximity. Like many parents in her region, she tried to shield her children from the danger that had become part of everyday life. Her daughter, Karen, was twenty when she disappeared.

On January 24, 2014, while working as a nanny in Texas, Miriam received a call at 4:00 a.m. from her eldest daughter, Azalea, who was crying and said something terrible had happened to Karen. By 8:00 a.m., Miriam was already on a bus heading back to San Fernando. Azalea told her what had taken place that night: their estranged father, Luis, had come to her door unexpectedly in the middle of the night. As he stepped inside, his phone rang, and a man on the other end told him they had his daughter and demanded a ransom of $77,000 for her release. Moments later, Karen's voice came through the line, pleading for him to pay, saying that if he didn't, this might be the last time they would hear from her.

The demand was impossible. The average annual salary in Mexico was around $15,000. They had until 3:00 p.m. the next day. By 10:00 a.m., the family had pooled their entire life savings and secured a business loan, amounting to less than $10,000. Luis went to drop the money off at a local health center while Miriam watched from a distance. A skinny teenage boy grabbed the bag and told Luis to meet him at the cemetery in twenty minutes to retrieve Karen. The boy jumped into a cherry-red Ford Explorer and sped off. At the cemetery, the family waited, but Karen never arrived.

The next day, the kidnappers called, claiming the rainstorm had prevented the exchange. Then, they broke into Miriam's house, where Karen lived, and stole some of her things. They called back and demanded more money. Miriam borrowed another $2,000 from everyone she could think of and paid it. It was everything they had. But Karen never came home.

For a month Miriam sank into a deep depression; the kidnapping had shattered everything she believed. She had taught her children that keeping their heads down and staying out of trouble would keep the cartels away, an unspoken bargain that now felt broken. The Zetas were no longer striking only the wealthy or their enemies — they were preying on anyone. On February 23, 2014, one month after Karen's abduction, Miriam rose, put on a full face of makeup for the first time in weeks, and went downstairs. She told Azalea that she no longer expected Karen to be returned, that she believed her daughter was dead, and that for the rest of her life she would hunt down the people responsible and make them pay.

Her investigation began almost accidentally. She started visiting the places Karen had gone before her abduction, talking to shopkeepers, taxi drivers, and anyone who might remember seeing her that day. Bit by bit, she began assembling fragments of the story. The kidnappers were part of a local Zeta cell, led by men who had once been neighbors, men she might have passed on the street. With every piece of information, Miriam grew bolder. She followed clues that the police ignored, calling phone numbers, comparing handwriting on ransom notes, and noting the details of cars and houses. But the real break came from Carlos, a friend of Karen's who had also been kidnapped that night but was later released. For months, Carlos was terrified to speak, but he eventually told Miriam what happened.

Carlos had gone to Karen's house to fix her car. When he arrived, two men came out of the house and invited him in to wait for her. Inside, he found Karen on the floor, her hands and feet bound, her face bloody and swollen. The men tied up Carlos and his cousin and proceeded to beat Karen, accusing her of working for the Gulf Cartel. She screamed that they had the wrong person, but they didn't listen, torturing her and suffocating her with a plastic bag.

The group was moved to a Zeta ranch, where they were lined up with other captives. A female Zeta member, seemingly enraged by Karen's appearance, grabbed her by the hair, straddled her back, and smashed her head against the floor, screaming, "This is for being so pretty!" The captives were forced to call their families for ransom. The next morning, the men were loaded into a truck. The two women, Karen and her friend Barbara, were dragged to a tree. Carlos saw the men tying a yellow rope around their necks, flinging it over a branch, and start beating them with sticks as if they were piñatas.

With this information, Miriam had a new target: the boy who had collected the ransom money. He was known as "the Florist." Miriam knew him; as a child, he was one of the hungry neighborhood kids she would often feed. He had later tried to give Karen flowers, which she always politely declined. Miriam tracked him down, tackled him, jammed her loaded pistol into his back, and whispered, "If you move, I will shoot you." He was her eleventh target.

Miriam's hunt was methodical and relentless. She was a master of disguise, changing her appearance, cutting her hair, and adopting different personas to get close to her targets. She tracked down one of the kidnappers, a young man named Cristiano, who had just turned eighteen. He had been the second man at the diner, the one who ate her sandwich. He was arrested and confessed, giving Miriam more names. During his interrogation, the boy kept asking for his mom and complaining that he was hungry. Miriam, watching from another room, walked in and handed him her own lunch. She later told the baffled police, "He's a child. No matter what he did, when I heard him saying he was hungry, it was like I heard my own child."

Her hunt became something of a running joke in the family: Miriam had always wanted to be a cop, but she wasn't corrupt enough to qualify. Fearless by nature, she had already confronted the Zetas once before. Years earlier, her son-in-law, Ernesto, had received a letter detailing his every move, followed by a phone number and a demand for ransom to prevent his kidnapping. Miriam took control of the negotiations, snapping at the Zeta on the phone that they didn't have that kind of money and calling him an idiot. She insisted on handling the drop-off herself. When Azalea tried to stop her, Miriam revealed a pistol tucked in her jacket, questioning what the criminals could want with an old woman like her, and instructing her daughter that if she wasn't back in fifteen minutes, she should pack up, take Karen, and flee to the U.S. At the abandoned gas station, Miriam tossed the bag of cash out the window and drove away, refusing to get out of the car.

This tenacity had always defined Miriam. When she was diagnosed with cancer while Karen was just four, she told the doctors that she couldn't die — there was a young child depending on her, and no one else would take care of her. She beat the cancer. Later, when her doctors warned that her weight posed a serious health risk, she underwent gastric bypass surgery, a procedure that would also help her in her quest. She spent her days hiking through abandoned ranches and staking out safe houses, relentlessly pursuing those responsible.

Miriam also turned her fight into activism, founding the "Vanishing Collective" to support other families of the disappeared. She taught them how to navigate the system, demand compensation, and pressure the government, becoming notorious for confronting and threatening officials while showing families that they had power in numbers. Through her relentless detective work, she brought Karen's killers to justice. She tracked down El Flo, who had left the cartel and was working in a factory, and found El Kike, the man alleged to have pulled the rope, arranging for his arrest at church. When the minister asked if she had mercy, Miriam met his gaze and asked where El Kike's mercy had been when he killed her daughter.

Her children begged her to stop. Authorities had recovered a few of Karen's rib bones from the ranch — just enough for a burial — but Miriam was far from finished. At the burial she opened the coffin, removed the small bag of bones, and held it aloft, telling those gathered that this was all she had left of her daughter and that she had no intention of stopping now.

In March 2017, three years after Karen's murder, twenty-nine inmates, many of them Zetas Miriam had put away, tunneled their way out of prison. For the first time, Miriam was terrified. She knew they would come for her. The police, who were legally required to protect her, offered no help. Her friends and family tried to reassure her, arguing that the Zetas were weakened and wouldn't be foolish enough to kill a high-profile national advocate like her. It would bring too much heat from the government. But Miriam knew better. "I can only hope," she told her children, "if those bastards come after me, they give me a chance to shoot back."

On May 10, 2017 — Mother's Day in Mexico — Azalea was waiting for her mother to meet her for coffee and cake. The call came from her father instead. Miriam had been getting out of her car in front of her ex-husband's house when a car drove by and fired thirteen rounds. She was hit eight times. Her son, Luis, found her with her hand in her purse, reaching for the pistol she always carried. She was pronounced dead at the hospital.

Miriam's death did not end her quest. Luis, who had never wanted to be part of her fight, found himself inheriting it. He took over the collective, and at his mother's funeral, a childhood friend gave him a tip, a name: "El Luche." Luis learned that the Zetas who escaped had not come for her themselves; they had hired a separate cell to kill her because she was causing them too much trouble. Luis, becoming more like his mother every day, began his own hunt. He helped authorities track down El Luche, who was killed before he could be arrested, and the other members of the hit squad. And finally, Luis found the last person on his mother's list: the woman who had beaten Karen for being pretty. He had her arrested.

Unlike his mother, Luis decided to stop. He had avenged his sister and his mother, but he wanted to protect what was left of his family. He now focuses on helping other victims' families through the collective his mother built, ending the cycle of vengeance that had consumed his mother and, for a time, himself.

42

"JESUS WAS AN ALIEN"

In the 1980s, a wave of fear known as the "Satanic Panic" swept across North America and parts of Europe, fueled by media reports and public anxiety about alleged ritual abuse, black magic, and the influence of dangerous cults. This moral panic, often amplified by evangelical Christian communities wary of rising occultism and alternative spiritualities, created an environment where suspicion and accusation could easily take root. While the panic was most prominent in the United States, its echoes reached far corners of the globe, including the remote towns nestled deep within the Brazilian Amazon. It was in this atmosphere of heightened fear and fascination with the dark side of spirituality that a small, obscure group known as the Superior Universal Alignment, led by a charismatic woman named Valentina de Andrade, would become entangled in one of the most horrific and disturbing series of crimes in Brazil's history.

Valentina de Andrade was born in the city of Carazinho in southern Brazil on September 28, 1931. Little is known about her early life beyond what she chose to reveal in her later biographical writings. She described a modest upbringing in a small town, lacking toys or bicycles, and claimed to be semi-illiterate, suggesting she intentionally avoided formal education to preserve her "authenticity." She portrayed herself as a romantic, an extrovert, loyal, affectionate, and possessing "unquestionable dignity." Crucially, she claimed never to have "practiced a single act of evilness." This self-constructed image of purity and innate wisdom laid the groundwork for her later claims to spiritual authority.

In 1981, at the age of fifty, Valentina experienced what she described as a life-altering spiritual awakening. She claimed to have been contacted by divine cosmic beings, extraterrestrials who delivered visions warning her of an impending doomsday. These beings, she asserted, promised to save her and her followers aboard a spaceship if she spread their message. This became the foundation of her belief system: she was a "materialized energy," a "cosmic entity of light, love, and truth," receiving divine knowledge from beyond Earth. Her teachings incorporated a wide array of esoteric concepts — reincarnation, recovering memories from past lives, energy fields, ghosts, life after death — alongside a central, controversial claim: Jesus was not God, but an extraterrestrial, and the traditional concept of God was a "big farce."

Valentina settled in the town of Altamira, located in the state of Pará deep within the Amazon region. There, her neighbors began to perceive her as having clairvoyant abilities. She became the local seer and fortune teller, charging people for insights into their future. Her popularity grew, especially after she published a book outlining her core beliefs, including the extraterrestrial nature of Jesus. Capitalizing on this local fame, she officially founded her group, the Superior Universal Alignment, in 1981.

Like many cult leaders promising salvation from apocalypse, Valentina claimed to know the exact date the world would end, a secret she shared only with her most devoted followers. A core tenet of her burgeoning cult was particularly disturbing: she declared that any child born after 1981 was a reincarnation of evil and needed to be "expunged." Prospective members with children were forced to abandon them, either giving them to family members or putting them up for adoption, as these children, deemed "unconscious instruments of the great scam called God," would not be allowed on the rescue spacecraft.

As Valentina cultivated her following, the inevitable happened: her prophesied doomsday dates came and went without incident. Rather than questioning her authority, however, her followers internalized the failure.

Manipulated by Valentina, they came to believe the spaceship hadn't arrived because *their* faith was insufficient, because *they* had not proven their loyalty. This dynamic deepened their dependence on her, reinforcing her control.

It was around 1989, amidst this environment of unwavering belief and Valentina's increasingly hostile stance toward children born after 1981, that a terrifying pattern began to emerge in Altamira. Young boys, primarily between the ages of eight and fourteen, started disappearing. Many came from impoverished families; some were orphans or homeless, scraping by shining shoes or doing odd jobs. The horror began not with death but with brutal assault.

On August 2, 1989, an eight-year-old boy named José was lured away by a strange man. Hours later, he was found alive but severely injured and showing signs of sexual abuse. Then, on November 16, ten-year-old Otoniel was invited by a man to share some mangoes he had just delivered. The man led him to an isolated area, incapacitated him with a chemical-soaked cloth, and when Otoniel awoke, he discovered he had been sexually abused and castrated. He survived but endured years of psychological trauma and dozens of painful, ultimately unsuccessful reconstructive surgeries. On July 23, 1990, nine-year-old Walda Clay encountered a man near the edge of town who asked for help getting a kite out of a tree. Lured into the woods, he too was rendered unconscious, sexually abused, and castrated. Like Otoniel, he faced a long road of surgeries and psychological recovery.

These initial survivors offered the first terrifying glimpses of the attacker, or attackers. They described a single man acting alone, using chemical cloths to subdue them before inflicting horrific mutilations. But soon, the attacks escalated from assault to murder. Between 1989 and 1993, nineteen boys disappeared in and around Altamira. As the bodies began to be found, a sickening pattern became undeniable.

The list of victims grew steadily, each discovery more horrifying than the last. Tito Mendes, thirteen, vanished on January 20, 1991, last seen with an unknown man near a stream. He was never found. Elton Fonseca, ten, went missing on May 5, 1991; his mutilated remains were found forty-six days later, only to mysteriously disappear from the morgue before an autopsy could be performed. Eleven-year-old J.C.B. disappeared in August 1991. On New Year's Day 1992, thirteen-year-old Judirley da Cunha's body was found days after he vanished; he was naked, castrated, sexually assaulted, and bore severe burn wounds. Ednaldo de Souza Teixeira, twelve, was found beaten to death beside a well in April 1992. Jaques de Silva Pessoã, thirteen, disappeared while tending cattle in October 1992; his body was found castrated, abused, tortured, with his eyes gouged out and hands chopped off. Clebson Varrêra Caídus, thirteen, was found murdered in November 1992, naked, castrated, and tortured. Fabrício Férris de Souza, twelve, vanished in December 1992 after being seen with a man on a red bicycle. The horror continued into 1993: Raylan Santos de Souza, nine, disappeared in January after being seen with two men near the Xingu River. Flávio Lopes de Silva, ten, went missing in March; his body was found tortured, his genitals mutilated, and covered in strange circular wounds later identified as human bite marks, suggesting possible cannibalism. R.F.S., an eleven-year-old shoeshiner, vanished in July 1993.

The community was gripped by terror. The local police, led by Chief Éder Mauro, struggled to connect the cases. Initial investigations were hampered by lack of evidence and, potentially, indifference toward the victims, most of whom came from poor backgrounds. An early suspect, a local drifter named Rotílio de Souza, was arrested but died suspiciously in custody only months later. When the disappearances continued, police had to admit he wasn't the sole perpetrator, if involved at all.

As the body count rose, investigators noted the precise, almost surgical nature of some mutilations, particularly the castration and the potential removal of internal organs in some cases. This led to a theory that the boys were being kidnapped for an organ trafficking ring. Suspicion fell on two doctors who had recently moved to Altamira, Anísio Ferreira de Souza and Césio Flávio Caldas Brandão. They were detained for questioning, but experts pointed out that the violent manner in which the bodies were mutilated would likely have rendered any organs unusable for transplant. With no evidence, the doctors were released.

The investigation stalled until one boy managed to escape his captors and identify them. His testimony implicated several high-ranking members of the Altamira community: a police officer, the two doctors previously suspected, the son of a wealthy land baron, and, crucially, Valentina de Andrade, the leader of the Superior Universal Alignment. Suddenly, the small, secretive cult was thrust into the center of the investigation.

Rumors, fueled by the ongoing Satanic Panic and Valentina's own anti-child rhetoric, began to spread like wildfire. Tales of ritualistic abuse, black magic, and cannibalism associated with the cult gripped the community and the media. Police, perhaps eager for a simple explanation or influenced by the prevailing panic, leaned heavily into the cult angle. They searched Valentina's estate, finding ritualistic hoods and videotapes of ceremonies. On one tape, police claimed Valentina entered a trance and ordered her followers to "kill little children." However, linguistic experts later reviewed the poor-quality audio and concluded she more likely said, "Yes, there are more experienced little children." The tape was deemed inadmissible.

Valentina maintained her innocence, claiming she hadn't even been in Altamira since 1987, years before the murders began. Despite the lack of physical evidence connecting her or the cult to the crimes, Chief Mauro seemed determined to pin the blame on them, publicly promoting the theory that the murders were committed during satanic rituals.

Parallel to the Altamira investigation, a similar horror unfolded miles away. On April 6, 1992, six-year-old Evandro Ramos Caetano went missing in Guaratuba, Paraná. Five days later, his mutilated body was found. His hair, toes, ears, genitals, and hands had been cut off, and his intestines, liver, and heart were missing. Investigators, echoing the Altamira theories, suspected human sacrifice. They accused Celina Abbage, the wife of the town's former mayor, and her daughter Beatriz, of paying cult members $2,000 to kill the boy as part of a black magic ritual to revive her husband's failing political career. Police claimed the women confessed, but they later retracted, alleging torture. Despite the lack of autopsy, forensic examination, or physical evidence, Celina and Beatriz spent nearly six years in prison before being acquitted in 1998. Beatriz was fully pardoned in 2016. This case, dubbed "The Witches of Guaratuba," highlighted the authorities' willingness to pursue ritualistic theories even in the absence of proof.

Back in Altamira, the case against the Superior Universal Alignment members continued, built almost entirely on questionable eyewitness testimony and coerced confessions. One key witness, Edmilson da Silva Frazão, claimed to have attended a ritual at Dr. Souza's house in 1991 where he saw Valentina. However, his testimony was inconsistent; he couldn't recall the date, initially saying 1989 or 1990, contradicting his earlier police statement which cited 1991. Despite these inconsistencies, the judge allowed his testimony.

Other former cult members testified, denying any ritualistic crimes but confirming Valentina's requirement that members abandon children born after 1981. They portrayed her as coercive but stopped short of accusing her of murder. Two of the surviving victims, Otoniel and another unnamed boy, identified one man as their attacker: Carlos Alberto Santos Lima, a military police officer who worked as a security guard for Amaílton Madeira Gomes, the son of the wealthy land baron, who was also implicated.

Despite the focus solely on Carlos Alberto by the victims, the prosecution pressed forward against all the indicted individuals connected to the cult. The investigation was riddled with flaws: no autopsies, no crime scene forensics, retracted confessions due to alleged police torture, and conflicting eyewitness accounts. The chief prosecutor himself argued for dismissal due to lack of evidence, but an assistant prosecutor pushed forward, and a judge ultimately pronounced the accused guilty in 1994.

The convictions were immediately appealed. A new prosecutor reviewed the case and accepted the appeal, citing the profound lack of evidence. This decision sparked public outrage, with protests erupting in Belém. Fearing for his life, the prosecutor fled Altamira. However, the courts eventually ordered a new hearing and nullified the convictions due to the investigation's egregious flaws. Dr. Brandão, after spending over two years in prison without trial, sued the state, claiming he was used as a scapegoat. All other defendants connected to the cult were released in 1995.

Valentina de Andrade, having had her name cleared early on and possessing an alibi placing her out of the country during the murders, had already fled Brazil. She moved to Argentina, continuing her cult activities with a diminished following, steadfastly maintaining her innocence regarding the Altamira horrors. Her current whereabouts, and whether she is still alive, remain unknown.

With the cult theory dismantled, the question remained: who killed the children of Altamira? The answer may lie with Francisco das Chagas Rodrigues de Brito. Born in 1965, Francisco endured a childhood of abandonment and abuse. He eventually settled in Altamira in the 1980s, working as a bicycle mechanic, precisely when the murders began. He fit the profile: a local man who could easily gain the trust of young boys working on the streets.

Francisco left Altamira and continued his horrific spree across Brazil, moving from city to city. His methods remained consistent: luring poor young boys, raping them, mutilating their genitals, ears, and fingers, and then killing them, often by strangulation or stabbing, sometimes burning their bodies. His victims were always boys, typically aged between four and fifteen.

He was finally caught in 2004 after the murder of fifteen-year-old Jonathan Viegas, who had told someone he was going to meet a bicycle mechanic just before disappearing. Police arrested Francisco, and a search of his home uncovered bones and clothing belonging to two victims. They found cut T-shirts matching those worn by other victims and realized his victims were always found within 600 feet (about 182 meters) of where he lived. Investigators connected him to the deaths of young boys dating back to 1989, spanning his time in Altamira. He was ultimately suspected of killing and mutilating up to forty-two boys across Brazil.

Francisco confessed to murdering seventeen boys but refused to provide details. Due to the botched initial investigations and lack of preserved physical evidence from the Altamira crime scenes years earlier, police could not definitively link him to those specific murders, even though his timeline and methods matched perfectly. The case against the cult had muddied the waters irrevocably. Francisco das Chagas Rodrigues de Brito was convicted for the murders he confessed to and sentenced to 580 years in prison, recognized as one of Brazil's most prolific serial killers.

The truth of what happened in Altamira remains obscured by incompetence, corruption, and the lingering shadow of the Satanic Panic. While

Francisco das Chagas appears to be the most likely perpetrator, the possibility of accomplices, or even a separate group operating concurrently, cannot be entirely dismissed. The sloppy police work and the rush to blame an unconventional religious group allowed a monster to continue killing for years. For the families of the victims, the lack of definitive answers and the system's failures represent a profound and enduring injustice.

43

THE WOMAN IN THE VALLEY OF DEATH

To an outsider, Isdalen, or the "Ice Valley," might seem an unusual place for a stroll. It's a desolate but starkly beautiful valley east of Bergen, Norway, where a large, dark lake fills the basin and pine forests climb the hillsides until they give way to barren rock and boulders. Its reputation is as treacherous as its terrain; another of its nicknames is the "Valley of Death," a nod to the many hiking accidents that have occurred on its hazardous trails and a darker, more ancient rumor that it was once a site where people in medieval times would walk to end their lives. November is a particularly cold and wet time of year in this part of the world, with only a few precious hours of sunlight each day. But on the morning of November 29, 1970, a university professor, familiar with the valley's paths, was out for a hike with his two young daughters, aged ten and twelve. They could not have imagined that their familiar walk was about to lead them to the heart of one of Norway's most profound and enduring mysteries.

As they navigated the trail, one of the girls spotted something unusual sticking out from behind a cluster of boulders. From a distance, her father thought it looked like a human foot, and his immediate concern was that a hiker had been injured. He hurried his children toward the spot, but as they drew closer, a repugnant and unsettling smell hit them — the unmistakable stench of burnt flesh hanging heavy in the crisp morning air. When they rounded the final boulder, the scene that confronted them was one of absolute horror. There was indeed a person there, a woman, but she was beyond any help. The professor quickly shielded his daughters' eyes, turned them around, and marched them out of the treacherous valley as quickly as he could to find a phone and call the police.

A small team of officers was dispatched to Isdalen, and they, too, were met with the same nauseating smell of burning as they approached the location. The woman lay on her back between the rocks, her body contorted into a disturbing posture known as a "boxer pose," with her fists clenched and her limbs flexed — a common, gruesome result of the dehydration and shrinkage of muscles in bodies exposed to intense heat. The entire front of her body was horrifically burned, the skin and clothing charred away, yet strangely, her back was completely untouched by the fire. There was no sign of a campfire or any other source for the blaze that had consumed her.

Scattered around her were a peculiar collection of belongings: a pair of rubber boots, two plastic water bottles that were partially melted, a purse, an umbrella, some jewelry, and a watch that was stopped, as if for display, at 10:10. Underneath her body, investigators found a fur hat that, when tested, revealed traces of petrol. This was the only hint of an accelerant, but there was no canister to be found. Even more bizarre was a deliberate and systematic effort to erase her identity. All the labels on her belongings had been meticulously removed or rubbed off, and every single tag on her clothing had been carefully cut away. This was no accident. The scene was immediately treated as a potential murder, but with a victim who was seemingly a ghost, burnt beyond easy recognition and stripped of any identifying marks, the police had no leads.

The woman's body was sent to a local university hospital for an autopsy, which only deepened the enigma. While the fire had clearly been a factor in her death — she had soot in her respiratory tract and signs of carbon monoxide poisoning — the toxicology report revealed another shocking detail. Her system was flooded with barbiturates. It was estimated she had ingested between fifty and seventy sleeping pills, a brand known to be sold in England and tragically popular among women who intended to commit suicide by overdose. Some of the pills were found undigested in her stomach, and according to one source, a few were still in her mouth when she died.

This finding threw the investigation into confusion. Was this a murder or a suicide? The sheer number of pills pointed toward a self-inflicted act, but the rest of the scene made little sense. Why would someone travel to such a remote and unusual location, consume a massive overdose of sleeping pills, and then set themselves on fire with petrol, all without leaving the container behind? The questions were piling up, with no answers in sight.

Three days later, the police got their first real break. A call came in from the luggage storage office at the Bergen train station. A week prior, on November 23rd, someone had checked in two suitcases and had never returned to collect them. When investigators opened the suitcases, the mystery of the Isdal Woman suddenly took on a life of its own. Inside, they found a fingerprint on a pair of non-prescription eyeglasses that matched the victim, confirming the luggage was hers. The contents revealed a woman who was well-traveled and meticulously prepared, yet fanatically secretive. The suitcases held wigs, fancy clothing, coats, cosmetics, and an eczema cream. But just as with the items at the death scene, every single label on her clothes and personal effects had been painstakingly removed or rubbed off.

There were, however, a few items that provided clues. They found 500 German Deutschmarks, a sewing kit from a hotel in Geneva, a spoon with the letters 'SCHP' engraved on it that was traced to an Austrian manufacturer, and a matchbook from a German erotic underwear company. Most importantly, they discovered a notebook that contained what at first appeared to be a sophisticated code — lines of numbers and letters. But the detail that would kick off the manhunt in earnest was a simple shopping bag from a shoe store in the city of Stavanger, south of Bergen.

Following this lead, investigators traveled to the shoe shop, where the owner vividly remembered the woman. He recalled serving her on November 18th, noting that she stood out. She was good-looking, he said, and spoke English with an accent he couldn't quite place. Another worker described her as being around five foot seven (about 1.67 meters) tall with dark hair, brown eyes, and a well-put-together appearance that seemed at odds with what the shopkeeper described as an unpleasant, garlic-like smell — something uncommon in Norway at the time. As he went to the basement to get her size, she called out to him in another language he thought might be German or French. The police now had a strong sense she was not from the area, so they began checking hotels in Stavanger.

They quickly found one right by the shoe shop. Staff there confirmed she had stayed for nine days, from November 9th to the 18th, in a small room without a bathroom. The bellboy remembered her, noting her heavy makeup and serious, rarely smiling demeanor. It was unusual for a lone woman to stay at the hotel for so long, especially in November, which was not a tourist season. When asked where she was from, she had told him Belgium. According to the hotel registration card she filled out, her name was Finella Lorck, and she was from Belgium. But when authorities checked, they found that no such person existed, and the passport number she had provided was a fake.

The Isdal Woman was a phantom, and her trail was a labyrinth of lies. The case had now attracted international attention, and Norway's secret police became involved — an unusual step for what was, on the surface, a local murder investigation. The mysterious notebook was sent to a military codebreaker, who soon realized it wasn't a sophisticated cipher at all, but rather a personal shorthand. Each line of letters and numbers represented a place and a date, documenting her extensive travels. Soon, police had a stack of hotel registration cards from all over Norway and even from other countries like France, all filled out in the same distinctive handwriting but all bearing different names and different Belgian birthplaces. The cards were mostly written in German, but with peculiar spelling errors and phrasing that suggested it was not her first language. She was juggling at least eight different fake identities, each with its own corresponding fake passport.

One hotel card, from the very last hotel she stayed in before she died, showed a distinct change in her penmanship. Handwriting experts confirmed it was the same person, but concluded that she had been deliberately trying to disguise her writing. This raised a chilling question: in her final days, was the Isdal Woman trying to hide from someone? The codebreaker was able to decipher all but the final line in her notebook: "M L 23 N M M." It was clear that "23 N" represented November 23rd, the day she checked her luggage at the station and was last seen alive, but the meaning of the initials "ML" and "MM" remains unknown to this day.

As investigators pieced together her movements, witness accounts began to emerge that placed her in the company of several unidentified men — details that were strangely absent from the official police reports. During a stay at the Hotel Neptune in Bergen in early November, a waitress remembered seeing her sitting alone one evening, looking sad. The following night, however, she was in the restaurant again, this time with an older, gray-haired man who the waitress believed might be Norwegian. The encounter was unsettlingly silent. The man read from a sheet of paper while the Isdal Woman sat stiffly, a serious look on her face, not saying a single word. The waitress was adamant that it felt like a serious meeting, not a romantic date.

Just a few days before her death, on the night of November 18th, after arriving in Bergen from Stavanger, she checked into the Hotel Rosenkrantz. That evening, a maid, believing the room to be empty, knocked briefly before entering to turn down the bed. She was startled to find the Isdal Woman lying in bed and, sitting in a chair across the room, a young man with blonde hair wearing a gray suit. The maid apologized and quickly made the bed while the pair watched her in complete, unnerving silence. Neither of them said a word. Again, this encounter with an unknown man was seemingly ignored in the police investigation, and neither of these men ever came forward after her death became public knowledge.

The next morning, she checked out and moved a short distance to the Hotel Hordenheimen — the hotel where she disguised her handwriting on the registration card. Her behavior there continued to be bizarre. She took a corner room, giving her a perfect view of both streets leading up to the hotel. Housekeepers noted that the "do not disturb" sign was almost always on her door, and when she wasn't in the room, she had a strange habit of moving an armchair from her room out into the hallway, only to bring it back inside when she returned. On November 23rd, she checked out, took a taxi to the train station, left her suitcases in a locker, and

vanished until her burnt body was discovered a week later in the Valley of
Death.

The involvement of the secret police, the systematic erasure of her identity, and her extensive, well-funded travels all pointed toward one tantalizing conclusion: the Isdal Woman was a spy. This theory gained
significant weight when a critical witness account finally came to light
years later. A fisherman from a small port near Stavanger claimed to have
seen her on the docks speaking for a long time with a naval officer aboard
a military vessel. The fisherman reported this to the police, but it's unclear
if he was ever formally interviewed before the case was abruptly closed.

What happened next, however, was even stranger. Just before Christmas,
as the fisherman and his family were about to board a train for a holiday
in London, two men in plain clothes approached him on the platform,
identified themselves as police, and took him aside for a twenty-minute
conversation. He later revealed to his family that the men — who never
showed any ID — had handed him a small handgun and a knife, telling
him to keep them on him at all times in London in case he needed to
protect himself. He was left terrified, with no idea who he was supposed to
be protecting himself from. This felt less like a police interview and more
like a thinly veiled threat to ensure his silence.

The reason a naval ship was in the docks that day was critical. The
Norwegian Navy was conducting top-secret tests of the new Penguin
missile system, a cutting-edge piece of Cold War technology that could be
launched from small ships and was of immense interest to the Soviet
Union. Norway was a founding member of the North Atlantic Treaty
Organization (NATO), and Russia was known to be closely monitoring its
highly developed arms industry, with Russian ships often spotted near the
test zones. The Isdal Woman's travels between Stavanger and Bergen
seemed to coincide perfectly with numerous tests of the missile system,
and she had even been spotted near the test sites on more than one
occasion.

It all seemed to add up, but if she was a spy, she was a clumsy one.
Experts in espionage point out that she stood out everywhere she went, a
fatal flaw for an undercover agent. A professional spy would have one or
two solid, well-researched false identities, not a chaotic tangle of eight or

more, and wouldn't need to cut the labels from their clothing. It's possible she wasn't a spy in the traditional sense, but perhaps an information courier, moving between operatives to pass along intelligence, which could explain her silent meetings with the various men.

Despite the compelling espionage theories, the Bergen police officially closed the investigation after only three weeks, declaring her death a tragic suicide. The decision was met with frustration from both the press and the police officers on the case, who felt that their hands had been tied by the secret police and that promising leads abroad were never pursued. In a final, somber act, the police themselves held a funeral for the unknown woman. In a small Bergen graveyard, sixteen men and two women from the force watched as a white, zinc-lined coffin — designed not to disintegrate, in case they ever needed to exhume her — was lowered into an unmarked grave.

In the years since, modern science has offered a few more clues. Isotope and DNA tests conducted on her remains suggest she grew up in Germany before moving near the French-Belgian border later in life. A carbon-14 test on her teeth also suggested she was closer to forty-five years old, not the twenty-five to thirty she consistently claimed on her hotel cards. After the *Death in Ice Valley* podcast brought new attention to the case, another witness came forward, claiming he saw a woman matching her description hiking near Isdalen just a few days before her body was found, trailed by two very serious-looking men in dark coats. But despite these advances, her true identity and what happened to her in the Valley of Death remain unknown. Her DNA is stored in international databases, holding out the slim hope that a relative might one day come forward and finally give a name to the ghost of the Ice Valley.

44

THE MAN WHO CUT OFF HER ARMS

The road stretched endlessly through the California desert — silent, sun-bleached, and empty. A van slowed to a stop beside a young hitchhiker standing alone on the shoulder. She was fifteen, tired, and just wanted to get home. The man behind the wheel smiled, the kind of harmless, grandfatherly smile that made him seem safe. She climbed in. It was a decision that would change her life forever.

Lawrence Singleton was born in Tampa, Florida, on July 28, 1927. Details about his early life are scarce, but it's known he grew up with numerous siblings. After leaving school, he served in the military during the Korean War, experiencing combat in what was described as a gruesome war zone. Following his military service, he spent most of his working life as a merchant marine, operating machinery below deck on cargo ships and traveling the world.

Singleton married twice, though specifics about these relationships are limited. What is known is that he struggled with alcoholism and exhibited violent tendencies, particularly when drunk. He suffered from depression and had difficulty controlling his anger. Both marriages ended relatively quickly. By his fifties, Singleton had retired from the Merchant Marine service and settled alone in Sparks, Nevada.

He had a daughter from his first marriage, but their relationship was deeply strained. His daughter reportedly disliked him intensely, an animosity fueled by his violent behavior. On one occasion, while drunk, Singleton slapped her hard. Following this incident, his daughter filed a complaint, successfully requested to be removed from his custody, and became estranged from him. This decision, in hindsight, likely saved her from further harm. Beyond these fragments, Lawrence Singleton's life before 1978 remains largely undocumented, offering few clues to the monstrous actions he would later commit.

In the summer of 1978, Mary Vincent's life in Las Vegas was unraveling. Fifteen years old and with six siblings, she had been a bright, talented dancer with aspirations of a professional career. However, her parents were undergoing a difficult divorce, and the turmoil at home led Mary to run away. She began living on the streets, sometimes sleeping in unlocked cars, adrift and vulnerable. For a time, she found companionship with a twenty-six-year-old man named Diego Montoya, but this association ended abruptly when Montoya was arrested for raping another fifteen-year-old girl. Alone again and desperate to escape street life, Mary decided to hitchhike to Los Angeles to stay with her grandfather.

Hitchhiking was common in the 1970s, often perceived as a relatively safe mode of travel. Mary's journey began uneventfully. She caught rides with several different people, making good progress. By September 29, 1978, she had reached Berkeley, California, a college town known for its transient population and frequent hitchhikers. She found herself at a spot colloquially known as "Hitchhiker's Corner," waiting with other young people also heading south.

It was there that Lawrence Singleton, now fifty-one years old, pulled up in his van. To Mary, he looked harmless, like a grandfatherly figure with a friendly smile. He offered her a ride, saying he was also heading south. As Mary climbed in, the other hitchhikers attempted to join her, but Singleton stopped them. He insisted he only had room for one, specifically Mary. This immediately raised red flags for the others at the corner; they warned Mary not to go, sensing something was wrong. But Mary, young, naive, and desperate to reach her destination, ignored their warnings. The fact that Singleton mentioned having a daughter close to her age further reassured her. She climbed into the van, believing the worst that could happen was minimal. It was a decision that would irrevocably alter her life.

Initially, the drive seemed normal. Singleton made small talk, reinforcing the harmless persona. At one point, Mary sneezed after lighting a cigarette. Singleton reached over and stroked her neck. Startled and creeped out, Mary pulled away. Singleton immediately withdrew his hand, and Mary tried to rationalize the odd gesture, telling herself he was perhaps just overly familiar or eccentric. Wanting to avoid confrontation while alone with him, she tried to put the incident out of her mind and eventually fell asleep.

When she awoke sometime later, she instantly knew something was wrong. They were no longer heading south toward Los Angeles; the van was traveling east, toward Nevada. Panic set in as she recalled the earlier warning signs: his insistence on taking only her, the creepy neck stroke, and now the wrong direction. Reaching under her seat, she found a long metal measuring stick. Brandishing it, she demanded Singleton turn around. Surprisingly, he didn't become aggressive. Instead, he acted confused, apologizing profusely, blaming his age and poor sense of direction. He immediately turned the van around and began heading south again. Mary, relieved, relaxed once more, believing she had asserted control.

They drove for some time, eventually reaching a long, deserted stretch of highway. It was now nighttime, and there was barely any other traffic. Suddenly, Singleton slammed on the brakes, announcing he needed to relieve himself. He got out of the van, and Mary exited as well to stretch her legs. Standing on the dark, empty road, a profound sense of unease washed over her. She felt exposed, vulnerable. The thought struck her: *What if he attacks me?* She assessed the situation — he was older, seemingly less fit than her. She believed she could outrun him. Looking down, she noticed her trainers' laces were untied. If she needed to run, she'd need them tied. As she bent down to secure her shoelaces, Lawrence Singleton crept up behind her and brought a sledgehammer down on her head with full force.

Mary lost consciousness instantly. When she came to herself moments later, Singleton was standing over her. He grabbed her hair and forced her to perform oral sex. He then dragged her to the back of the van, tied her up, and proceeded to rape her repeatedly throughout the night. Mary remained conscious through the entire ordeal, screaming, pleading with him to stop, promising she wouldn't tell anyone if he just let her go. He ignored her cries, forcing her to drink an alcoholic substance between assaults, likely to keep her subdued. By sunrise, she was battered, bruised, and bleeding, convinced she was going to die and, in her agony, wishing for it.

As dawn broke, Singleton dragged Mary out of the van and threw her onto the dusty ground beside the deserted road. She continued to plead for her life. "You want to be set free?" Singleton reportedly sneered. "I'll set you free." He went to the back of his van and retrieved a small axe from his toolbox. He returned to Mary, grabbed her left arm, and swung the axe down, severing her forearm just below the elbow in a single, clean blow.

Mary, in shock, felt herself falling backward even as she instinctively tried to hold onto Singleton. Looking down, she saw her left arm was gone. But Singleton wasn't finished. He grabbed her right arm. It took three swings this time, but the result was the same. He chopped off her right forearm. Mary remained conscious, witnessing the horrific act, feeling the searing pain. As she lay on the ground, she looked up and saw her own severed right hand still clamped onto Singleton's arm — her muscles had locked in a death grip at the moment of impact. She watched him frantically shake his arm, trying to dislodge the gruesome appendage.

Once free of her severed hand, Singleton dragged Mary's mutilated body to a nearby ravine and threw her over the edge, a drop of some thirty feet (about nine meters). Still not satisfied, he carefully climbed down the embankment to where she lay. To ensure she wouldn't be found, he shoved her broken body into a concrete drainage pipe, assuming she would bleed out and her remains would remain hidden. Then, he climbed back up, got in his van, and drove away, leaving the fifteen-year-old girl for dead.

Against all odds, Mary Vincent did not die. Lying in the cold concrete pipe, bleeding profusely, weak, and freezing as night fell again, she fought the overwhelming urge to succumb to sleep. A voice in her head, she later recalled, urged her to stay awake, telling her she had to survive to stop this man from hurting anyone else. Fueled by this thought, she somehow found the strength to push herself out of the pipe.

Once free, her survival instincts took over. Realizing she would bleed to death if she didn't stop the flow from her severed arms, she did something remarkable. She plunged the stumps of her arms into the surrounding mud. The mixture of blood and earth created a crude paste, which she packed into the wounds, effectively creating clots that slowed, then stopped the bleeding. It also, she later said, kept her muscles from protruding from the raw ends of her arms.

Her next challenge was the cliff. Without hands or forearms, weak from blood loss and trauma, she began the arduous climb. Using the bones protruding from her arms and her feet, she dragged herself up the steep embankment. It took her an entire day, an agonizing, inch-by-inch struggle against gravity and exhaustion, but she made it to the top.

Back on the deserted road, she could hear the faint sound of traffic in the distance. She began walking toward the sound, another journey that took miles and hours in her ravaged state. Finally, she reached the side of a slightly busier road, though still remote. She stood there, battered, covered in dried blood and mud, armless, hoping for rescue.

The first car that approached, a red convertible, slowed down, the occupants clearly seeing her horrific condition, but then sped away. Mary later expressed understanding, acknowledging she must have looked like something from a nightmare. But shortly after, another convertible appeared. This couple, on their honeymoon and lost, did stop. They bundled Mary into their car, tried to tend to her wounds, and raced to find a phone. Paramedics arrived, and Mary was airlifted to a hospital equipped to handle her catastrophic injuries. Doctors determined she had lost nearly half the blood in her body, and what remained had reached toxic levels. Incredibly, she survived.

Mary's physical recovery was long and grueling. Surgeons grafted muscle from her legs to reconstruct parts of her arms. She was fitted with prosthetic arms ending in hooks. During the investigation, in a bizarre postscript, police found one of Mary's severed arms washed up near the

Golden Gate Bridge in San Francisco, over a hundred miles from the attack site, far too late for reattachment.

Initially, Mary was too traumatized to speak coherently about the attack. Police employed forensic hypnosis to help her recall the details. Gradually, she provided an accurate description of Lawrence Singleton. The resulting composite sketch was so precise that Singleton's own neighbor recognized him and called the police. On October 9, 1978, just two weeks after the attack, Lawrence Singleton was arrested. Mary identified him in a lineup.

Confronted by police, Singleton denied everything. He concocted a story about picking up Mary along with two other male hitchhikers named "Pedro" and "Larry." He claimed they all went to a bar, smoked marijuana, and then paid Mary $10 each for sex, calling her a "cheap prostitute." He denied raping her or cutting off her arms, blaming the fictitious Pedro and Larry. Police saw through the lies immediately.

A search of Singleton's home revealed remnants of Mary's burnt clothing and a pack of her cigarettes. He had ripped out the carpet in his van and meticulously cleaned it, attempting to remove all traces of blood. Investigators also learned he had attempted suicide shortly after the attack, which they interpreted as a sign of guilt.

The trial took place in March 1979. Mary Vincent faced her attacker in court, taking the stand just feet away from him. As she walked past Singleton after delivering her harrowing testimony, he leaned toward her and whispered a chilling threat: "If it's the last thing I do, I will finish the job."

The jury found Lawrence Singleton guilty on all charges: kidnapping, mutilation, attempted murder, forcible rape, sodomy, and forced oral copulation. Despite the severity and number of convictions, the sentence was shockingly lenient. Due to sentencing laws in California at the time, the maximum penalty he could receive was just fourteen years. He was sent to San Quentin State Prison.

Mary tried to rebuild her life, but the trauma, coupled with the knowledge that her attacker would eventually be released, cast a long shadow. Sadly, her family struggled to cope with her injuries and the aftermath of the attack, and she eventually became estranged from them. She got engaged and had two children, but the approach of Singleton's potential release date caused her immense stress. Then, on her wedding day, she received devastating news: Lawrence Singleton was being released after serving only eight years. He had earned early release for "good behavior" and through a work incentive program designed to alleviate prison overcrowding. A psychological evaluation conducted just before his release deemed him "out of touch with his hostility and anger" and an "elevated threat," yet he was freed anyway.

Singleton's release sparked public outrage. No community in California wanted him. Protests erupted wherever parole officials tried to place him. Residents picketed his temporary residences, firebombed his brother's house where he briefly stayed, and demanded he leave. Eventually, officials resorted to housing him in a trailer on the grounds of San Quentin for the duration of his one-year parole. The public outcry led to the passage of the "Singleton Bill" in California, increasing penalties for crimes involving torture and limiting early release for such offenders, though it couldn't be applied retroactively to Singleton himself.

After his parole ended, Singleton moved back to his hometown of Tampa, Florida. He faced similar rejection there but eventually found a place to live, largely keeping his past hidden. Mary, meanwhile, struggled. Her marriage ended, she fell into debt, her health suffered, and she could no longer afford upkeep on her prosthetics. In a display of staggering audacity, Singleton sued Mary from Florida, absurdly claiming *he* was the victim of kidnapping by her and the fictional Pedro and Larry. The suit went nowhere. Mary countersued and won a $2.56 million judgment, but Singleton only had $200 to his name.

Over the next decade, Singleton lived a mostly quiet, lonely life in Florida, punctuated by minor crimes, including a brief return to prison for stealing a $3 hat. Neighbors described him as a raging alcoholic, rumored to drink two gallons of vodka a day. His health declined, and he reportedly battled cancer. In February 1997, a neighbor found him attempting suicide and intervened, saving his life — an act the neighbor would later bitterly regret.

Just days after the suicide attempt, on February 19, 1997, Lawrence Singleton, now sixty-nine, picked up Roxanne Hayes, a thirty-one-year-old mother of three working as a sex worker to fund a drug addiction. Roxanne had endured a difficult life, surviving childhood sexual and physical abuse and the death of her mother. Despite her struggles, she was known as a witty, caring person devoted to her children.

Singleton took Roxanne back to his home. Around 6:00 p.m., the neighbor who had recently saved Singleton's life came by to discuss some work. Peering through the window after getting no answer at the door, he witnessed a horrifying scene: Singleton, naked and covered in blood, standing over Roxanne, beating and strangling her. Roxanne was still alive and screaming for help. The neighbor banged on the window, momentarily distracting Singleton, who stared blankly at him before turning back to continue the assault. The neighbor immediately called 911.

When a deputy arrived, Singleton answered the door, still naked and blood-soaked. He claimed he had cut his finger while chopping vegetables. The deputy stepped inside and found Roxanne Hayes's lifeless body on the living room floor. She had been beaten, strangled, and stabbed multiple times.

Lawrence Singleton was arrested and charged with first-degree murder. This time, he didn't deny the killing but tried to justify it, claiming Roxanne had tried to steal from him. Many theorized, however, that the murder was a surrogate act — unable to fulfill his threat against Mary Vincent, he unleashed his rage on a woman who bore a striking resemblance to her. His approach was also different: brazen, in his own home, with no attempt at concealment, suggesting perhaps he no longer cared about getting caught.

At Singleton's trial for the murder of Roxanne Hayes, Mary Vincent emerged from hiding. She took the stand once more, testifying about her own horrific experience at his hands. Coupled with the neighbor's eyewitness account and the overwhelming physical evidence, the testimony ensured Singleton's conviction. This time, his sentence was death.

Lawrence Singleton died of cancer on Florida's death row in 2001 before his execution could be carried out. Mary Vincent, upon hearing the news, found closure not in his death itself, but in the relief she saw on her children's faces. Singleton could no longer harm them. She remarried and dedicated herself to advocacy, setting up a foundation for victims of traumatic crime and sharing her story publicly to inspire others. She also discovered a talent for painting, selling her artwork.

While Mary found a path to healing and purpose, Roxanne Hayes's life was tragically cut short, leaving behind three children. Investigators suspected Singleton likely had other victims over the years, perhaps during his decades traveling as a merchant marine, but no definitive links were ever established. His documented acts against Mary Vincent and Roxanne Hayes remain a chilling testament to his capacity for extreme, inexplicable violence.

<h1 style="text-align:center">45</h1>

THE ANGELS OF INSURANCE

In a quiet corner of Kansas, just north of Wichita, lay a ten-acre (about 40,500 square meters) farm known as Angel's Landing. To outsiders, it was a place of surprising wealth and idyllic freedom. The commune hosted lavish parties, with guests swimming in the large pool or riding ATVs on a private track. A fleet of expensive cars — Dodge Vipers, Corvettes, and multiple SUVs with personalized "Angel" license plates — shuttled members around town. The children living there seemed to have everything, including multiple horses.

At the center of this makeshift family was Lou Castro, a man who was, by his own account, a centuries-old angel. He was a jack-of-all-trades in the supernatural realm: he claimed to be possessed by three separate angels, he could predict the future, and he even held the power to bring the dead back to life. But this lavish lifestyle had a dark price, one paid by Lou's own followers. Every few years, like clockwork, a member of the commune would die in a bizarre and tragic accident. As the body count grew, this supposed paradise began to look less like a sanctuary and more like a hunting ground.

The path to Angel's Landing began for one family in 2001, in a suburb of Kansas City, Missouri. The Hudson family was living a typical, happy life.

Jennifer Hudson was a real estate agent, often selling the houses her husband built. They had two daughters: Sarah, a seventeen-year-old self-proclaimed daddy's girl with a rebellious streak, and Emily, a ten-year-old top student. The girls were close despite their age gap, and the family ate dinner together every night. Their life was stable and unremarkable until the summer of 2001, when Jennifer took on a new client named Lou Castro.

Lou and his companions, a married couple named Trish and Brian Hughes, and another woman known only as KL, were looking for a large property to accommodate their group. Lou described them as a makeshift family of free spirits, living in harmony. Jennifer, herself a very spiritual person with a fascination for angels, was immediately captivated. Lou was charming, soft-spoken, and exuded a calm, dignified air. He told her he was independently wealthy from the stock market and owning cattle, which explained his expensive cars and mansion.

As their friendship progressed, Lou revealed his truth: he was a centuries-old angel and seer. He claimed he could see the future, know the date of a person's death, change the weather, and was a relative of Geronimo. His followers backed up every claim. Trish Hughes, his second in command, swore to Jennifer that she had personally witnessed Lou bring an animal, and even himself, back from the dead. Trish told Jennifer, "People say you can't pick your family, but that's exactly what we've done," and invited her to join.

The allure of this new life quickly fractured the old one. Jennifer's once-solid marriage began to crumble, and soon, she and her husband divorced. Lou and his group moved to a ten-acre (about 40,500 square meters) property in Kansas, and Jennifer, telling her daughters she couldn't stand to be far from him, announced they were moving. She promised the girls that Lou, being an angel, would protect them. In the fall of 2001, Jennifer packed up her two daughters and drove them to Angel's Landing to start a new life. Their father, devastated, eventually moved to Kansas just to be closer to his children.

The commune was a small group. At the top was Lou Castro, who claimed to be possessed by three angels: Arthur, the bad angel; Daniel, the nice one; and Amber, the angel of death. Trish Hughes was second in command, a happy, laughing woman who had known Lou for years. Her husband, Brian, was a diesel mechanic, deeply devoted to his wife and their daughter. Then there was KL, a woman who had met Lou in 1996 when she was just fifteen and he was forty-six, a relationship that had begun as illegal abuse but which she, at the time, believed was consensual.

At first, Sarah and Emily were miserable. Sarah, seventeen, despised Lou for breaking up her family. Emily, at ten, was easier to win over. Lou showered them with gifts, a tactic known as love bombing. Emily was given three horses; anything the girls wanted, Lou provided. As time went on, Sarah's guard came down. She saw how happy her mother was and how much everyone else loved and trusted Lou, and she too grew to care for him. Jennifer found a real estate job in the area, and in her absence, Trish stepped in as a second mother to the girls, helping them all settle into one big, seemingly happy family.

But the idyllic facade hid a nightmarish reality. Almost immediately, Lou began sexually abusing ten-year-old Emily. He manipulated her with a terrifying story: as an ancient angel, he could only survive by being sexual with a young girl. He told her she was special and gave him the power he needed to stay alive. He recited Bible scriptures to justify his actions, convincing the child that if she refused, this man she had grown to love would die, and it would be her fault. Just weeks after arriving, Emily began sharing Lou's bed every night, a routine that continued for years.

She was not his only victim. He also manipulated and abused seventeen-year-old Sarah. He told her she was "broken" and that if she ever wanted a family of her own, she had to have sex with him so he could "fix" her. He enforced her silence by threatening that if she ever told anyone, something terrible would happen to her father, the man she adored. He was also abusing KL, and at times would force all three girls to engage in activities with each other. He referred to this abuse as "feeding," claiming it was time for him to feed. He pitted the sisters against each other, straining their relationship, and would fly into violent rages, blaming the "bad angel" Arthur for his actions.

The other adults in the commune claimed to know nothing. Emily later said that because she and Lou were so close, no one found it strange when they disappeared together. But the fact that Jennifer allowed her ten-year-old daughter to sleep in a grown man's bed every night suggests the depth of Lou's control, or her own complicity. It's likely Lou targeted Jennifer from the beginning, seducing her into the group to gain unlimited access to her daughters.

This pattern of abuse and control was funded by a far more lethal operation. Before the Hudsons ever arrived, Lou's inner circle had already experienced its first "tragedy." In February 2001, a woman named Mona Griffith, a single mother of two named Cody and Lindsay, died in a plane crash. Mona had become close friends with Trish and Lou in the mid-90s in Corpus Christi, Texas, and moved with them to South Dakota. She, her daughter Lindsay, and her new boyfriend, a fifty-year-old real estate agent named Jim Chase, were on a trip to Nebraska in Jim's private plane when it vanished. The wreckage was found six weeks later; there were no survivors.

After the crash, Lou came into a large sum of money. At his direction, Mona had taken out a $750,000 life insurance policy on herself, naming her daughter Lindsay as the beneficiary. She had also, at Lou's direction, named Trish Hughes as Lindsay's guardian. With both Mona and Lindsay dead, the money was awarded to Trish and promptly handed over to Lou. This was his true business: he wasn't a stock trader; he was a con artist who funded his lavish lifestyle through insurance payouts. He had every adult in the cult take out large policies on themselves, carefully instructing them who to name as beneficiaries so that his own name was never attached.

By the summer of 2003, just two years after Mona's death, Lou's bank account was running low. Around this time, a narcotics detective named Ron Goodwin had already begun looking into Angel's Landing. The unexplained wealth smelled like a drug case, but Goodwin was baffled to find no record of a "Lou Castro" anywhere. The houses and cars were all registered in the names of other cult members. Goodwin suspected "Lou Castro" was an alias and made it his mission to find out who the man really was.

He didn't know that Lou was already planning his next windfall. One night, Lou approached Trish, her toddler daughter, and eleven-year-old

Emily with a solemn announcement: he had a vision. Amber, the angel of death, had shown him that it was Trish's time to die. Emily was hysterical, but Trish, a deep believer, remained perfectly calm. She assured Emily that it was fine, that Lou would simply bring her back to life after she died, healthier than ever.

A week later, the group went out to lunch. When they returned to Angel's Landing, Lou instructed Trish and Emily to clean the pool. He and Sarah, meanwhile, would go car shopping, securing his alibi. While Sarah was inside getting ready, Lou walked Emily, Trish, and Trish's toddler to the pool. He told Emily the time had come and instructed her to take the baby into a nearby workshop and wait. Emily, crying, hugged Trish goodbye on the diving board. A few minutes after Emily was in the workshop, she heard a splash and a scream. It is believed Lou hit Trish over the head, knocking her into the pool, and then held her underwater until she drowned. The small bruises found on her forehead during the autopsy were not from the fall, but from Lou's fingers pressing into her skin.

A few minutes later, Lou entered the workshop, out of breath and with wet arms, and gave Emily her instructions. She was to wait twenty minutes, then get in the pool with the baby so they would both be wet. She was to call 911 and tell them Trish's daughter had fallen in, and that Trish had slipped, hit her head, and drowned while trying to save her. Emily, terrified, did exactly as she was told, getting into the water where her surrogate mother's body was floating face down. When Lou and Sarah raced back, police were already there. Trish's death was ruled a tragic accident. Lou collected over $1 million in insurance payouts. Three months later, he donated $19,000 to the local police department for a new patrol car, with the sole request that it bear a sticker in memory of Patricia Hughes.

The cycle repeated. Three years later, in late 2006, the money was low again. The next to die was Brian Hughes, Trish's grieving husband. Lou had spent months manipulating the despondent man, telling him that "crossing over" was the ultimate, peaceful goal. While visiting family in South Dakota, Brian, a diesel mechanic known for his obsessive attention to safety, was crushed to death when a jack allegedly gave out and a vehicle fell on him. He hadn't used cinder blocks under the tires, something he normally always did. Lou, back in Kansas, had been heard commenting that he did not expect Brian to return from the trip. It was believed Lou had convinced Brian it was his time, allowing him one last trip to see his family before staging his own death.

Two years later, in 2008, the accounts were low again. This time, Lou's vision was for Jennifer Hudson. When he told Sarah and Emily, they protested, but their mother, still a true believer, calmly told them it was okay and not to worry. Not long after, Jennifer Hudson died on impact when she slammed her car at high speed into a gravel truck. Witnesses all said the same thing: it looked as though she had deliberately swerved into oncoming traffic. The girls knew their mother was never coming back; they had waited for years for Trish and Brian to be resurrected, and they never were.

In 2009, Lou moved the remnants of his cult to a large colonial house in Columbia, Tennessee. Sarah, now twenty-four, refused to go, choosing to stay in Kansas near her father. Lou left with Emily, then seventeen, and his other followers. Finally free from Lou's constant control, Sarah began to breathe. She started dating a man named Daniel McGrath, and as she slowly revealed the story of her life, he became justifiably alarmed. Without telling Sarah, Daniel McGrath wrote a secret email to the FBI, detailing the years of abuse, the mysterious deaths, the insurance payouts, and Lou's new location in Tennessee.

This was the break investigators had been waiting for. The FBI began surveillance on the Tennessee home and saw a vehicle registered to a "Joe Venegas." They monitored Lou's bank accounts, watching money transfer from Kansas to Tennessee. At the Tennessee bank, security footage captured Lou and Emily opening an account under the false name Joe Venegas. It was identity fraud, and it was enough. In April 2010, detectives arrested Lou at his home. He was arrogant, but his fingerprints, when run, came up empty. He was booked as a John Doe, pleaded guilty to identity fraud, and was sentenced to two years in prison, likely believing this would end the investigation.

It only gave detectives the time they needed. They focused on Trish Hughes, who had known Lou the longest. They called her family in

Beeville, Texas, and her sister told them about a man Trish had dated in the 90s named Daniel Perez, who had reportedly died. On a hunch, detectives requested records for Daniel Perez. As Detective Goodwin stood by the fax machine, a mugshot printed out. Staring back at him was Lou Castro.

They finally had his real identity. Daniel Perez, born in 1959, was a former army plane mechanic — a detail that made the 2001 plane crash infinitely more suspicious. They also learned *why* he had "died." In the mid-90s, Perez had pleaded no contest to the sexual assault of two young girls, but the charges were dropped when he was reported dead after a beating. He had faked his death, and Trish, who was just a teenager when she met him, was his first follower. Together, they became Lou and Trish and began collecting new members and new insurance policies.

With Lou in prison, his psychological hold began to break. Sarah gave investigators a full account, including a story of how Lou had threatened to kill her father unless she secretly videotaped an eight-year-old girl undressing. Emily, however, remained loyal. Her loyalty finally shattered when she wrote Lou a letter in prison, telling him she was happy and doing well. Lou wrote back, furiously berating her for daring to find happiness without him. That cruelty was the final snap. Emily started talk-ing, telling detectives the true, step-by-step story of how Lou Castro murdered Trish Hughes.

When Daniel Perez was released from prison for identity fraud, he was immediately rearrested and charged with twenty-eight new felonies, including the exploitation of a child, assault, and the first-degree murder of Trish Hughes. His trial began in early 2015. Sarah, Emily, and four other women, all unconnected to each other, took the stand and told nearly identical stories of abuse at his hands. Lou took the stand in his own defense, spinning a web of bizarre lies. He claimed he hadn't faked his death but had been beaten, suffered amnesia, and it was Trish who convinced him his name was Lou. He claimed he never abused anyone but had consensual sex with them as adults. He said Amber, Arthur, and Daniel weren't angels, just names he liked to be called during intimacy.

The jury did not believe him. He was found guilty on all charges and sentenced to eighty years in prison without the possibility of parole. He is currently serving his time at the Lansing Correctional Facility in Kansas. In the wake of the trial, both Sarah and Emily Hudson have gotten married and are focused on healing from the youth that was stolen from them.

46

CHILDREN OF THUNDER

At 5:00 a.m. on August 2nd, 2000, the sound of gunfire echoed through the small town of Woodacre, California. Police were dispatched to a small studio apartment, a unit tucked away behind the garage of a main house, difficult to find unless one already knew it was there. Inside, officers found a grisly scene. Ginny Villarin, forty-five, was dead on the bed. Her boyfriend, fifty-four-year-old Jim Gamble, was on the floor beside her. Both were naked and had been shot multiple times. The room was soaked in blood, and 6.9-mm shell casings littered the floor. Yet, two separate stashes of money were found untouched in the apartment. This was not a robbery; it was an execution.

The victims had been house-sitting. The apartment belonged to Ginny's twenty-three-year-old daughter, Selena Bishop. Ginny and Jim had gone there to sleep after Ginny finished her late shift at a local bar, the Paper Mill Creek Saloon. Ginny Villarin was a beloved figure, the long-ago girlfriend of famed musician Elvin Bishop, who had famously written the song "Fooled Around and Fell in Love" about her. Though they had split in the early 80s, Ginny remained the vibrant center of her family. Jim Gamble was a retired and charismatic man from Napa Valley, a longtime friend who had driven to Pennsylvania in 1999 to help Ginny move back to California. Their old friendship had recently turned into a romance.

The investigation immediately focused on the apartment's absent tenant, Selena Bishop. She was supposedly on a camping trip in Yosemite with a mysterious new boyfriend known only as "Jordan," a man she had kept hidden from her friends and family. Selena's journal entries revealed her deep unease with this new man: "There is so much of your life hidden from me," she wrote. "Your name, your past, your wife... I realize I don't know you from a can of paint... I won't want to be with you when your big plan goes down. I don't want to be rich."

When Selena failed to show up for her 10:30 a.m. shift at the Two Bird Cafe on Friday, August 5th, she was officially declared a missing person. The case broke open when her coworkers found a pager she had forgotten at the cafe. Detectives scrolling through the numbers found one with a Concord, California area code, registered to a man named Justin Helser. Investigators learned that Justin lived with his older brother, Taylor Helser, and that Justin had recently purchased a 9-mm handgun — the same caliber used to murder Ginny and Jim. When police showed a bartender at a place Selena frequented a photo of Taylor Helser, he immediately identified him. "Jordan," he said.

Glenn Taylor Helser and his younger brother Justin were raised in a devout Mormon household, but the family dynamic was deeply unhealthy. Their mother, Karma, who was believed to have undiagnosed mental health issues, became convinced that her eldest son, Taylor, was a prophet. She encouraged the entire family to defer to him, and Justin, who was more introverted, grew up idolizing and obeying his older brother. Taylor was charismatic and a rising star in the church, setting conversion records on his mission trip to Brazil in 1989. But the trip also radicalized him; he became obsessed with the "moral decay" of the world, the coming apocalypse, and his own belief that he had a direct line to God.

When Taylor returned home in 1991, his mother introduced him to a controversial self-help program called Harmony Impact Training. The program's mantra was that there was "no right and no wrong," only "results." It used cult-like tactics, including sleep deprivation, public humiliation, and intense psychological games, to break members down before building them back up. Taylor, who had married his high school girlfriend and become a stockbroker, embraced this new philosophy. He grew bored with his family, telling a psychiatrist he resented his wife for not being as sexually submissive as the women he saw in pornography and confessing his fantasy of gathering a group of Brazilian women to be his sex slaves.

In 1996, Taylor left his wife and children and moved in with Justin, immediately forcing his brother to attend the Harmony training. After Taylor was excommunicated from the Mormon church for drug use and his extreme beliefs, his delusions fully crystallized. He and Justin would save the world by taking over the Mormon church, which they would accomplish by training an army of Brazilian orphan assassins to kill the church leaders. To fund this plan, Taylor estimated he would need $20 million.

Taylor and Justin formed a small cult with a new recruit, Dawn Godman, a vulnerable woman with a history of meth addiction and homelessness whom Taylor had met at a church function. He charmed her, took her to the parking lot of a Mormon temple, and told her he was a prophet; she believed him. Taylor named the trio the "Children of Thunder," with himself in the role of Jesus. He armed them with his "Twelve Principles of Magic," including the tenets: "I am already perfect and therefore can do nothing wrong" and "I am always right."

Their plan for raising money was extortion. First, they needed a clean bank account. Taylor, using the alias "Jordan," met twenty-two-year-old Selena Bishop at a rave. He love-bombed her and fed her a story about needing to hide a $100,000 inheritance from his "ex-wife." Believing him, Selena opened a new bank account in her name on June 30, 2000.

The cult's first targets were eighty-five-year-old Ivan and seventy-eight-year-old Annette Steinman, a wealthy, elderly couple who had been Taylor's clients during his stockbroker days. On July 30, 2000, the Children of Thunder declared war on Satan in a group prayer, and then Taylor and Justin went to the Steinmans' home. The couple let them in, and Justin pulled the 9-mm handgun. The brothers forced the terrified couple into their own minivan and drove them to the cult's house in Concord.

There, the trio forced the Steinmans to ingest Rohypnol and handcuffed them. They were forced to write checks — Ivan for $33,000 and Annette for $67,000 — made out to Selena Bishop. When Annette began to nod off from the drugs, Taylor forced her to smoke meth, blowing the smoke into her face to keep her conscious enough to sign the check. Believing the drugs would kill the couple, the cult members waited, but the elderly couple proved resilient. Impatient, Taylor ordered the group to strip to their underwear to avoid bloodstains. He and Justin began bashing the couple's heads against the bathroom floor, but they both fought back. Taylor then slit Annette's throat with a hunting knife; when she still struggled, he pulled her head back and drowned her in her own blood. Ivan continued to fight as Dawn sat on his chest until he suffered a fatal heart attack. The cult members then dismembered the bodies and packed them into duffel bags.

The plan unraveled the next day, July 31st. Dawn went to the bank in an outlandish disguise — a bright green sweatsuit, pigtails, a cowboy hat, and a wheelchair — to deposit the checks. She told the bank manager, Vicki Sexton, a convoluted story about Selena needing emergency heart surgery. Sexton, highly suspicious, put a hold on the checks and tried to call the Steinmans but got no answer. Dawn left empty-handed. The cult realized they had made a critical error: they had killed the Steinmans before the checks had cleared.

They now had to eliminate the only remaining loose end: Selena Bishop. On August 2nd, Selena came to Taylor's house, believing she was about to leave for her camping trip. Taylor told her to lie down for a back rub. As she lay on the floor, Justin crept into the room and repeatedly struck her in the head with a hammer. As Dawn began to clean the blood, she noticed Selena's legs were still moving. Taylor dragged the dying woman to the bathroom, put her in the tub, slit her throat, and held her head underwater until she was dead.

But Taylor wasn't finished. He decided Selena's mother, Ginny, also had to die, as she had briefly seen him once at Selena's apartment. That same night, he and Dawn drove to Woodacre. Taylor, dressed in a long black coat and carrying two guns, used his key to enter Selena's apartment. He was startled to find Jim Gamble in bed with Ginny, and he immediately opened fire, killing them both. He and Dawn then returned to Concord, where Taylor cut the tattoo from Selena's shoulder and fed it to his Rottweiler to hinder identification. The remains of Selena and the Steinmans were packed into nine duffel bags and dumped into the Sacramento River Delta.

On August 7th, after bank manager Vicki Sexton linked the Steinman checks to the missing Selena, and Selena's pager led police to the Helser brothers, authorities raided the Concord home. They arrested Justin and Dawn, and captured Taylor after he fled, broke into a neighbor's home, and threatened a woman with a knife. That same day, a jet skier on the Sacramento River Delta discovered the first of the nine duffel bags containing the dismembered victims.

Once in custody, Dawn Godman was worked with by a cult deprogrammer. Realizing she had been brainwashed, she testified against the brothers and was sentenced to thirty-eight years in prison. Taylor Helser, who remained defiant, described the murders as "collateral damage" and the work of a soldier in a holy war. He was given five death sentences and remains on death row. Justin Helser was given three death sentences. In 2013, after several previous attempts, including stabbing himself in the eyes with pencils, Justin Helser was found hanging in his cell, dead by suicide.

47

THE GIRL IN DARK CANYON

In August 2010, nearly a year after twenty-four-year-old Mitrice Richardson vanished, park rangers were hiking through Dark Canyon, an incredibly steep and remote area in the Malibu hills. The terrain was so difficult that it was not recommended for hikers. There, they discovered a human skull with dark, curly hair still attached. Nearby were women's clothes. The remains were soon confirmed to be those of Mitrice. The discovery, however, raised far more questions than it answered. Her body was found in a state that baffled investigators: her shirts, underwear, socks, and shoes were missing, yet her remains, which had lain exposed for almost a year in an area full of coyotes and scavengers, were almost completely undisturbed by animals.

Before she was a set of remains in a canyon, Mitrice Richardson was a bright and ambitious woman. Born in 1985, she was raised by her mother, Latice Sutton, and her great-grandmother, Mildred. Her biological father, Michael Richardson, had been incarcerated for drug dealing when she was four. Seeking a quieter life away from the 1993 LA riots, the family moved to the suburbs of Covina, where Mitrice thrived. She was a high-achieving student who found school almost too easy. She was a cheer-leader and loved to dance, known for a happy, contagious energy. She was the first in her family to attend college, graduating with honors from Cal

State Fullerton in 2008 with a degree in psychology. She planned to pursue her master's degree while living with her great-grandmother and working as a "go-go" dancer under the name "Hazel" at a local nightclub.

In the summer of 2009, Mitrice's behavior began to change. Friends and family noticed she seemed stressed and withdrawn, possibly due to a complicated relationship with a woman named Vanessa. She stopped calling friends and instead sent bizarre, disjointed text messages. Her social media was filled with random, philosophical statements posted at all hours. In one text to her mother, she claimed she wanted to be "Miss Mother Nature" and needed to talk to Michelle Obama about creating a position for her in the White House. On September 16, 2009, she went to her shipping company job, seemed fine, but left at lunch and never returned. That evening, she skipped her regular Wednesday dinner with her great-grandmother, saying the ocean was "calling her name" and she was driving to Malibu.

Mitrice arrived in Malibu and pulled into the parking lot of Geoffrey's, an expensive, valet-only restaurant. Her behavior was immediately erratic. She climbed into a valet's personal car, telling the confused employee it was "subliminal" and that she was there to "avenge the death of Michael Jackson." She walked into the restaurant wearing a Bob Marley T-shirt and a Rastafarian hat. After ordering a $65 Kobe steak and a cocktail, she joined a table of seven strangers, telling them she was from another planet. When her meal was finished, she attempted to walk out with the group, leaving her $90 bill unpaid. Stopped by the manager, she emptied her pockets and said, "I'm busted. What are we gonna do?" The restaurant staff, believing she was on drugs or having a mental crisis, called the police. Mitrice's great-grandmother, Mildred, called and offered to pay the bill over the phone, but the restaurant refused to accept it without her being physically present.

When deputies from the LA Sheriff's station arrived, Mitrice passed a sobriety test. They searched her car and found her driver's license and a small, non-arrestable amount of marijuana. Her wallet, phone, and debit card were all in the messy vehicle. The restaurant owner, however, insisted on pressing charges for defrauding an innkeeper. Mitrice was handcuffed and taken to the station. Her mother, Latice, called the station and was explicitly told that Mitrice would be held overnight; the officer assured her they would have Mitrice call in the morning. Relieved, Latice went to sleep, believing her daughter was, at the very least, safe. Despite Mitrice's bizarre behavior, deputies made no notes about her mental state, a decision that would later be debated as a way to avoid paperwork. At 12:15 a.m. on September 17, Mitrice was released. She was alone, in the dark, with no car, no money, and no phone. Her impounded car was fifteen miles (about twenty-four kilometers) away. The department later claimed she had refused offers to stay in the lobby.

At 5:20 a.m., Latice called the station, only to be told her daughter had been released hours earlier. Panicked, she tried to file a missing persons report but was told to wait twenty-four hours. An hour later, at 6:30 a.m., a retired reporter named Bill Smith, living in the remote Monte Nido canyon area six miles (about ten kilometers) from the station, called 911. He reported a slim Black woman with an afro in his backyard, who said she was "just resting" before disappearing. A deputy was dispatched but found no one. The first official search didn't happen for another forty-eight hours, according to the family. A tracking dog picked up Mitrice's scent at Smith's home but quickly lost it.

The investigation was immediately fraught with tension. The Sheriff's department denied any negligence, drawing public fury when it was pointed out that actor Mel Gibson had been arrested at the same station for a driving under influence (DUI) charge and was given a courtesy ride back to his car. For months, the department insisted that there was no surveillance footage of Mitrice in her cell, claiming the cameras didn't record. Only after her family's attorney applied heavy pressure did the footage "magically" appear, showing Mitrice acting agitated in her cell, and, crucially, a deputy exiting the station at the exact moment she was released, contradicting the official report.

The discovery of her remains in August 2010 only deepened the mystery. The scene was so remote that the coroner could not access it, and the body had to be airlifted. The only scene photographs were taken on a park ranger's cell phone. The official cause of death was ruled "undetermined," with no signs of trauma. This conclusion was fiercely disputed. Mitrice's family hired a forensic anthropologist who pointed out glaring inconsistencies. The Sheriff's department claimed the body was "untouched," yet her skull was detached and five of her neck bones were missing. Her left arm was flexed in a position that defied gravity, suggesting homicide, not an accidental death. Her teeth had a pinkish hue, a potential sign of strangulation, but the missing neck bones made confirmation impossible. An earring she was not reported to be wearing was found tangled in her hair, but it was never examined.

Mitrice's parents, Latice Sutton and Michael Richardson, both filed separate lawsuits against the LA Sheriff's Department for negligence and were awarded settlements. The department, however, never admitted any wrongdoing. A subsequent investigation by the California Attorney General's office found insufficient evidence to charge any deputies with a crime, in part because the statute of limitations had already expired. The case remains unsolved, suspended between theories of a tragic accident fueled by a mental health crisis, or a homicide cover-up, all of which began the moment deputies released a vulnerable woman into the pitch-black, unfamiliar canyon roads with no way to get home.

48

THE MISSING SECRETARY

Mary Shotwell Little was twenty-five years old and settling into a new life. A secretary at the Citizens & Southern National Bank in Atlanta, Georgia, she had been married for just six weeks to Roy Little, a bank auditor. On the morning of October 14, 1965, her husband was out of town, having traveled sixty miles (about ninety-six kilometers) south of the city for a work training course, leaving Mary at their home alone. Her day proceeded as expected: she completed her shift at the bank, went grocery shopping, and then, with her evening free, made plans to meet a friend.

She drove her 1965 metallic pearl gray Comet to the Lenox Square Shopping Center, one of Atlanta's more affluent destinations, known for its expensive shops and "posh" restaurants. It was not the kind of place where residents feared for their safety. Mary met a co-worker at the Piccadilly Cafeteria, and they shared a pleasant dinner. The co-worker later recalled that Mary was in high spirits, talking happily about her new married life and seeming to be in a very happy place.

At approximately 8:00 p.m., the women left the restaurant and walked back into the car park. The area was well-lit and still busy with other patrons leaving for the evening. Since they were parked in different areas, the friends parted ways. Mary's last words to her co-worker were a simple "see you," which the friend assumed meant she would see her at work the next day. It was the last time anyone is known to have seen her.

The next morning, October 15, Mary did not show up for work. This was immediately alarming; she was known for being punctual, and her failure to arrive was completely out of character. Her worried boss first tried calling her home, but the line rang unanswered. He then contacted her landlady, who checked the apartment and reported that Mary's morning newspaper was still on the doorstep, a strong indication that she had never made it home the previous night.

After speaking with the co-worker Mary had dined with, the boss called Lenox Square security and asked them to search the car park for Mary's gray Comet. The security guards, who had started their shift at 6:00 a.m., reported that the car was not there. A patrol police officer who had also driven through the lot that morning confirmed their account: the car was gone. Frustrated and increasingly concerned, Mary's boss drove to Lenox Square himself around midday. He began his own search of the car park and, within minutes, found it. Mary's 1965 Comet was parked in the lot in plain sight. The discovery posed an immediate and baffling question: Had the security guards and the police officer somehow missed the car, or had it been taken and returned sometime between 6:00 a.m. and midday?

Police were dispatched to the scene, and Roy Little was finally contacted at his training course and rushed back to Atlanta. The scene inside the car was bizarre and deeply unsettling. The vehicle's exterior was coated in a thin layer of red dust, suggesting it had recently been driven at high speed down a dirt road. Inside, Mary's four bags of groceries from the previous night sat undisturbed. Also present were bottles of Coke and a pack of Kent cigarettes, her preferred brand.

The most disturbing evidence, however, was a small pile of clothing. Mary's slip, panties, and girdle had been neatly folded and placed on the center console between the two front seats. On the floorboard lay her bra and one of her stockings. The stocking appeared to have been cut with a knife. The undergarments, which were confirmed to belong to Mary and to have been recently worn, were speckled with blood. More blood was found smeared on the steering wheel, the driver's side door handle, and the passenger side window.

Forensic analysis determined the blood was almost certainly Mary's, but the quantity was small, not enough to suggest a fatal wound, perhaps as little as would come from a small nosebleed. The way the blood was smeared, combined with the unnaturally tidy stack of underwear, led many officers to believe the entire scene had been intentionally staged. An unidentified fingerprint was found in the blood on the steering wheel, but police were never able to match it to Mary or any known suspect. Mary's purse, her car keys, and all of her outer clothing were missing.

The initial investigation was stumped. Police were puzzled as to how an abduction, one that apparently involved forcing a woman to strip, could have occurred in a busy, well-lit car park without a single witness. The theory that she had been taken elsewhere and the car returned seemed more plausible, but it raised its own set of confusing questions. Why would an attacker risk being caught by returning the car to the scene, and why would they leave such a strange tableau of evidence behind?

Investigators turned to Mary's personal life and discovered it was more complicated than her happy, newlywed status suggested. She had recently received roses from an unknown "secret admirer" and had been bothered by "worrying" phone calls. Co-workers had overheard parts of these calls. On one occasion, she was heard saying, "I'm a married woman now." In another, even more cryptic exchange, she told the caller, "You can come over to my house anytime you like, I can't come over there." This statement suggested to some that she was not having an affair, as she would likely be sneaking to the other person's location; rather, it hinted that she was afraid of the caller and wanted any meeting to be on her own territory, perhaps when her husband was present. This fear was reinforced by a conversation she had with a friend weeks earlier, in which she admitted she was worried about being home alone and, specifically, being in her car alone.

Her husband, Roy Little, was briefly scrutinized. He had a rock-solid alibi, as he was sixty miles (about ninety-six kilometers) away and seen by numerous people at his work training. Police never considered him a suspect. His behavior, however, was noted by many as strange. He appeared publicly unemotional, expressed more concern about getting his car back than about the search for his wife, and refused to take multiple lie detector tests. While suspicious to a modern eye, some context has been offered regarding the cultural expectations of male stoicism in the 1960s.

For a month, the case was a complete dead end. Then, the investigation was thrown wide open when evidence emerged that Mary had been taken across state lines, making it a federal offense and bringing in the FBI. Mary's credit card had been used. The first charge was made in the early morning hours of October 15, around 2:00 a.m., at a gas station in Charlotte, North Carolina. The second charge appeared later that same day, around midday, at another gas station in Raleigh, North Carolina.

Detectives raced to North Carolina and retrieved the receipts. The signature on the slip from Charlotte read "Mrs. Roy H. Little Jr." and was confidently identified as Mary's handwriting. The gas station attendants from both locations were interviewed and clearly remembered the encounters. The attendant in Charlotte recalled a woman with a bleeding cut on her head, who was trying to hide her face while a man with her "barked orders" at her. The attendant in Raleigh described an even more grim scene: the woman was covered in blood, including blood running down her legs, and she was in the company of two men, both of whom were ordering her around.

This new information created an impossible, contradictory timeline. At the exact same time Mary was reportedly being seen with two men in Raleigh — midday on October 15 — her car was being discovered by her boss back in the Atlanta car park. This implied a highly complex crime involving at least three individuals: the two men with Mary in North Carolina, and a third accomplice who drove her car forty-one unaccounted-for miles (about sixty-five kilometers) before returning it to the Lenox Square lot.

The choice of location was just as baffling. Charlotte, North Carolina, was Mary's hometown, the place where her parents still lived. Taking an abductee to the one place she was most likely to be recognized was an audacious risk. It suggested the attackers were either astonishingly reckless or, perhaps, knew exactly where she was from and were taunting her. This link to Charlotte was strengthened by another clue: a license plate, stolen from Charlotte, was reportedly found on the car the group was using in North Carolina. The psychological profile of the lead attacker was terrifying: a man who took bizarre risks, was clever, and was utterly unafraid of being caught.

In the years that followed, the case grew colder but stranger. In 1966, an inmate in a Georgia prison told the FBI that two men had confessed to him that they were paid $5,000 to kidnap Mary. They claimed they took her to a small greenhouse in Mount Holly, killed her, and buried her there. Investigators located a property that matched the description, but it had recently been demolished, leaving them with another dead end.

Then, in May 1967, the case took another sinister turn. A woman named Diane Shields, the secretary who had been hired to take over Mary's job at the C&S Bank, was found murdered. Her body was discovered in the trunk of her car; she had been suffocated with a scarf and paper shoved down her throat. She was fully clothed, and her diamond engagement ring was still on her finger, ruling out sexual assault and robbery as motives. The case remains unsolved, but police have long speculated it was linked to Mary's disappearance.

This potential link fueled theories that the disappearances were connected to a scandal at the bank. Around the time Mary went missing, the bank had a former FBI agent investigating rumors of a small prostitution ring and "lesbian sexual assaults" among the staff. Mary's boss insisted she knew nothing about it, but other sources claimed she did. The fact that both Mary and her replacement were murdered suggested they may have known something that made them a threat. In a final, inexplicable twist, after a detective publicly suggested the two cases were linked, Mary's mother called him. A year and a half after her daughter had vanished, she told the detective to "leave it" and that she did not want Mary's case looked into anymore.

Other potential leads, like a $20,000 ransom call that was deemed a hoax and a report of another woman being lured in the same car park just ten minutes before Mary's disappearance, all led nowhere. A full review of the case in 2009, using modern forensic technology, made no progress. The files related to Mary Shotwell Little's disappearance have reportedly since been lost. The staged car, the cryptic phone calls, the contradictory time-line, and the chilling North Carolina sightings have hardened into one of Atlanta's most enduring and perplexing unsolved mysteries.

CONCLUSION

As you close this book, you are left with a chilling realization: evil rarely announces itself with a roar. More often, it moves in silence, hiding behind a neighbor's door or beneath the mask of an ordinary life. Through these twenty-four stories, I have traced the darkest outlines of the human experience — from the scams that exploited blind ambition to the cults that devoured the will, and the crimes that time very nearly managed to erase.

Finishing these chapters does not mean the danger has passed. The cases presented here serve as stark reminders that justice is often a winding path, and truth is frequently more terrifying than any urban legend. These accounts force us to ask an uncomfortable question: how many more secrets remain buried in forgotten files, waiting for the light of day?

I hope this journey into the unknown has prompted you to look at the world through a different lens. The next time you hear an unexplained creak in the floorboards, spot an unfamiliar van idling in your neighborhood, or read a headline that seems too strange to be true, remember that behind every anomaly lies a story just as cold as the ones you've just finished.

Thank you for walking beside me through the shadows. Keep the lights on, stay vigilant, and above all, never assume you truly know those around you. The world is far more complex — and much darker — than most of us dare to admit.

A SPECIAL THANK YOU FOR YOUR SUPPORT!

Thank you so much for purchasing this book and joining me on this journey into the shadows. As a token of my appreciation, I'd love to send you a special bonus — the digital versions of two of my best-selling books, completely free:

- 1,144 Random, Interesting & Fun Facts You Need to Know – The Knowledge Encyclopedia to Win Trivia
- Why Do We Say That? 101 Idioms, Phrases, Sayings & Facts! A Brief History on Where They Come From!

Scan the QR code below and enter your email, and I'll send the files directly to your inbox. Happy reading!

Thank You for Reading!

Thank you for joining me on this journey into the darkest corners of human nature. I hope this exploration of the mysteries behind these cases has challenged your theories and provided a clearer understanding of the search for justice.

If these haunting accounts have left an impression, I would be deeply grateful if you could leave a review on Amazon. Simply scan the QR code below to share your perspective. Reviews are the lifeblood of the true crime community, helping fellow armchair detectives and curious minds find the cases that deserve to be told.

Even a brief reflection makes a significant impact — and I truly appreciate your support in the pursuit of the truth.

See you in the next case file.

Scott

www.ingramcontent.com/pod-product-compliance
Lightning Source LLC
Chambersburg PA
CBHW051410050726
47595CB00010B/4004